Russia and Asia, No.1

G.-F. Müller and Siberia, 1733 — 1743

J.L. Black
Carleton University
and
D.K. Buse
Laurentian University

Translation of German materials
by Victoria Joan Moessner
University of Alaska, Fairbanks

THE LIMESTONE PRESS
Kingston, Ontario : Fairbanks, Alaska

Russia and Asia Series, No. 1. Editor, Richard A. Pierce

International Standard Book Number: 0-919642-23-3

This book has been published with the aid of a grant from the
Canadian Federation for the Humanities, using funds provided by
the Social Sciences and Humanities Research Council of Canada.

Printed and bound in Canada by:
Brown & Martin Limited, Kingston, Ontario.

CONTENTS

ntroduction   v - xii

.-F. Müller and Siberia   1

ocument 1 - Instructions given to G.-F. Müller   47

ocument 2 - Allowances for Participants in the Kamchatka
            Expedition   48

ocument 3 - A.F. Büsching: Müller's Great, Long Siberian
            Journey   49

ocument 4 - G.F. Müller: Travels in Siberia, 1733-1740   63

ocument 5 - Reports and Memoranda   113

ocument 6 - [G.-F. Müller]: Letter from a Russian
            Sea-Officer to a Person of Distinction
            at the Court of St. Petersburg   122

ILLUSTRATIONS

Gerhard Friedrich Müller (Russian: Fedor Ivanovich Miller). Silhouette, in the State Historical Museum, Moscow.   30

Title page of Müller's <u>Description of the Siberian Kingdom and all occurrences there, from the beginning and particularly from its conquest by the Russian State</u>. St. Petersburg, 1750. First edition.   36

Tiumen. A page from the Remezov Chronicle of the Conquest of Siberia, discovered by Müller.   43

Title page of Müller's <u>Voyages from Asia to America</u>, London, 1761.   44

Title page of first issue of <u>Monthly Compositions for Profit and Entertainment</u>, edited by Müller, 1755-1764.   45

Title page of G.-F. Müller, <u>Description of the heathen peoples inhabiting Kazan gubernia</u>... St. Petersburg, 1791.   46

Gold objects from Enisei burials, obtained by Müller's expedition.   62

Müller's travels in Siberia, map   Endpapers

INTRODUCTION

From the 15th through the 18th centuries Europeans explored the globe. A common pattern prevailed, in that for the most part they probed the edges of continents, charted the seas, and followed large river systems. In their preoccupation with sea routes, especially passages to the east, Europeans reconnoitered only a few land masses, usually with the hope of obtaining riches rather than establishing trade. Aside from the colonies of North and South America where settlers slowly pushed inland, the one area in which the least extensive land explorations occurred is also the area about which the least information appears in general studies on European expansion, namely Siberia. The expansion of Muscovy appears as an aside in most such studies, though it features prominently in monographs on "Russian" history. Historians of Europe have been preoccupied with the Dutch getting to the eastern Asian islands, the English captains (such as James Cook) arriving in Australia and Canada, and the Spanish crossing to the Pacific Ocean. Yet simultaneously with those movements, Russian and Russian-sponsored explorers, traders, conquerors and colonizers made their way eastward through the vast tracts of Siberia towards China, Japan and North America.

Historically, the territories of Central Asia and Siberia had been a subject of European interest for centuries and, of course, had been traversed for the purpose of trade and conquest from peoples of the Mediterranean and Asia as well. The Hellenic armies of Alexander the Great in the 4th century B.C., the great Viking expansion of the 8th and 9th centuries, and the "pax Mongolica" established by the Mongolian Khans of the 13th century over an area from the Pacific Ocean to the region which became Muscovy, were among the great expansionist movements of early history which took in parts or much of these vast regions and "connected" them to Europe.

The Portuguese voyages of exploration in the 15th century, first of the coasts of Africa and then by the 1480s towards India, soon followed by the Spanish exploration and conquest of Central and South America, combined missionary zeal with a search for gold and silver. Thereby, they began the extension of European influence throughout the world and opened the way for the more scientific exploration of a later period. The governments and merchants of Holland, France and England, stimulated by the development of commercial capitalism and ambition for empire completed the process. The opening of Siberia was part of this world-wide phenomenon. During the 1580s cossacks led by Ermak Timofeevich destroyed the Tatar fort of Sibir, near the conjunction of the Ob and Irtysh rivers, and set the stage for Russian movement into the area which came to be called Siberia. The city of Tobol'sk was founded, and by the early 17th century Russians had built their own forts along the Enisei and had reached the Lena. Another cossack founded Iakutsk

on the Lena in 1632 and military governors (voevody) were poste
there to establish Russian authority.

One of the most memorable adventures undertaken in thes
regions during the 17th century was the voyage of Semen Dezhnev
a cossack, and Fedot Alekseev, an employee of a Moscovit
merchant. In June 1648 in seven small flat-bottomed vessel
(kochi), they sailed east from the mouth of the Kolyma, in th
Arctic Ocean, and passed through the straits which a long tim
later would be named after Vitus Bering. Typically, their goa
was not to explore, map, convert native peoples, or even t
expand the official frontiers of the Russian state; rather the
were searching for new spoils in the form of sable pelts. Onl
one of the seven craft, Dezhnev's, reached the Anadyr, on th
Pacific Ocean; Alekseev's vessels disappeared. The story c
Dezhnev's accomplishment, did not become generally known unti
G.-F. Müller publicized it in 1758, well after Bering's tw
voyages to Kamchatka.

The details of Dezhnev's discovery, Müller's informatic
about it, and the voyage's significance in the history of 17t
century exploration are discussed thoroughly in Raymond F
Fisher, The Voyage of Semen Dezhnev in 1648: Bering's Precurso
(London: The Hakluyt Society, 1981). Fisher's account provide
valuable background to the information contained in thi
collection about Müller's own experiences in Siberia, and als
clearly demonstrates the way in which the exploration of Siberi
was related to the overall pattern of European discovery.

One phase of the Russian eastward expansion, the tw
expeditions led by Vitus Bering from 1725 and 1741, was bot
well-known to contemporaries and has been described thoroughly k
modern historians of exploration and discovery. The fact tha
Bering's second voyage was only part of a large and practicall
autonomous scientific enterprise is less well known and studiec
It is to be hoped that this small collection will illustrate tha
dimension of the Second Kamchatka Expedition. Thus Bering'
exploits will mainly be left aside here, and our attention wil
be focused almost exclusively on that part of the Academy c
Sciences contingent headed by his co-explorers, Müller and J.-C
Gmelin.

The term "expedition" is appropriate to their enterprise nc
only because contemporaries utilized it, but because of the scoﾟ
and size of the group involved. The large party of ethnographers
geologists, mineralogists, historians, and cartographers wei
away from St. Petersburg for more than a decade. Although it wa
not a voyage into an unknown void, its participants had onl
vague notions, mixed with some precise reports from traders ar
military governors, about the region they were cataloguing. The
were fitted out handsomely with experts and supplies, and ha
well-defined tasks to perform. In this manner, the Berir
undertaking was similar to that of Meriwether Lewis and Willia
Clark, i.e., the first American expedition to the Pacific, whic

vi

was sponsored by the American government for military and commercial purposes during the first decade of the 19th century.

Like Alexander von Humboldt and Aimé Bonpland's expedition into the jungles and partially-known lands of South America at the end of the 18th century, the expedition in which Müller participated sought geographic exactitude, determined astronomical positions, mapped rivers and collected botanical specimens. The universality of the explorers' realm is demonstrated by the fact that von Humboldt was hired later by the Russian government to investigate mineral resources throughout many of the areas previously studied by Müller and Gmelin. His voyage through the territory of the Irtysh and Ob Rivers in 1829, to the Chinese frontier at Narym, also had significant scientific results.

The documents in this collection help to clarify the purpose of Bering's voyages and the scientific part of his expedition. The Russian state was interested in facilitating trade, defining and protecting its borders, discovering minerals and precious metals, and establishing authority over its non-Russian population. It hoped to find routes to Japan and America and to explore the Arctic coast, and also to surround such discoveries with a cloak of secrecy. In fact, the sea-going components of the Kamchatka Expedition explored and mapped most of the Arctic Coast of Russia and Siberia, and located and charted part of the coast of Alaska, the Aleutian chain, Kamchatka and the Kurile Islands.

Müller and his group went as far east as Iakutsk on the Lena, south to Kiakhta on the Chinese border and Nerchinsk on the Amur. Towards the southwest, they visited Ust'-Kamenogorsk on the upper Irtysh. The most northerly part of their trek was Berezovo on the Ob. The documents also illustrate the difficulties encountered by the adventurers. The cold, vast distances, winding rivers, glorious and wild scenery, friendly, indifferent or hostile tribes, novel customs and religions, all struck explorers of Siberia much as similar phenomena fascinated Europeans in other parts of the world. The Müller account contained here illustrates these things, and throws some light on the operations of the Russian Academy of Sciences, the relationship between central and provincial authorities and local tribesmen, on Imperial Russia's strategy vis-à-vis China, and on trade and mining in the region.

An historical comparison highlights the significance of the academic part of this enterprise. If one looks at some better-known explorations of North America or elsewhere, it is surprising how well prepared and scientifically oriented this group was. When, also during the 1730s, the Sieur de La Vérendrye and his sons wanted to find profitable fur trade routes in the interior of what became Canada, he received no financial support from the French state or governors, in spite of their intense competition with the English Hudson's Bay Company. La

Vérendrye's explorations and the forts which he built to protect
his trading monopoly demonstrate heroism but poor organization.
Later explorations by Alexander Mackenzie, the first man to cross
the North American continent, in 1793, and David Thompson, who
gathered information on the vast area between the Great Lakes and
the Pacific on behalf of rival trading companies, achieved much
but could not rival the Second Kamchatka Expedition in scope or
scientific accomplishment. Only Captain James Cook's famous
traverse of the entire South Pacific, 1768-1771, accompanied by
naturalists and astronomers, was of the same scientific calibre
as the Second Kamchatka Expedition.

Cook's voyages left us the names of Joseph Banks, who later
became president of the Royal Society, and George Forster, as men
of science who helped discover a new world and present its
novelties to a curious European world. Their expeditions were
well-organized and their leaders were highly skilled and
intensely interested in the scientific dimensions of their
enterprises. Forster's work on Cook's second voyage stimulated a
young von Humboldt, whose later exploits marked a pinnacle of
scientific exploration.

By Humboldt's time, such expeditions had become standard and
were part of the 18th century intellectuals' desire to chart and
catalogue the entire world. Even Napoleon tried to outfit a
massive exploratory voyage under the leadership of Louis Antoine
de Bougainville, but his wars undercut the necessary investment.
It is noteworthy, then, that among the earliest, largest and most
thorough exploratory voyages were those carried out by the
tsarist state in Siberia. The documents included below help
demonstrate Russia's crucial role in the history of European
expansion, and illustrate G.-F. Müller's right to be ranked among
Europe's great scientific explorers.

Of the recollections left by scholars and explorers who took
part in the second Kamchatka Expedition, S.P. Krasheninnikov's
has received the most attention. Krasheninnikov was a student
under Müller's tutelage during the expedition and from Okhotsk
and Kamchatka reported regularly to Müller and to J.-G. Gmelin.
His description of the peninsula has been printed and translated
many times. The first Russian printing was edited by Müller
himself in 1755. An English translation appeared in 1763/64;
three French editions appeared during the 18th century; the
original German version was published in 1766 and there were
three other issues in the same century. In 1966 the Academy of
Sciences republished Krasheninnikov's previously unpublished
Kamchatka materials.[1]

Another member of the Academy section of the expedition, G.W.
Steller, who spent two months with Müller and Gmelin in 1737
before he went on to join Krasheninnikov and Bering, left a
logbook of his journey which was first published in Leipzig in
1774. P.S. Pallas then printed it in two volumes of his <u>Neue
Nordischer Beytrage</u> (1791-93) and separately in 1793; William

Coxe added a partial English translation of it to the 1803 edition of his book on Russian discoveries. A complete English translation was included in Frank A. Golder's <u>Bering's Voyages</u> (Vol.II, 1925), and a new translation, by O.W. Frost, is pending publication. The first printing of Steller's work contained a collection of materials on Kamchatka which Müller compiled at Iakutsk in 1737 and gave to Krasheninnikov.[2] J.E. Fischer, who was sent to Siberia in 1738 to replace Müller for the Kamchatka stage of the long voyage, wrote a history and description of Siberia. But the book, which was written between 1752 and 1757, did not appear in print until 1768 and was based entirely on research undertaken by Müller. A Russian translation appeared in 1774.[3] Müller's constant companion, Gmelin, wrote a four-part memoir of his ten years in Siberia. It was published in Göttingen in 1751/52, was translated into French in 1767, and attracted wide attention throughout Europe.[4] It has never been printed in Russian or English. The French-language version of Gmelin's memoir, an abridgement, was quite harsh in its indictment of the Russian administration of Siberia and of the living conditions which prevailed there. In 1768 the Abbé Chappe D'Auteroche's notorious <u>Voyage en Siberie</u>, also published in Paris, depicted Russia as a backward and barbaric land. Since d'Auteroche was a French academician and astronomer whom the Russian government had assisted generously, Catherine II was enraged by the book. She went to press anonymously with a response, <u>L'Antidote</u> (1770), and the Academy instructed Müller to publicize the accomplishments of Russia's explorers in European journals.[5]

Lieutenant Sven Waxel, who accompanied Martin Spangenberg (Bering's second-in-command) to the Japanese coast in 1738/39 and then went with Bering to America in 1741, also left a journal which appeared in Russian in 1940, and twice later in English (1952, 1962).[6] Even an account by the rather unsavory Francesco Locatelli, who travelled under false pretenses with Müller and Gmelin from St. Petersburg to Kazan in 1733, appeared in French, German, and English editions in the 1730s.[7] Only the memoirs prepared by Müller, although he was the best known member of the Academy of Sciences contingent, have remained virtually ignored by Russian, French, and English translators.

Other 18th century explorers of Siberia have had their works published in several languages. The first large-scale expedition sponsored by the Russian government was led by Daniel Messerschmidt in 1720. The results of his seven-year tour were printed in part by P.S. Pallas in 1782 and have recently been published in full in Berlin.[8] But the work of a member of Messerschmidt's entourage, Ph. I.T. Strahlenberg, appeared in 1730 in Stockholm (in German), was translated into English in 1738, and into French in 1757.[9] Later representatives of the Academy of Sciences in St. Petersburg who were sent on exploratory treks also had their reports widely circulated. Among these were Pallas, Ivan Lepekhin, Samuel Gmelin, J.P. Falk, J.P. Georgi, and J.A. Guldenstadt, each of whom was associated

with Müller in one way or another.[10] Europeans who travelled in
the Russian Empire found a ready market for their travel
accounts, some of which were translated into Russian. Among
these was John Bell, a Scottish doctor who journeyed from St.
Petersburg through Siberia to Pekin - and back - during the years
1719/22. His Travels from St. Petersburg in Russia to Diverse
Parts of Asia was printed in two volumes in Scotland in 1763. A
French translation appeared in the 1770s and it was reprinted
regularly in English until the mid-nineteenth century. M. Popov
translated it into Russian in 1776 for an Academy edition in St.
Petersburg.[11] Popov cited Müller in his foreword in order to
verify several names used by Bell - but no attempt was made to
bring Müller's own long account to the attention of Russian
readers.

None of these individuals spent more time than Müller mapping
and describing the vast stretches of the Russian Empire. Nor did
any of them file as many documents and notes on towns, natural
history, geographical phenomena, and ethnographical information
as Müller. Imperial Russian and Soviet writers have given Müller
credit for the enormous value of his Siberian source collecting,
and his European contemporaries regarded him as the foremost
expert on Siberia. Nevertheless, Müller's chronicle of that
incredible journey remains available only in German as scattered
paragraphs within his own incomplete history of the Academy of
Sciences, 1725-1743, which was published in St. Petersburg in
1890.[12]

Müller's brief outline of Russian voyages from Asia to
America, which he printed himself in both German and Russian in
1758, was very quickly translated into English and French during
the 1760s and was reprinted twice more in German during the
seventies.[13] But that work tells only a fraction of the tale of
his expedition. The purpose of the present volume, then, is to
make available Müller's more detailed narration and to supplement
it with other documents of and about the Second Kamchatka
Expedition so that English-language readers can gain a fuller
appreciation of Müller's remarkable contribution to the opening
up of Siberia.

In light of the fact that 1983 marked the 200th anniversary
of Müller's death and 250th anniversary of his embarkation on the
Second Kamchatka Expedition this collection can serve both as a
reminder and as a belated celebration of his noteworthy
accomplishments.

As an appendix we include the anonymous "Letter of a Russian
naval officer," published in French in Berlin in 1753 and in
English translation in London in 1754, commonly attributed to
Müller. The letter provides the official Russian position on
Bering's voyages and presents Müller as a publicist.

J.L. Black, Ottawa
D.K. Buse, Sudbury

x

1. Krasheninnikov, S.P. _Opisanie zemli Kamchatki_, I-II (St. Petersburg, 1755); _Opisanie zemli Kamchatki_ (Moscow, 1949); _S.P. Krasheninnikov v Sibiri: neopublikovannye materialy_ (Moscow-Leningrad, 1966). _The History of Kamtschatka and the Kurilski Islands with the Countries Adjacent_, trans. James Grieve, I-II (Gloucester, 1763-6). This was reprinted in Chicago, 1962; _Beschreibung des Landes Kamtschatka_ (Lemgo, 1766); _Explorations of Kamchatka. Report of a Journey Made to Explore Eastern Siberia in 1735-1741_. Trans. and edited by E.A.P. Crownhart-Vaughan (Portland, Oregon, 1972); _Histoire et description du Kamtchatka_, I-II (Amsterdam, 1770).

2. Steller, G. _Beschreibung von dem Lande Kamtschatka_, (Leipzig, 1774); _Reise von Kamschatka nach Amerika mit dem Commandeur-Capitän Bering_ (St. Petersburg, 1793); Coxe, _Account of the Russian Discoveries between Asia and America_, 4th edition (London, 1803), pp. 30-93; Golder, _Bering's Voyages_, II (New York, 1925).

3. Fischer, J. _Sibirischen Geschichte von der Entdeckung Sibiriens bis auf die Eroberung dieses Lands durch die russische Waffen_, Pts. I-V (St. Petersburg, 1768); _Sibirskaia istoriia s samago otkrytiia Sibiri do zavoevaniia sei zemli rossiiskim oruzhiem_ (St. Petersburg, 1774). In a foreword to the German edition, Müller's predominant role in the work was mentioned, but his name does not appear in the Russian version. Fischer never got to Kamchatka, and contributed nothing of note to the Kamchatka Expedition.

4. Gmelin, J.-G. _Reise durch Sibirien von dem Jahr 1733-1743_, I-IV (Göttingen, 1751-52); _Voyage en Sibérie_, I-II (Paris, 1767).

5. Chappe d'Auteroche, Abbe. _Voyage en Sibérie fait par ordre du roi en 1761_, I-IV (Paris, 1768); Catherine II, "L'Antidote," _Sochineniia_, VII, (ed.) A.M. Pypin (St. Petersburg, 1901).

6. Waxell, S. _Vtoraia Kamchatskaia ekspeditsiia Vitusa Beringa_ (Moscow-Leningrad, 1940); a translation of the original manuscript, in German. A Danish translation was the basis of _The American Expedition_ (New York, 1952), reprinted as _The Russian Expedition to America_ (New York, 1962).

7. Locatelli's book was printed as _Lettres Moscovites_ (Königsberg, 1736); _Lettres moscovites: or, Moscovian Letters_ (London, 1736); and _Die so gennante Moscowitische Brieffe_ (Frankfort, 1738). Only small parts of it dealt with the expedition.

8. "Nachricht von D. Daniel Gottlieb Messerschmidts Siebenjähriger Reise in Sibirien," Neue Nordische Beyträge, III (St. Petersburg und Leipzig, 1782), pp. 97-157; Forschungsreise durch Sibirien, 1720-1727. Edited by E. Winter and N.A. Figurovsky, I-V (Berlin, 1962-68).

9. Strahlenberg, P.J.T. von. Das Nord-und östliche Theil von Europa und Asien (Stockholm, 1730); An Historico-geographical Description of the Northern and Eastern Parts of Europe and Asia (London, 1738); this was reprinted in 1970; Description historique de l'émpire russien, I-II (Amsterdam, 1757).

10. Pallas, P.S. Reise durch verschiedene Provinzen des russischen Reichs, I-III (St. Petersburg, 1771-76); a second edition was printed in St. Petersburg in 1776-77, and another appeared in Frankfurt and Leipzig, 1776-78. A Russian printing appeared in 1773-88; Pallas' work was also translated into English, French and Italian; Georgi, Bemerkungen einer Reise im Russischen Reichs, I-II (St. Petersburg, 1772-75); Falk, Beyträge zur topographischen Kenntnis des russischen Reichs, edited by Georgi, I-III (St. Petersburg, 1765-86; Güldenstädt, Reisen durch Russland und im Caucasischen Gebürge, edited by Pallas, I-II (St. Petersburg, 1787-91); Lepekhin, Tagebuch der Reise durch verschiedene Provinzen des Russischen Reiches, 1768-69, I-IV (St. Petersburg, 1771-1805); a Russian translation appeared in 1795-1814; Samuel Gmelin, Reise durch Russland zur Untersuchung der drei Natur-Reiches, Pts. I-IV (St. Petersburg, 1770-84); Samuel Gmelin was Johann's nephew. His book also appeared in a Russian translation, 1771-85. See generally, Lomonosov, Schlözer, Pallas: deutsch-russische Wissenschaftsbeziehungen im 18. Jährhundert (Berlin, 1962), and Gert Robel, "Der Wandel des deutschen Sibirienbildes im 18. Jährhundert", Canadian/American Slavic Studies, 14, no. 3 (Fall 1980), pp. 406-26.

11. Belevye puteshestviia chrez' Rossiiu i raznyia aziatskiia zemli: a immeno; v Ispagan, v Pekin, v Derbent i Konstantinopol, I-II (St. Petersburg, 1776); "Predislovie", p. 1.

12. Materialy dlia istorii imperatorskoi akademii nauk, VI (St. Petersburg, 1890).

13. On Müller's publications on Russian sea voyages and their translation into most West European languages, see bibliography. See also Carol Urness, Bering's Voyages: The Reports from Russia by Gerhard Friedrich Müller (Fairbanks, Alaska, 1986). Urness' collection does not incude any of the Müller material about Siberia.

G.-F. MÜLLER AND SIBERIA *

I

Gerhard-Friedrich Müller was born on 18 October 1705, in Herford, Westphalia. His father was a rector of the local gymnasium.[1] After completing a gymnasium education, Müller studied in Rinteln for a year and in 1723 was admitted to the University of Leipzig. There his main instructors were Johann Gottsched, a junior professor who was to become one of Germany's most respected journalists, and J.-B. Mencke, Privy Councillor of Saxony and one of the senior scholars at Leipzig. Müller was given employment with J.-P. Kohl, a church historian who was responsible for the university library. On Mencke's recommendation in 1725, Kohl and Müller were offered contracts by the Imperial Russian Academy of Sciences - which was founded in that year. Kohl was hired as a professor of rhetoric and church history; Müller agreed to accompany him to Russia as his student and as a teacher of history, geography, and Latin at the Academy gymnasium. Two years later, Müller was promoted to the Academy as adjunct.

In June 1728 Müller was asked to edit the St. Petersburg Gazette for the Academy. The next year a special supplement to the Gazette, called at first the Historical, Genealogical, and Geographical Notes, and later the Supplement, was also put in his charge. At the same time he took over the printing of Commentarii Academiei:, and its abbreviated Russian language version which appeared first in 1728.[2] As if these chores were not enough, Müller undertook the duties of vice-secretary of the Academy Conference, acted as assistant to the Academy librarian, and for the first six months of 1730 actually managed the affairs of the Chancellery of the Academy when its secretary, J.-D. Schumacher, was called to Moscow. As a result of all this labour, the Academy Conference unanimously agreed to name Müller Professor of History and ordinary member of the Academy.[3] At the age of twenty-five, Müller's star was clearly rising.

But his rapid ascendancy halted abruptly in the latter half of 1730. As Schumacher's protégé Müller incurred the enmity of several academicians; so in part to escape a hostile atmosphere and in part because of his father's death, he returned to Germany in August. To justify his leaving St. Petersburg while still under contract to the Academy, Schumacher commissioned Müller to order books and scientific equipment, and to recruit personnel for

---

*   Much of the material in this introductory essay was drawn from information scattered through the eight chapters of my book, G.-F. Müller and the Russian Academy of Sciences (Montréal/ Kingston, 1986). This essay, however, is focussed on Müller and Siberia, and draws much more heavily on Gmelin's account than does the earlier study - in which Müller's Siberian interests received only secondary attention.

1

the Academy in England, Holland, and in his homeland. After a very successful voyage, Müller arrived back in the Russian capital in September 1731 only to find that for some reason Schumacher had turned against him. Thus, having lost one avenue to a successful career, that is, as Schumacher's assistant, Müller decided to make his way as a scholar of "Russian history, which I intended not only to study industriously myself but to make known in compositions from the best sources. A daring undertaking! I had so far done nothing in this subject and was still not altogether skilled in the Russian language."[4]

With the help of G.-S. Bayer, the only Academy historian of ancient Russian, Müller pored over Russian sources (using translators until his Russian improved). With Bayer's help, in 1732 he founded and edited the Sammlung russischer Geschichte (Collection of Russian History), through which he hoped to make enough Russian sources available to make it possible to prepare a full Russian history. In spite of these labours, however, Müller was so harried by Schumacher that in 1733 he volunteered to join Captain-Commander Vitus J. Bering's second expedition to Kamchatka.[5] As one of three Academy representatives on the trip, Müller spent the next decade travelling through Siberia gathering historical documents and carrying out ethnographical and astronomical projects. Although illness prevented him from going on to Kamchatka, his ten years of research in Siberia have benefited all future studies of the area and its peoples.[6]

II

In 1716, G.W. Leibniz, planner of the Berlin Academy of Sciences, proposed to Peter the Great that "the extensive lands of the Russian Empire ... offer excellent opportunities ... for new discoveries by which the sciences are advanced." He further suggested that Peter might "render a great service" by ordering the exploration of the northern seas and the geographical relationship between Asia and America. Leibniz also observed that the huge empire would undoubtedly "yield many plants, animals, minerals, and other natural objects that have not yet been discovered."[7]

These suggestions were timely, if not decisive in Peter's decision to explore and open up the vast potential of his domain. In fact, Leibniz had broached the subject regularly since 1697 when he first mentioned it to François Lefort, Peter's adviser. One of Peter's own subjects, F.S. Saltykov, made similar recommendations in 1714.[8] But Peter had taken the initiative himself already in 1699 when he ordered a survey of the Caspian Sea. The first attempt failed, so in 1703 Captain Jeremiah Meyer of Hamburg was sent off to complete the project. Meyer was killed in Astrakhan in 1705, but left a map of the Caspian which was printed in 1723.[9] There were various other schemes to map the Caspian and Russia's borders with both Persia and Turkey, but in the long run the most important were those in which F.I. Soimonov and J.G. Gerber were involved. Soimonov went to Astrakhan in 1719

nd helped Karl van Werden and Johan Rentel prepare a detailed map
f the entire coastline of the Caspian. This map was taken to
aris by Schumacher in 1721 and published by Joseph Nicolas
elisle, who shortly afterwards agreed to come to St. Petersburg
s the Russian Academy's first astronomer.[10] Gerber began a survey
f the west coast of the Caspian inland in 1722. His work was
rinted in 1735. Both Gerber and Soimonov were to play
ignificant roles in Müller's career.

While the Caspian region was being successfully charted,
eter began looking towards the wide expanse of Siberia,
amchatka, and even the potential of trade with Japan and America.
ut it was only after regular reports of disorder, lawlessness,
nd finally rebellion on the part of the cossacks and native
eoples in Eastern Siberia between 1710 and 1714, that Peter was
ersuaded to appoint the Great Kamchatka Command in 1716. Although
hat expedition never took place, it set the stage for others. The
ext year Peter discussed the geography of Siberia with Guillaume
elisle, Joseph Nicolas' older brother and even more prominent
ember of the Academie de Sciences in Paris, who in 1706 had
rinted a map which implied there might be a chain of mountains
onnecting Siberia and "quelque autre Continent."[11]

In 1719 the geodesists Fedor Luzhin and Ivan Evreinov
ravelled to Kamchatka and prepared maps and reports on the region
nd on the Kurile Islands.[12] They had secret instructions to
iscover whether Asia and America were joined, but this they were
revented from doing because of a sea accident. While the
oastline was being explored, Peter also called for major
ompaigns to chart the resources of inland Siberia. In 1718
aniel G. Messerschmidt was contracted to explore western and
entral Siberia, with orders to list its plants, its human
esources, and to outline its natural history. The next year he
ent to Tobol'sk, which remained his headquarters for the next
even years. During that time, Messerschmidt gathered large
ollections of rocks, plants and animal specimens, made
omparisons of local languages, drew maps, and in 1727 was able to
eposit an unprecedented quantity of material in the Kunstkamera
Museum) in St. Petersburg. P.J.T. von Strahlenberg, a Swedish
fficer who lived in Tobol'sk from 1711 to 1721 as a prisoner of
ar, accompanied Messerschmidt in 1721-22, and in 1730 published
n Stockholm the first historical and geographical accounting of
iberia.[13] All these scattered projects were incorporated into
he law of the land in February, 1720, when as part of a general
kaz on the organization of Colleges (Ministries), Peter ordered
eodesists to describe "all boundaries, rivers, cities, towns,
hurches, villages, forests, and so on", in the empire. A
upplemental order of 1721 called for even more detailed
escriptions of Peter's realm.[14]

Earlier attempts to discover whether Asia and America were
oined by land having failed, in December 1724 Peter commissioned
ering to lead the Great Northern, or what is better known as The
irst Kamchatka Expedition to the easternmost tip of the Russian
mpire. Bering set out from St. Petersburg by land in January

1725, with his lieutenants Aleksei Chirikov and Martin Spangenberg, and a huge team of geodesists, navigators, seamen shipbuilders, and soldiers. Bering had a number of specific tasks to perform: to find out whether there was a north-eastern route by land between Asia and America; to prepare detailed maps of the empire; to enumerate its resources; and, above all, to reconnoiter the coast of America.[15] During five years of extreme hardship he reached Okhotsk, built a ship, transported goods to the west side of Kamchatka, provoked a bloody rebellion on the part of the Kamchadals (1730-31), constructed another ship at Nizhne-Kamchatsk and sailed as far north as Cape Chukotka.

In March 1730 Bering returned to St. Petersburg. Müller was responsible for printing an official notice about Bering's exploits in the St. Petersburg Gazette,[16] but at that time he was not much interested in Siberia or Kamchatka. After his return from Europe in 1731, however, Müller's newly found interest in the history and geography of the Russian Empire attracted him immediately to the proposals Bering made for another more grandiose trek to Kamchatka.

After more than a year of discussion, the Russian Senate issued several orders under Empress Anna's imprint. Together they called for a vastly complex and expensive project of exploration, re-organization, and mapping of Eastern Siberia and Kamchatka; the charting of the Arctic coast of Siberia; and visits to the coasts of America and Japan for the purpose of setting up trade relations. In June, the Senate formally approved a proposal to involve the Academy of Sciences directly in the expedition, and appointed a group of professors to undertake scientific research in Siberia and Kamchatka.[17] It had not been easy to persuade the government to sponsor a second Bering expedition. Aside from the general malaise caused by the advent of a new monarch and new favourites in 1730, there was no longer the interest in discovery which had been a feature of the petrine court. Moreover, Joseph Nicolas Delisle persuaded the Admiralty College that Bering's charts were inaccurate. But Bering was able to win the support of Ivan K. Kirilov, senior secretary to the Senate, who was himself an enthusiastic statistician and geographer. In turn, Kirilov swayed Count Ostermann to favour Bering by emphasizing the potential such an enterprise represented for trade, missionary work, and profit from natural resources.

While official discussion and constant rumours about what was known variously as the Great Northern or Second Kamchatka Expedition, were going on, Müller developed a concern for eastern subjects. Since Bayer and his translator, J.-W. Pus, were eastern specialists and Müller himself had read books by Nicolas Witsen on Tatars, by J.G. Gerber on towns in the Caucasus, and Bayer's own study of Azov, his intersts were easily channeled towards Siberia. Müller fully intended to expand a study of the Kalmyks which he began in 1732, and actually printed essays on the Samoyeds in both the Notes and the Sammlung.[18] Indeed, Müller became directly involved with the expedition when Kirilov asked him to translate communiques on the subject for Anna's chief adviser, Duke Ernst iron. But in the long run, Müller said it was "Bering - to whom was very well known, who stimulated in me a desire to join the voyage even when there seemed to be no chance of my going."[19]

The original Academy appointments to the expedition were J.-. Gmelin and Louis Delisle de la Croyère, Nicolas Delisle's half-brother. Providentially for Müller, Gmelin grew ill and was excused from participation, so Müller "offered his services to describe the civil history of Siberia and its antiquities, with the manner and customs of the people, and also the occurrences of the voyage, which was likewise approved of by the Senate." Kirilov and Ostermann both supported his application, which Müller claimed was put forward by Bering himself. Official sanction was given Müller on 23 March 1733. Then Gmelin's health improved--allegedly after drinking two full bottles of the "best Rhine wine"--and he was reinstated to the expedition with no prejudice to Müller's participation.[20]

On 5 July 1733, Müller, Gmelin, and de la Croyère were given their general instructions from the Chancellory. De la Croyère was told to make astronomical observations and Gmelin was expected to report on "everything that concerns natural history."[21] Müller's job was to describe the history of those peoples whose paths he crossed while in the company of Bering. He was also to observe and comment upon their religions, village life, customs, commerce, military and political forms, language, the regions in which they dwelt, costumes, "and especially to observe in detail the origin, morals, customs, and so on of those peoples who live on the north side of the Amur River, because it is rumoured that a Russian Nation lived there in ancient times." [See Document 1] Müller was also to keep "an accurate journal in the Latin language." As Gmelin put it in the memoir which he published some twenty years later, their job was to "generally learn everything that has scientific interest."[22] A tall order indeed!

About six hundred persons were assigned to the Second Kamchatka Expedition.[23] They were divided into three detachments --the Academy unit was to go overland to Eastern Siberia with Bering; another group was to proceed by the northern sea route; and a third party was to go overland, build ships in Siberia and sail to the coast of Japan. Two landscape artists, a physician, an interpreter, an instrument-maker, four surveyors, five students to assist the professors, and fourteen guards accompanied the academicians.

Nine wagonloads of instruments, including two large telescopes, a substantial library (to which they constantly added titles), writing paper, paints, drafting material, and other items considered necessary for scientific endeavours were dragged along by some forty packhorses. The academics carried official documentation which gave the right to examine any archive collection and to requisition interpreters and guides at local expense. They received an enormous raise in salary (from 600 to 660 rubles each) and permission to purchase items at Academy expense.[24] Furthermore, Müller and his two colleagues were

granted the privilege of private quarters, the right to deman
assistance from Bering for their exploratory side trips, an
freedom from his authority. All in all, this amounted to quite
coup for the newly appointed professors. Müller was then twenty
eight years old and Gmelin only twenty-four. They had littl
idea, however, of how rough and potentially dangerous Siberi
could be; nor did they have any notion of how their presence an
privileges complicated Bering's administrative chores.

The expedition departed St. Petersburg in stages. Captai
Spangenberg, Bering's second-in-command, left with the heavies
equipment in February. Bering followed in April, going first t
Novgorod, then to Tver, Kazan, Ekaterinburg, and Tobol'sk. Th
Academy contingent, which was to take the same route, did no
leave until 8 August. Because of the size of their entourage an
the bulk of their supplies, the academics achieved "often not mor
that 12 or 15 versts per day" (that is eight to ten miles), an
did not reach Tver until the second week of September. Unforesee
incidents delayed them as well - the breakdown of Müller's wagon
and a "small crisis" when the student Ivanov somehow shot a woma
who lived in the house where he was quartered.[25] In a detaile
report to St. Petersburg from Tver, the Academy was informed tha
Gmelin already had found "new or unnamed grasses and trees", an
also had listed all known plants and their locations along th
way.   In Novgorod Gmelin and Müller visited monasteries while d
la Croyère set up his astronomy equipment and recorde
observations. As well, Müller studied epitaphs and other source
of genealogical information about Russia's nobility. A patter
was thus set which they tried to follow throughout their lon
voyage to Siberia.[26]

Terrible weather during their two weeks at Tver prevente
Gmelin and de la Croyère from compiling botanical and astronomica
reports, but Müller had some success when he discovered a fe
documents pertaining to the lives of former great princes. Thei
first realization that orders from St. Petersburg might carry les
and less authority as they moved east in the Russian Empir
occurred in Tver.   There the artist Johann Berkan had bee
arrested when priests from the church he was sketching becam
suspicious of his motives and had the local constabulary take hi
in.   By the time Müller obtained his release night had fallen
Berkan never completed his sketches because on the followin
morning they boarded the large, well supplied barque left them b
Bering, and proceeded in relative comfort to Kazan. They arrive
on 18 October.

The voyage from Tver proved very fruitful. At Mologa, Gmeli
discovered more new rocks and collected samples to send back t
the Kunstkamera. He and de la Croyère twice daily kept track o
barometric and meteorological conditions, and made corrections o
their maps of the Volga.   Müller listed and described th
tributaries, islands, rapids, towns, and villages of the grea
river. At Uglich, he found genealogical information on princes o
that town and of Rostov.   While in Iaroslavl, however, he wa
prevented from pursuing such investigations by church authoritie

who simply ignored his orders from the Senate.[27]   At Nizhnii
Novgorod, Müller found a much more co-operative cleric who showed
him documents on nineteen members of the Russian great princely
families.   But farther down the river, at Cheboksary, he and
Gmelin tried for three days in the company of an interpreter and
two soldiers (who were Chuvash themselves) to get information
from Chuvash villagers.   Müller said that they had very little
success in this venture.   But Gmelin was able to describe their
dwellings, religious customs, and some of their social practices.
Apparently they worshipped one God, Tora; believed in the sanctity
of the sun, and prayed to many small idols which were set up in
their villages.   One of their favourite pastimes, Gmelin reported,
was to steal horses from the Russians.   Quoting an unnamed
voevoda, he added that even though Orthodox missionaries had
baptized many of the Chuvash, their conversion was only
superficial.   Müller could not have published such information in
St. Petersburg.[28]

Both their successes and failures proved exciting to Müller
and Gmelin.   Even though Müller's most thoughtful recollection of
this voyage was put to paper some forty years later, the
excitement he felt while travelling along the Volga and when he
first sighted the towns of Uglich, Iaroslavl, Kostroma, Nizhnii
Novgorod, and Makar'ev, the "Cheremises and Chuvash in their
environment", and the great monasteries, still stands out.   Within
three days of their arrival in Kazan, the rivers froze over, so
they had time to examine that "remarkable city".   Although the
commandant of Kazan, P.I. Musin-Pushkin, assisted them only
reluctantly, Müller was able to report on its Tatar features, the
remnants of ancient Tatar townsites, churches and seminary which
he visited, conversations with individuals who had travelled from
Kazan to Astrakhan and Persia, and the effects of Russian
schooling on speakers of Tatar, Chuvash, and other indigenous
languages.   Assisted by a Major La Mothe, he also watched Tatars
and Votiaks taking oaths on the Koran as they were inducted into
the Imperial Russian army.

Gmelin spent much of his extra time observing the rites of
the Tatar religion, while Müller compiled a simple vocabulary of
non-Russian languages of the Kazan region.   Among the peoples he
referred to specifically were the Tatars, Chuvash, Mordvins,
Cheremises (now Mari), and the Votiaks (now Udmurts).   He took key
words, most of which reflected their way of life, and gave them
Latin equivalents.   He used and added to this list for the next
ten years.   While Müller set about recording the local languages,
his artists depicted costumes, dwellings, religious sites, and
villages.   He was also shown ancient Tatar coins and had drawings
made of them.   By the end of 1733 Müller had organized his
research on the people of Kazan into a paper for publication.   He
sent this to St. Petersburg but it was not printed until 1756.[29]

To a certain extent, the staggering multiformity of Müller's
interests was forced on him, and on his companions, by the Academy
Chancellory.   In October 1733 the Academy insisted that Latin and
Russian language copies of all "astronomical and magnetic

8   G.-F. MÜLLER AND SIBERIA

observations, the history and inscriptions from the Cathedral,
churches, and monasteries of Novgorod, descriptions of the
mountains near Bronnitsy and its different plants, either in
drawings or actually impressed in paper; and two charts, one of
Novgorod, the other of the mountains ... ", be sent back to St.
Petersburg. In their turn, the professors pestered the Academy
for medicines (which the Senate ordered Bering to release from his
own supply), Academy publications, scientific books, and money to
pay local coachmen and scribes.[30]

     To facilitate communications between the Expedition and the
Capital, Bering had been instructed to establish a monthly postal
service from points east of Moscow. He was to arrange this system
in consultation with local officials, but the dearth of men,
horses, roads, and the vast uninhabited distances which the
couriers had to cover, assured this scheme's failure.[31]
Increasingly, communications between St. Petersburg's Senate, the
Admiralty, the Academy and their respective charges in Siberia
were characterized by long and frustrating delays. The situation
was made worse for Bering in that he had not been granted
authority over the academicians or even over regional officials.

     De la Croyère, who had continued to take astronomical and
"magnetic" observations at Kazan, left there on 8 December. Müller
and Gmelin set out three days later. They proceeded by sledge
along the Kama River to Sarapul and Osa, and then overland to
Kungur and Ekaterinburg, where they caught up to de la Croyère on
29 December. At Ekaterinburg they were hosted by General-
Lieutenant George von Hennin, who was more amenable to their
wishes than had been his counterpart in Kazan. Hennin had resided
in the region since 1722 when he had been sent to Kungur as
director of mining and manufacturing for the Urals and Siberia.
He was an avid collector of historical and current information on
Siberia, and proved to be especially useful to Müller and
Gmelin.[32]

     On 9 January de la Croyère left for Tobol'sk, leaving Müller
and Gmelin to visit several local mining sites. A letter from
Bering, however urging them to make haste to Tobol'sk prompted
Müller to leave a week later. Gmelin, who had not completed his
observations, followed shortly thereafter. Thus the academic
expedition came to be scattered into separate, and therefore more
expensive, groups across the Siberian expanse. They straggled
into Tobol'sk between 15 and 30 January 1734, Gmelin having
stopped for some time at the Kamenskii zavod, the oldest iron
works in Siberia, and at the Irbit annual fair.[33]

     Müller and his colleagues had the good fortune to find in
Tobol'sk governor Alexei L'vovich Pleshcheev, an official anxious
to assist them in any way he could. Himself an author of an
historical-geographical manuscript on Siberia, Pleshcheev was
well-qualified to direct their activity. But the Tobol'sk
archives did not contain any documentation of the Russian conquest
of Siberia. Müller did find, though, an old Siberian illustrated
chronicle, the authenticity of which he was certain. He sent this

back to St. Petersburg "as especially precious", and later included it in the first part of his Siberian history.[34]

Many other items were catalogued and copied by Müller's assistants. His four and a half months' experience in Tobol'sk proved to be of inestimable value, for it afforded him both the time and the necessary co-operation from the authorities to work out a methodology for his later searches. Müller was concerned primarily with historical documents. His general approach was first to re-arrange the old records - or rolls (stolbtsy), and books chronologically, noting their contents, and designating those to be copied. This work usually followed questions he submitted to regional chancellories, placing the onus on them to locate documents for him, and to provide both translators and clerks to make extracts.

Brandishing the authority granted him by the Senate, Müller and his staff prepared descriptions of towns, islands, mining sites, trade patterns, settlements, religions, and other dimensions of regions they visited. He and Gmelin sought out artifacts and relics, purchased drawings, idols, weapons, items from grave sites, gathered samples of clothing, and collected coins from the native peoples. In 1734 Müller began to prepare maps of Siberia and within a year was able to send charts of the Irtysh and Ob River regions to the Academy. It was in Tobol'sk that the young explorers first witnessed orgies of drunkenness, extreme passion, and sporadic fits of gluttony which Gmelin at least came to believe was characteristic of the Siberian - and Russian - way of life. Gmelin was later to describe such incidents in detail - from a safe desk in Tübingen - while Müller never mentioned them. Gmelin also found the inhabitants of Tobol'sk to be an interesting mixture. A quarter of them were Tatars. The rest were Russian, nearly all of whom were exiles or children of exiles. He and Müller had great difficulty in finding people willing to work for them, a fact which Gmelin attributed to the apparent abundance of food, inexpensive bread, and more cattle than he observed in any other Siberian town.[35]

Their Tobol'sk stay was especially productive academically. Before he left the region, Müller had posted a list of ancient Tatar and Armenian grave inscriptions, translated into Russian; a history of the origins of Kungur; notes on Siberian and Kazan history; vocabularies for the Tatar and Vogul languages; and a translation of a prayer book into Vogul. Gmelin sent observations on natural history, which included depictions of caves at Kungur, notes on the water of the Silvo River, descriptions of Kalmyk cows, sables, and an account of the Irbit fair.[36]

In May 1734, they left Tobol'sk and journeyed south on the Irtysh to Tara, Omsk, Zhelezinskaia, Iamyshevskaia, Semipalatinsk, and Ust'-Kamenogorsk. En route they visited the site of what was alleged to be the ancient city of Sibir, where they found some old, collapsed walls. De la Croyère left them at Omsk and accompanied one of Bering's captains to Iakutsk, arriving there in the summer of 1735. Bering had gone to Iakutsk in the spring of

1734, after a year in Tobol'sk supervising the construction of a
vessel (the Tobol) large enough to carry the first task force
north on the Irtysh to the Arctic Ocean. There were many delays,
not the least being that caused by the leisurely manner in which
our heroes had made their way to Tobol'sk. They had with them the
surveyors and instruments Bering needed to make final plans for
his voyage.

A few days after the Tobol left port, Bering went to Iakutsk.
There he found that no provision had been made for him, and his
supplies did not arrive until the following spring. Nevertheless,
Bering was able to build two more ships. He also sent these to
the Arctic, this time along the Lena River, One ship was to turn
west and chart the coast to the Enisei, the other was to turn east
and survey the coast to the Kamchatka Peninsula. Bering remained
in Iakutsk in order to construct more ships, dwellings, iron
foundries and an entire complex from which to supply and organize
the various parts of his expedition. But administrative
roadblocks caused long delays. They were the consequence in part
of the incompetence and spitefulness of Major-General Pisarev,
harbour-master and de facto governor of Okhotsk, a town from which
the final stages of the expedition were to be launched. The
bureaucratic obstructionism, and increasing rancour between Bering
and local officials eventually eroded Müller's and Gmelin's
enthusiasm for Kamchatka.

Later in the spring of 1734 Gmelin and Müller set out
northwest for Tomsk, Eniseisk and Krasnoiarsk. As Müller later
wrote, the joy of discovery was still upon them and "everything
that we saw was new to us." They still had not faced the
discomfort, lack of supplies and even dangers which were to
confront them in subsequent years. They found Tomsk unpleasant,
however, because an epidemic of some sort had killed "all but ten
cows [of more than 100] and left only two or three horses", the
summer before their arrival. Gmelin said that there were more
mice there than he had ever seen in one place before, and that
even the local cats could not keep them under control. Moreover,
he guessed that at least one person in each household suffered
from syphilis, because of the loose living which predominated.
Throughout the spring and summer of 1734 they also had their first
real experience with mosquitoes, which Gmelin said were so vicious
in Ilimsk that they tormented cattle to death. They were forced
to sleep under hot screening, to wear veils on their faces and
gloves on their hands at all times. At Eniseisk they encountered
a cold spell in December which was so drastic that "birds fell out
of the sky as though dead and froze if not immediately taken into
a warm room." But they continued undaunted to compile
information. A caravan of some 200 camels driven by Russians,
Tatars, and Bukharans arrived in Tomsk while they were there, so
that Müller was able to gather considerable data on trade. At
Kransnoiarsk Müller again was informed about trade routes by means
of long discussions with Kalmyk and Buryat merchants who formed
part of the caravan system of that region.

March of 1735 found Müller and Gmelin en route to Irkutsk.

There they had difficulty persuading the vice-governor, Andrei Pleshcheev, to grant them access to the archives, or even to arrange supplies for their retinue. Pleshcheev demanded immediate payment for any services rendered and countered their complaints by saying that it was they who worked for him - he was under no obligation to them. In June they moved east to Nerchinsk, pausing on the way to Selenginsk and Kiakhta, the way station for Russian trade with China.

On this tour Gmelin and Müller had their first extended experience with deserts, where they found the dry heat to be nearly intolerable.[37]   At Kiakhta, Müller dicussed matters of trade with Brigadier Ivan D. Bukholz, who had been responsible for border security and commerce in the city since 1728. Müller also observed both private trading and the organization of a government caravan.   At Nerchinsk he completed a long report on the Tungus language and customs (which appeared in the Commentarii in 1747). He and Gmelin also spent some time in consultation with two of Bering's land surveyors who had been in Nerchinsk for nearly a year trying to obtain guides and supplies for a mapping expedition to the Ud River.   Their purpose was to find a practical route from Nerchinsk to the Pacific, and it was in part from their subsequent lack of success that Müller was to conclude that Russia's trade interests would be served best by taking control of the Amur.[38] Gmelin once again was struck by what in his opinion seemed to be a prevalence of "shameful vices", disease, and a general laziness among the people.[39]   He also labelled the local voevoda corrupt and incompetent.

Returning to Irkutsk in September, Müller and Gmelin found Pleshcheev somewhat more amenable and so they remained there until January 1736.   It was so cold at Irkutsk, Gmelin said, that they spent most of their time in bed;   ironically, he also wrote that the local population "loved idleness, wine, and women to excess." From Irkutsk they went north on the Angara to Ilimsk.   There Müller adopted a new system for searching out archival material. Instead of randomly examining registry lists and checking those items he wished to see, he now divided documents chronologically, concentrating on materal from specific eras, such as the "Time of Troubles", and leaving other well-defined categories to his assistants.

The year 1735 was an especially fruitful one for the Academy contingent in general, and for Müller in particular.   Among the many articles he sent back to St. Petersburg were ancient and more recent Chinese coins; a description of an old townsite which had been called Sibir and in Müller's time featured a saltpeter works; some historical documents from Tobol'sk; chronological notes on an old calendar which dated everything from Creation; two stones, one with the head of a bear, the other a ram; copies of documents from the Tara archives which referred to Russian history; genealogical notes about the Romanov family; calculations of the distances from Tobol'sk to Tara, Tara to Tomsk, Tomsk to Verkhne-Irtyshshkie; vocabularies of the Kalmyk and Bukharan languages; measurements of the Iamyshevskii salt lake; and notes on grave sites and towns

along the Irtysh. As well, some fifty other items were crated and
shipped that year. All were then noted in a report which Müller
compiled for the Senate in 1746.   Gmelin's reports were as
extensive, if not so varied.

Müller and Gmelin spent the winter of 1735-36 in Iakutsk with
Bering, de la Croyère, and the remainder of the Kamchatka
Expedition (which had now grown to 800 persons). This was their
first protracted association with the harassed Bering and the
proximity was not to their liking. Müller later wrote that Bering
and Spangenberg "had little success in whatever they undertook.
Everything went on so slowly that one could not foresee when the
trip to kamchatka would begin."[40] Pleading a lack of necessary
academic supplies, Müller and Gmelin avoided making the trip to
Kamchatka when the opportunity finally arose. In their stead they
sent the student Krasheninnikov, armed with a detailed report on
the geography and conditions of Kamchatka prepared by Müller.[41]
Fierce cold, high winds, and generally harsh living conditions had
dissipated their passion for further northern travel. Gmelin
reported that by September 1735 the Lena was covered with ice a
yard and a half thick, that his windows, constructed of ice, let
in too little light to work by, and that he had to wear furs from
head to toe when outside.[42] Moreover, Gmelin and Müller had been
contracted to the Expedition for five years, and felt that if they
moved farther north-east, they could not return to the capital
within the allotted time.   Perhaps to justify in part their
failure to complete their mission to Kamchatka, Müller and Gmelin
sent reports back to St. Petersburg in which their respective
illnesses were featured prominently alongside tales of Bering's
incompetence and overbearing attitude.

A fire at Iakutsk destroyed half of Müller's money supply and
most of Gmelin's notes, books, and equipment They therefore had
to re-trace their steps north on the Lena in order to record again
Gmelin's observations. In September 1737, they journeyed together
to Kirenskii ostrog. Gmelin spent the winter there while Müller
went on to Irkutsk. Müller's health was instrumental in this
decision, for they knew a physician was wintering with a caravan
in that city. In spite of increasing ill health, Müller had found
the time in Iakutsk to prepare a series of notes on Kamchatka,
detailing the surrounding geography, plus the customs, commerce,
and settlements of the Kamchadals, Koriaks, and Kurils. These
reports, compiled from interviews and from materials located in
the Iakutsk archives, were passed on to Krasheninnikov in June.
The selection of Krasheninnikov to go to Kamchatka had been a
unanimous decision.   The student had already completed several
minor expeditions on his own and both Gmelin and Müller respected
his abilities. In turn, he reported to them regularly during his
three months in Okhotsk before he left Kamchatka.[43]

Müller was more seriously ill that winter, and in December
applied to St. Petersburg to be relieved of all further duties in
Siberia. While awaiting orders he continued to work on his
historical and ethnographical projects, but used his pending
request to avoid any commitment to Bering. Müller did present

Bering with a report based on information gleaned from explorers, sailors, and the Iakutsk archives on the "frozen sea" which allegedly separated Asia from America. He also found reports of seventeenth century voyages from the Lena to the Kolyma River. One revealed that a small boat captained by S.I. Dezhnev had sailed around the Chukotka Peninsula to Kamchatka in 1648, thereby preceding the Danish navigator through the Bering Straits by nearly a century.[44] The northeastern tip of Asia was now named Cape Dezhnev.

Müller later wrote, with some sarcasm, that even though he had posted this information to St. Petersburg, Bering still felt it necessary to prove geographical phenomena which he, Müller, had already demonstrated. His disgust is understandable, if somewhat misdirected. Müller and other academicians were convinced that the primary purpose of Bering's explorations was to discover whether Asia and America were connected, and had no idea of the degree to which the Admiralty and Senate also were concerned with exploration and obtaining trade reports about the American coast.

The two young professors wintered at Eniseisk in 1738 and investigated the languages, customs, and history of the Buriats and Tungus. On 31 March 1739, they received a senatorial decree allowing Müller to return to the capital if he continued his researches on the way home. The Academy ordered G.W. Steller, who had been assigned to the expedition in 1737 and was with them for several weeks at Eniseisk in 1739, to act as Gmelin's assistant. J.-E. Fischer was sent to replace Müller, and Jacob Lindenau, who was to become a prominent ethnographer, joined them as translator.[45] Gmelin's plea to return to St. Petersburg was denied, and Müller was ordered to turn over all his documentation and folios to Fischer. Though they were pleased to have Steller, neither Müller or Gmelin were satisfied with the results of their respective petitions. On 8 May, however, they were both instructed instead to prepare a "complete description of the Siberian provinces ... its geography and natural history ... in order that the Russian state may reap some benefits from the Kamchatka Expedition." Three copyists and two geodesists were sent to assist them.[46]

The reasons for the Academy and Senate decision are not known, but the fact that Schumacher was involved may in part explain their perverseness. He suspected that Gmelin, and especially Müller, were malingering. A 1738 memorandum to the Senate signed by Schumacher and Baron J.-A. Korff (president from 1734 to 1740) acknowledged their agents' poor health, but implied that it was Steller and Krasheninnikov who were doing the real work for the Academy in Siberia, and for much less pay than the professors. Later, in 1740, Schumacher filed a note to the effect that if Müller were to stay in Siberia, his expenses should be covered by local government agencies and not by the Academy.[47] But a more compelling reason for the Senate to demand some return for its huge investment was the fact that it was beginning to despair of the Bering expedition altogether. Reports from Siberian officials who disliked Bering had placed the entire project in

14   G.-F. MÜLLER AND SIBERIA

jeopardy again, as Martin Spangenberg learned to his distress in
1740. Spangenberg's successful voyage to Japan in 1738 had so
depleted the Okhotsk detachment's supplies that their long-awaited
departure for Kamchatka had to be postponed. But they were not
even allowed to rejoice in Spangenberg's noteworthy accomplishments, which included the charting of the Kurile Islands. While
on his way to St. Petersburg to report his findings personally to
the Senate, Spangenberg was intercepted in July 1740 at Kirenski
ostrog, accused of deception, and ordered to repeat his voyage to
Japan.[48] Thus Bering's departure for Kamchatka was delayed once
again.

     In fact, court and Academy intrigue had caught up with the
Kamchatka expedition. The office of president was in constant
state of flux, and the academicians still battled Schumacher. In
November 1734, Baron Korff replaced Baron H. K. Keyzerling (1733-
34); in 1736 he took on the imposing title of Supreme Commander.
When Korff was appointed minister to Denmark in 1740, he was
replaced by another of Anna's Baltic German officials, Karl von
Brevern. Brevern's term was cut short by the coup undertaken in
the name of Elizabeth, Peter's daughter, who promptly dismissed
almost all Germans from high office. Academy affairs were still
left to Schumacher, who had been appointed a director in 1738.[49]
By 1742, however, even his position became uncertain.

     This situation compounded Bering's difficulties. Always at
odds with Siberian officials who neither wished nor could afford
to deplete resources to assist the expedition, and left to manage
a vast enterprise with too little authority, Bering lost control
of his finances. Costs soared. His first estimates to Anna's
Chancellory had called for a sum which ranged between 10,000 and
12,000 rubles, apart from salaries, provisions and shipbuilding
materials.. By 1737, however, actual costs had gone beyond
300,000 rubles and Bering had nothing to show for it.[50] Some
members of the Senate suggested that the entire project be
abandoned; Soimonov proposed that Spangenberg replace Bering; and
the Admiralty pressured Bering to start out for Kamchatka. In
1737 he was deprived of his supplementary salary, with the warning
that it would not be renewed until the expedition got underway
again.

     Bering was finally ready to leave Okhotsk in the summer of
1740, but a number of unforeseen incidents - the change in orders
delivered by Spangenberg at the last moment; an accident which
cost them valuable supplies; and a revolt by harshly overworked
native peoples - resulted in his not reaching Kamchatka until
September. By then it was too late in the year to undertake the
voyage to America. Only in June of 1741 were Bering's two ships,
the St. Paul and St. Peter, able to set sail from Petropavlovsk.
After suffering through six months of storm, cold, shipwreck and
disease which killed many of his crew, the sixty year old Bering
died. The famous Danish explorer was buried on a desolate island
which later bore his name. His captain, Chirikov, suffered from
scurvy and died shortly after his return to St. Petersburg.
Officially terminated in 1743, the Great Northern Expedition

ctually limped on until 1749 under two of Bering's captains, but
ith little exploration or discovery after 1742.

In the meantime, Müller and Gmelin were still studying
iberia. In June 1739 they travelled north to Novaia Mangazeia
nd were so fascinated by the fact that there was little
ifference between night and day that they spent an entire night
atching the sun. They returned to Eniseisk in time to attend the
reat trade fair which took place annually in August.[51] In
eptember the academicians made their way south to Krasnoiarsk and
et up headquarters for a series of tours by horseback around the
egion between that city and Abakanskoe. They bribed Tatars to
lunder the tombs of their ancestors for artifacts and gold and
ilver ornamants and jewllery. Back in Krasnoiarsk they observed
n two separate occasions the punishment of women who had murdered
heir husbands. They were buried alive up to their necks and
llowed slowly to die of thirst - if sun stroke or insect bites
id not kill them first. One of the women had already languished
n prison for twelve years before this final retribution.[52]

In February 1740, leaving Gmelin in Krasnoiarsk, Müller
eparted for Tomsk. There, to his suprise, he found that the
rchives contained not one historical act. Indeed, the entire
ollection consisted of current documents. Although informed at
irst that the earlier materials had been destroyed by fire, he
iscovered to his horror that shortly before his arrival the local
oevoda had thrown all the old documents into the Tom River.[53]
rom Tomsk, Müller sailed up the Ob to Narym and Surgut, where he
et Fischer in June. He had already written the Academy a year
arlier expressing his concern over the decision to have Fischer
ake over his manuscripts. In that letter he had stressed the
ifficulties of his task, stating categorically that he could not
omplete his research without constant access to the material he
ad already collected.[54] Müller also pointed out that Fischer was
 novice in historical and ethnographical studies and so could not
ossibly make good use of his documentation. Although there is no
vidence to suggest that Müller had a reply from the Academy by
he time he confronted Fischer, he kept much of the folio material
or himself anyway and sent the rest to St. Petersburg.

Fischer's lack of preparation worried Müller, and Gmelin's
laim that Fischer was an unwilling worker[55] heightened his
nxiety. As a result, Müller rushed to complete a detailed series
f instructions for Fischer to use while gathering information on
he history and peoples of Siberia. The instructions included a
umber of briefly stated points, over 1,200 in all, categorized
nder six specific heading: authoritative journals; geographical
escriptions; The present circumstances of towns and regions;
ethods for examining archives and accounts of Siberian history;
ccounts of antiquity; describing the morals and customs of
eoples. The prospectus also included instructions on preparation
f maps and drawings, what items to collect for the Kunstkamera,
nd how to add words to the dictionary Müller had started in 1733.
üller had been preparing this guide since 1734, so Fischer's
oming was not responsible for its inception. Indeed, in 1740

Müller found and used a similar but shorter instruction which V.N.
Tatishchev had left in Krasnoiarsk in 1735.[56]

After Surgut, Müller proceeded northward on the Ob. In
Berezov he found several important historical documents and heard
enough "oral testimony", to prepare a description of peoples who
lived in the Arctic Ocean area. During the autumn of 1740 he went
again to Tobol'sk. There he wrote the Academy that his tour had
been especially beneficial, because of the information on the
"customs and way of life of the Ostiaks[now Khanty], Voguls [now
Mansi]", and the Samoyeds. He also complained that the Tobol'sk
archives had fallen into "such disorder that many rolls, or so-
called stolbtsy," which had been there in 1734, could no longer be
found. Müller grumbled further about the "coolness and slowness"
on the part of local officials. A letter to Euler of June, 1740
suggests that he had his fill of Siberia: "God grant that my
Siberian business will soon come to an end ... I do not wish to
complain, ... but there is hardly a town or part of Siberia in
which I have not been."[57]

In March 1741, Müller went to Tiumen, then to Irbit, and in
July reached Ekaterinburg. During the summer and fall he studied
thoroughly the surrounding areas, going as far south as
Cheliabinsk. He was reunited with Gmelin on the river Iset in
September, and together they returned to Tobol'sk. From Gmelin,
Müller discovered how fortunate they both had been insofar as
physical dangers were concerned. A few weeks earlier, Gmelin had
passed through two deserted villages and learned that every man,
woman and child had either been killed, tortured or taken away as
prisoners by a band of renegade cossacks.[58] Apparently such
large-scale acts of violence were becoming increasingly common.
Bands made up of cossacks, Russian exiles and criminals, and
Tatars were causing a situation of near civil war. In general the
brigands were after horses and trade goods and the frontier troops
seemed unable to stop them.

Müller and Gmelin stayed in Tobol'sk until January 1742, when
they set out for Turinsk. There Müller prepared a long report for
the Academy outlining the extent of his historical findings to
date. He claimed to have found enough material to "bring into
clarity the history of Siberia."[59] He pointed out, however, that
he could find nothing in this region on Siberian history prior to
1593, nor was there any information about Ermak's conquest of
Siberia in the 1570s.

While in Turinsk, Müller was stricken with pneumonia, and was
unable to resume research until that summer. At that time he
sailed north on the Tura River to Verkhotur'e. There he met and
married the widow of a German surgeon. Having now gathered almost
everything he needed, including a wife, Müller spent much of his
time during 1742 writing. He probably completed the first four
chapters of his history of Siberia before he got back to St.
Petersburg. Perhaps aware that they might never again have the
opportunity to travel eastward in the Russian Empire, Müller and
his bride returned to St. Petersburg in a relaxed manner. They

pent several weeks in Solikamsk where they and Gmelin were
mpressed by the family of N.A. Demidov, son of the State
hancellor:

> We were especially enthusiastic about the practices of
> Demidov, son of the Chancellor of State [wrote Gmelin]
> ... His wife is no less civil than he; their children
> are raised in a way that is rare in this country; by
> their manners, their politeness, their knowledge and
> their ability, they are far ahead of what is normal for
> children of their age. This Demidov is versed in
> natural history ... he has a very beautiful garden and a
> truly regal orangery in view of the rigorous climate.[60]

teller and Fischer also admired this garden in 1746.[61] Leaving
melin in Solikamsk, the Müllers passed through Vologda and
elozersk and reached the Russian capital on 14 February 1743.
melin followed three days later. According to Müller's own
alculations, he had travelled 31,362 versts (about 24,000 miles)
uring this decade in Siberia.

Between 1735 and 1738 Müller submitted to the Chancellory
ully prepared descriptions of the Kuznetsk (1735), Eniseisk,
angazeisk, Krasnoiarsk, Selenginsk (1736), and Nerchinsk (1737)
egions. He also sent information about the industries in the
ountains of Siberia and Perm, silver mines in Irkutsk, and the
orts along the Irtysh River (1735). In 1740 he forwarded a
atalogue of natural history specimens, and was commissioned by
he Senate to prepare a full study of the Amur River area for the
ice-governor of Irkutsk, Lorents Lange. Lange was preparing to
egotiate with the Chinese over trade rights and access to the
mur. Müller's "Nachrichten von dem Amur-Flusse", was completed
n early January 1741 and sent to St. Petersburg where it was
mmediately translated into Russian. In it Müller extolled the
irtues of the Amur as one of the most important waterways in
sia. He saw it as the means to eliminate many of the
ifficulties faced by Russians wishing to travel to Japan,
merica, and even to India. He referred to the Treaty of
erchinsk (1689), which gave the Chinese full control of the
iver, as illegal and deserving of repeal. Later he wrote that in
aking this report he was fulfilling his "full patriotic duty".
üller also wrote a short history of Irkutsk province and sent it
o the capital in 1736, was published in the Notes to the Gazette
n 1742. Such reports (the Nerchinsk treatise was 115 pages) were
ade possible through the use of questionnaires sent ahead to the
fficials of the region he wished to study.

All in all, Müller's accomplishments in Siberia were
emarkable. His collection of documents, abstracts from old
ecords, and artifacts, many acquired through the services of
rave robbers, have proved invaluable to later scholars of
iberia. His Folios contained enough raw material to enable him
o publish books and articles on Siberia for the next thirty-five
ears.

Müller's ethnographical work was vast, but his efforts t
catalogue, copy, and rearrange the historical documents in Siberi
were even more prodigious. The Siberian archives contained
great number of official documents sent from Moscow in the lat
sixteenth and throughout the seventeenth centuries to provincia
authorities, military commanders, and Church representatives.   I
many cases the originals had disappeared in western Russia.   I
Tobol'sk, Eniseisk, Iakutsk, and Verkhotur'e, the holdings wer
contained in large wooden buildings; in Tomsk they were stored i
a damp stone room. Most were in a state of acute disorder a
well, so Müller and his assistants first attempted to rearrang
them into some kind of chronological order. The information i
records later lost to fire and rot was saved for posterity. Th
fact that many documents in Tobol'sk and Tomsk disappeared durin
the six years between Müller's first and return visits testifie
to their high rate of loss.

Müller later insisted that local officials were reluctant t
help if their assistance cost them money. So he became more an
more demanding, proclaiming his rights in the name of the Senate
Nevertheless, even though he sent requests and questionnaire
ahead of him, much time was wasted while Müller waited for loca
copyists. He had brought competent assistants from St. Petersbur
- his translator Iakhontov, and the students Tret'iakov
Krasheninnikov, and Gorlanov. Iakhontov died at Eniseisk in 173
but the last two, and the artist Berkan left him to go t
Kamchatka. Berkan was replaced by Johann Decker who, Müller said
"was good as a copyist but had no talent for drawing animals."[6]
Generally, though, he had to rely upon personnel provided by loca
authorities and he complained repeatedly about the quality o
their work.

In spite of such difficulties, Müller arrived at the Academ
feeling, rightly, that he had accomplished something of importanc
for that institution. His completed and catalogued collection
included forty-two books of documents on the history and geograph
of Siberia, four books of Siberian and Kazan' chronicles, te
books of descriptions of Siberia prepared by Müller himelf, thre
books prepard by students and overseen by Müller, and a larg
quantity of maps, drawings, and city plans. He even delivere
fifteen books of reports, documents, letters, orders, and othe
forms of communications between his group and St. Petersbur
between 1733 and 1743. Müller promised soon to hand over th
journals of his and Gmelin's voyages, a history of Siberia,
geographical description of Siberia and its provinces, correcte
maps of Siberia, and a detailed account of the trade
administration, society, and customs of contemporary Siberia.[63]

III

Feeling the ill effects of his long bouts with pneumonia an
depression, Müller stayed away from the Academy Conference for
full month after his return to St. Petersburg. His long report t
the Senate, which included a register of all items he had poste

to the capital during his travels, was not ready until August. Müller's frequent illness had been regarded with suspicion by Schumacher, but the effect of the hardships of Siberia on body and mind could not be underestimated. Bitter cold, raging storms, oppressive heat, and swarming mosquitoes had taken their toll of the expedition. Bering suffered recurring spells of depression long before his death. De la Croyère died of scurvy aboard ship in 1741; Steller passed away of a "fever" at Tiumen in 1746, aged thirty-seven; Krasheninnikov's health was so impaired that he died in 1755 aged forty-two; Gmelin died in the same year of "exhaustion" after a long illness.[64]

Müller's absence from the Academy may also have been due to the fact that the institution was still in turmoil caused by the palace coup two years before. Schumacher had been accused of fraudulent practices and removed from office. Andrei Nartov, his replacement, charged Schumacher also with anti-Russian attitudes. Even though Schumacher was exonerated by the end of 1743, suffering only financial penalties for a few minor infractions, the situation at the Academy remained uncertain. Several staff members lost their positions, and the court issued directives which made it difficult for non-Russians to gain access to the Academy library, archives, and typography.[65]

Coupled with the Schumacher incident was a crisis sparked by a recently appointed (January 1742) Russian adjunct in chemistry, M.V. Lomonosov. When Müller returned to St. Petersburg, Lomonosov was already under ban for arriving at the Conference drunk and threatening violence to one of its members. Further fights and arguments caused several members, among them Müller, to ask that Lomonosov be removed from the Academy permanently. Lomonosov never forgave Müller for his participation in this matter,[66] and a highly charged rivalry began between the two lasted until Lomonosov's death in 1765. Besides the tension among the Academy personnel, Müller continued to find it difficult to collect monies owed him both for salary and expenses incurred during his decade in Siberia. Only in 1745 were he and Gmelin awarded payment for their debts.

Meanwhile, however, Müller labored over a new map of Siberia, using documentation from the Geographical Division and his own notes. But even this task proved to be more trouble than it was worth, for in April 1746 he was ordered to cease all such efforts. Apparently the government already had approved a proposal to create a map of the Second Kamchatka Expedition based on information compiled by Steller and Chirikov. Moreover, Schumacher had allowed the Geography Department of the Academy to publish a full atlas of Russia (Atlas rossiiskoi) in 1745. Even though the Atlas was filled with errors and criticized by the Academy Conference, its appearance forestalled the acceptance of a general map of Siberia prepared by Müller.

While the Atlas may have been printed by Schumacher in part to spite Müller, the charting of the Second Kamchatka Expedition had political overtones. Soon after seeing the Atlas, Müller

wrote the Imperial Cabinet directly and asked permission to use
maps of the Siberian coast and waterways recently drawn up by
naval officers. But when the chairman of cabinet ordered that the
maps be turned over to Müller by the Admiralty College, Vice-
Admiral Z.D. Mishukov balked at doing so. It was clear that
members of the Admiralty College did not wish to trust such
information to the Germans at the Academy. Mishukov stalled the
Cabinet for nearly a month and then requested that the project be
turned over to the Naval Academy. The court agreed and the
Academy Chancellery was ordered to gather together all maps
created by participants in the Kamchatka expedition and send them
to the cabinet. Thirty-six maps and plans, including Müller's
efforts, were assembled. The map of the Second Kamchatka
Expedition was completed by the Naval Academy in May. In that
way, Müller's efforts were forestalled and his own maps were not
returned to him until 1752. Only one scion of Russia's
officialdom recognized Müller's expertise. In 1744 Prince Boris
G. Iusupov ordered him to prepare a memorandum on trade in Siberia
for the College of Commerce. This was done, and the report was
later to be part of one of Müller's most important studies on
Siberia.

     Müller's own interest, however, still lay primarily with
history.   In a long proposal which he submitted to the new
president of the Academy, Count Kyril G. Razumovskii, in August
1746, Müller called for the establishment of a special historical
division at the Academy. The task of this new branch would be to
prepare for the writing of a definitive history of the Russian
Empire by collecting and organizing all available historical
materials.[67] Müller offered to oversee the new organization and
to finish his own history of Siberia while materials for the
larger study were being gathered.

     The first part of Müller's treatise on the history and nature
of Siberia had already been submitted to Elizabeth in 1744, and in
1746 Razumovskii had assigned Golubtsov the task of translating it
into Russian. It was obvious, however, that the Academy planned
to keep a vigilant eye on this German who was writing Russian
history. In August, the Chancellory asked Müller to outline his
"method" for writing history, and urged him to complete it as soon
as possible.[68] In February 1747 Razumovskii responded to Müller's
proposal about a History Division by ordering him to stick to his
task of finishing the history of Siberia and a geography of
Kamchatka.[69]

     Müller replied to Razumovskii's order by insisting that he
had too much else to do. He had already been involved for a year
in a crisis which developed after he was accused by Peter Krekshin
of seeking out historical information which was detrimental to
Russia.   These charges came after Müller had criticized
genealogical charts of Russia's royalty prepared by Krekshin.
After two months, Müller was cleared of any wrong-doing, but he
had lost a lot of research and writing time. Other jobs on which
he worked in 1747 were a geography of Siberia, its provinces and
districts; a geographical survey of Siberia; and a study of

Siberian trade, including data concerning Russian state interests there. He presented a series of lectures on the Tungus to the conference and then rewrote them for publication in the tenth volume of <u>Commentarii</u> (1747).[70] But most of his written papers remained in bureaucratic limbo for at least another decade.

Delays in the completion of Müller's many projects did not concern him particularly, for more exciting things were going on at the Academy. In July the Academy was granted a charter which for the first time carefully outlined the duties of its members. In November Müller signed a new, permanent contract; shortly thereafter he became a Russian citizen; and early in 1748 his proposal for an historical department finally was acted upon. The contract committed Müller to completing the Siberian history, "in which there shall be an accurate description of the geographical position of all Siberia, its religion, the language of all its native peoples, and Siberian antiquities." He was to be assisted by Fischer and was expected to print at least one volume of the study each year until the work was done. Only then was Müller to undertake a history of the Russian Empire, and for that task the contract named him Imperial Historiographer and director of the History Division. He was also appointed rector of the Academy university.[71]

The new Academy Charter endorsed Razumovskii as its first president since 1741, and gave real executive powers to a redefined Chancellory which was still directed by Schumacher.[72] The Charter also separated the university from the Academy insofar as the duties and ranks of its members were concerned. Müller was therefore no longer subject to the whims of the Academy Conference, but it cannot be said that he was free to work without outside interference. The Historical Division was authorized on 27 January 1748, with Fischer as Müller's assistant. But it was not the institution envisioned by Müller a few years earlier. The Senate decided to create also an Historical Assembly of professors to act as an advisory board to the Division. The Historical Assembly included all members of the Academy who were deemed expert in history and the "Humanities", (Poetry, Criticism, Philosophy). Thus, besides Müller and Fischer, the Assembly was joined by P.L. Le Roy (History) F.H. Strube de Piermont (Jurisprudence), V.K. Trediakovskii (Eloquence), Joseph Braun (Philosophy), Christian Crusius (Antiquity and Historical Literature), and Lomonosov. Razumovskii's own personal assistant, G.N. Teplov, combined the positions of assessor in the Academy Chancellory and manager of the financial affairs of the Historical Division.

The Historical Assembly proved to be a greater hindrance than help in the publication of Müller's Siberian history. It met on a weekly basis and was ordered to examine carefully anthing published in the domain of the Humanities. In short, it acted as a censorship board. Fischer checked every page of Müller's work and usually found something with which he could argue. To compound matters, in May 1748 Fischer decided to produce something of his own, and offered to write a compendium, or "lexicon" of

all materials on the history and geography of Siberia housed a
the Academy.   Müller immediately appealed to the Historica
Assembly and then to Razumovskii, saying that a student coul
perform that service easily; that he would not allow Fischer t
enumerate the unpublished items in his own collection; and tha
according to his contract, Fischer was supposed to be helping hi
with the Siberian history. Fischer countered by insisting that
student would not be qualified for such a task, that Müller had n
right to keep a fellow Academy historian from his collection, tha
his own contract said nothing about helping Müller, and that he
as a professor, should not be subordinate to another professor
Fischer decided not to go ahead with the lexicon, but relation
between him and Müller remained cool.

        Fischer and Müller had a particularly sharp exchange over th
latter's methods of preparing the history of Siberia fo
publication.   Fischer rather rudely suggested that Müller do mor
selecting and editing on the great number of documents which h
hoped to include verbatim in the study. Müller replied with som
heat that Fischer "hopes to turn me into a literary thief", an
referred to his erstwhile colleague as a "novelist" and as "Mr
Censor".[73]

        Lomonosov did his best to interfere with the printing o
Müller's Siberian history as well, challenging any section whicl
he suspected of disparaging Russia's heritage. In April a specia
Commission was organized solely to examine the Kamchatka material
independently of both Müller and Fischer, and to report it
findings to Trediakovskii, secretary to the Historical Assembly.[7]
Further delays brought accusations that Müller was withholdin
page proofs, to which Müller responded by criticizing hi
translator's efforts. In fact, Golubtsov's translating was deeme
unsatisfactory even by Lomonosov. Lomonosov was instrumental i
having a friend, V.I. Lebedev, assigned the task in June 1748. O
finishing the translation in August, Lebedev again turned th
manuscript over to Lomonosov, who noted only a few stylisti
errors and recommended its publication in Russian.[75]

        Now it was Teplov's turn to hold up procedures until Mülle
agreed to the few minor changes in the Russian suggested b
Lomonosov, A.S. Barsov and N.I. Popov.[76] When the first fiv
chapters were handed over to the Historical Assembly for it
approval in June 1748, there arose a wild debate over the rol
played by Ermak in the conquest of Siberia during the sixteentl
century.   In describing Ermak's activities, Müller called him
"Rauber" (robber) and accused him of "Verbrechen" (crimes
against the native peoples. Lomonosov was outraged and insiste
that "in view of his conquest of Siberia, [Ermak] should not b
accused of brigandage."   Stählin, Strube de Piermont, and Brau
all endorsed Lomonosov in this matter. Teplov agreed with them
albeit for political rather than patriotic reasons. Fischer an
Trediakovskii hedged.   Their contribution to the discussion wa
best represented by Trediakovskii who acknowledged that a
historian must never say anything that is untrue but, "on th
other hand, seemliness, and some precautions ... suggest that on

ould not offend readers, and especially Russians, by calling
rmak dishonest ..."[77]

Lomonosov added that, "it is not known whether Ermak
onquered Siberia for himself or for the All-Russian autocracy;
owever, it is true that he turned it over to the All-Russian
onarch ... [if the unfavourable items] ... cannot be changed,
en it is better to exclude everything." Only Crusius supported
ller. Caught between the Russian patriots and the politically
nsecure historians. Müller decided to follow Lomonosov's
uggestion by omitting his description of Ermak's conquests
together. "In all truth", Müller said, "it is not possible to
ll him good."[78]

Thus, when the first five chapters of his Description of the
berian Kingdom (Opisanie Sibirskago tsarstva) finally appeared
print in 1750, it was a much truncated version of Müllers
riginal manuscript. Even his foreward was eliminated at the
quest of Schumacher, who told Teplov that "it is intended more
cover him [Müller] with glory than to bring honour to the
resident and to the Academy. He even makes it sound as if he was
e originator of the Kamchatka academic expedition himself. "Two
ronicles Müller had hoped to include in the book were removed by
humacher, who said that too much in them was "false, fables,
raculous, and about church matters..."[79]

In July 1750 Müller was ordered to submit all further parts
the Siberian history in German to the Chancellory, which would
en take full charge of its translation into Russian. This was a
ow to Müller. He had written in his introduction that a
anslator must think in the same manner as the author if he is to
justice to the work. The second volume was ready in September
50, but met with still more resistance from the Historical
sembly. Even Lomonosov became so disenchanted with the
uabbling over Müller's work that he asked for and was granted
lease from the Historical Assembly in November 1751 in order to
turn to his scientific pursuits. In that very year, however,
monosov drew up his first outline for a Russian history of his
n.[80]

In recalling these hectic sessions fourteen years later,
monosov blamed the slow appearance of the Siberian history on
ller's own "stubborness". Trediakovskii went so far as to lay
e blame for most of the "misfortunes" suffered by Russia's
ademicians on Müller's "insolence and pride".[81] Although
ither Trediakovskii or Lomonosov can be regarded as impartial
tnesses, their recollections of Müller's intransigence have a
ng of truth to them. The fact of the matter is that Müller was
set from all sides during the years 1748 to 1750. He played a
ntral role in a series of minor arguments and major crises which
gether very nearly ended his recently renewed career in Russia.

One of these scenarios had Gmelin as its leading character.
elin had signed a four year contract with the Academy in January
47, which included permission to travel to Germany for reasons

of Health - on half salary. Müller and Lomonosov, Gmelin's be:
friends in the Russian capital, underwrote his contract.   B'
Gmelin failed to return and took a post at Tübingen instea‹
thereby making Müller and Lomonosov responsible for half of h
salary.   Not until 1750, after careful mediation by Leonha
Euler, who had left Russia in 1741 for the Berlin Academy
Sciences, was a compromise reached. Gmelin repaid money which ‹
owed the Academy and agreed to have his most famous work, <u>Flo</u>
<u>sibirica</u>, the first volume of which had appeared in 174
published in St. Petersburg.[82]

Although the Academy was satisfied, the matter caused Müll‹
considerable hardship. Gmelin explained away his behaviour '
accusing Müller of giving him bad advice, in that w‹
corroborating doubts which Schumacher and the Academy Chancelle
already had of Müller's loyalty. He was suspected again   wh‹
rumours reached St. Petersburg that Joseph Nicholas Delisle, w'
had left Russia under a cloud in 1747, planned an expose of t.
Academy.   Schumacher readily assumed that Müller was Delisle
agent in the Russian capital. The fact that diplomatic relatio‹
between Russia and France, where Delisle was now a leadi‹
astronomer, were at a particularly low ebb at the time aggravat‹
the situation.

On 18 October 1748, the Chancellery accused Müller
conspiring with Delisle to "abuse the honour of the Academy". H
private papers were confiscated and Müller was confined to h
quarters and told not to contact the president until the matt‹
was resolved. Lomonosov and Trediakovskii were assigned the cho‹
of examining Müller's papers. It seems that Delisle had se‹
Müller a letter from Riga in an attempt to enlist his aid in
campaign against the Academy administration. The letter referr‹
to papers on the history of the Academy which he intended
return to Müller. Although Schumacher took this to mean th‹
Müller had sent proscribed information to the Frenchman, Müll‹
insisted that he had not even replied to Delisle and had never se‹
him Academy materials. A commission was established to investiga‹
the matter and within a month Müller was again cleared of a‹
misbehaviour. But the final report, filed by Lomonosov, left ro‹
for doubt in the Delisle affair and depicted Müller as
troublemaker within the Academy.[83]

As if these incidents were not enough to destroy Müller‹
position at the Academy, in the autumn of 1749 Lomonosov w‹
handed another opportunity to wreak his vengeance upon h
bloodied opponent. In March of that year both Müller a‹
Lomonosov were asked to present papers to a public meeting
September. Müller chose to speak on the origin of the Russi‹
people and their name, and gave his speech a trial run before t‹
Academy and the Historical Assembly on 23 August. Lomonosov w‹
present at that meeting, which approved Müller's paper and allow‹
it to be printed in Latin and Russian. In the first week
September, however, the president postponed the public performan‹
for two months on the grounds that it would then coincide with t‹
anniversary of Elizabeth's accession to the throne. But the re‹

eason for the delay seems to have been a series of actions
nitiated by Krekshin and Schumacher, who contacted Teplov and
azumovskii (who were in Moscow) and warned them of dire political
mplications in Müller's paper. The Chancellory was then ordered
o send copies of the paper to a select group of Academy
istorians, including Lomonosov who returned a very harsh
riticism of it dated 16 September.

Details of the subsequent furor are well-known;[84] suffice it
o say here that after a long investigation, first by a special
ommittee chaired by Teplov and then by a full session of the
cademy, Müller was severely reprimanded, lost his position as
ector of the university, was demoted to adjunct at the Academy,
as ordered to lecture daily at the university, and had his salary
ut by nearly two-thirds. Existing copies of his paper were
rdered destroyed.[85]

The final report on the matter was written for the Academic
onference by Lomonosov, who was especially irate about Müller's
laim that the early Russian princes were Swedish rather than
lavic. With this assertion he started the first major skirmish
n the battle over "Normanism" which goes on to this day. But
hat was only the most irritating of Müller's judgements.
omonosov also strongly objected to Müller's rejection of the
raditional view that Russians could trace their origins and name
o the "Roxalani", who were allegedly Slavic and settled the
nieper-Don region in the eighth century; and he was furious over
üller's scorn for the old tale that the Slavs derived their name
tymologically from the word slava (glory). In a closing report
f 21 June 1750, Lomonosov stressed the political dangers of an
pproach like that taken up by Müller, implying that it might turn
he public against the Academy.[86]

The charges against Müller were fully outlined in a lengthy
eport tabled by Razumovskii on 6 October 1750. The question of
üller's dealings with Delisle was dredged up once again. Müller
as also denounced for "feigning illness" so as to avoid going to
amchatka and of malingering in his obligation to finish the
istory of Siberia. Razumovskii accused Müller of purposely
asting his colleagues' time with his "prejudicial" dissertation
f 1749, of falsely charging his colleagues with collusion, and of
abusing" Teplov by calling him a "liar". According to the
resident, Schumacher also had been a victim of Müller's
ilification, and both members of the Chancellory had apologies
oming to them. Seemingly fully vindicateed, Schumacher wrote
uler gleefully in December 1750: "Mr. Müller is incorrigible. I
hank God that I now have him off my neck."[87]

But the whirlwind into which his impolitic dissertation had
ast him seemed to leave Müller relatively unruffled. He
omplained vehemently about the daily lectures, arguing that his
ealth would not stand up to such rigorous activity, that he had
ot lectured regularly for nearly eighteen years, and that they
ould prevent him from working on the Siberian history. Although
is pleas were ignored, Müller showed that he understood the

situation at the Academy better than any other, for he solved th
problem himself simply by not lecturing.   Krasheninnikov, wh
replaced him as rector, reported in October and again in Novermbe
that all the professors but Müller were performing their duties
Müller had not yet shown up in a lecture hall.[88]   His delayin
tactics seemed to work well.   On 21 February 1751, Razumovski
demonstrated the whimsical nature of Academy, Senate, and cour
relations with this statement:

> Since the adjunct Müller, according to his own
> admission, which he made in a petition to me in his own
> hand dated 21 February, feels himself to be deserving of
> that punishment which he brought upon himself, therefore
> in the hope of his usefulness to the Academy and in an
> expectation of many accomplishments from him for which
> not a few expenses have already been provided by her
> Imperial Majesty, his former rank and professional
> duties are returned to him, and a salary of one thousand
> rubles per year will be paid him, as of 21 February; and
> his is to be freed from all duties other than his work
> on the history of Siberia, and as soon as it is written
> by him in the German language, it will be turned over to
> the Chancellory for translating into Russian.[89]

One of the reasons for this remarkable turn about in Müller'
fortunes was the appearance in early 1751 of the first parts o
Gmelin's memoir on the decade he had spent in Siberia.   In spit
of the fact that members of the Expedition had been sworn t
secrecy, Gmelin's work was printed in Göttingen with n
consultation whatsoever with the Russian Academy.   Schumacher an
Teplov were furious about his unfavourable comments on th
Chancellory's role on the Kamchatka expediation.   The Russia
government was concerned about the fact that the memoir carrie
vivid descriptions of the drunkenness, harsh living conditions
and official brutality as normal facts of Siberian life an
history.   Gmelin also made derogatory remarks about Ermak's rol
in the conquest of Siberia, which may have given Müller som
satisfaction, and noted Chuvash and Tatar resentment of th
Russian occupation.   The Academy community was shocked again th
following year.   In 1752 Nicholas Delisle published a map an
description of the North Pacific that contradicted earlier map
printed by the Russian Academy and claimed for himself and de l
Croyere discoveries which were not theirs.   Müller was now calle
upon to act as the Academy's chief defender against Gmelin th
memoirist and Delisle the map-maker.

To counter Gmelin, Müller suggested in 1752 that Fische
write a single volume on Siberia and its peoples, while Mülle
undertook a description of his own Siberian travels.   Even thoug
Razumovskii was convinced that this was another Müller ploy t
procrastinate on the Siberian history, he agreed reluctantly t
the plan.   Fischer's book was completed by 1757, though no
printed for another decade.[90]   In order to refute Delisle, Mülle
was allowed to resurrect his old charts which the Academy had onc
ignored, work up new ones, and prepare a detailed response for

European audience.   His essay, entitled "Lettre d'un officier de la marine russienne a un seigneur de la Cour concernant la carte des nouvelles decouvertes au Nord de la Mer du Sud, et le Memoire qui y sert d'explication publie par M. Delisle a Paris en 1752", was published with the assistance of Euler in Nouvelle bibliotheque germanique in 1753.   [See Document 4.]   It was not signed.   Müller's maps were printed between 1754 and 1758.[91]

In 1755 Müller edited the richly detailed account of Kamchatka and the Kuriles written by Krasheninnikov, who had died before his manuscript was ready for the press.   In an introduction Müller praised the author and congratulated three unnamed "professors of the Academy" for their assistance to Krasheninnikov, and excused those same professors for not going to Kamchatka themselves.   But Müller's enthusiasm for his own history of Siberia waned considerably.   He had no control over its translation into Russian and every page was subjected to careful scrutiny by people he regarded as enemies.   Only when an opportunity arose for him to become independent of the Historical Assembly did Müller return to writing about Siberia.

Müller's co-operation in countering the damage done to the Academy's reputation by the publication of Gmelin's memoir and Delisle's map provided him with just such an opportunity.   In February 1754, much to the dismay of Lomonosov and undoubtedly of others, Razumovskii appointed Müller permanent secretary of the Academy Conference.   Less than a year later he was also assigned duties as the sole editor of a new Academy publication, Monthly Compositions for Profit and Entertainment.   He now had a forum in which he could print the results of his research on Siberia without fear of interference from the Historical Assembly.

Monthly Compositions was printed in twenty volumes from January 1755 to December 1764, and doubtless was one of the most important monthly magazines published in eighteenth century Russia.   It carried translations from most of the leading European journals, and original essays on science, medicine, education, history, geography, and international politics.   Of its twenty-three articles on history, geography, and statistics, some of which were serialized over ten issues, seventeen were written by Müller himself.   For the purpose of the present study, however, reference will be made only to the journal's frequent references to Siberia.[92]

The first results of Müller's ten year expedition to appear in the pages of Monthly Compositions were his exhaustive reports on trade in Siberia, which were featured in five numbers between September 1755 and May 1756.   They were printed in a separate book in 1756 and reappeared in German four years later in the Sammlung russischer Geschichte - which had gone into abeyance in 1737 and was revived by Müller in 1758.[93]   The series included detailed information on Siberian, Kalmyk, Bukharan, and Chinese traders, and noted the main periods of contact between Russians and the peoples of Siberia.   He took the opportunity to advocate a revision of the Treaty of Kiakhta, a trade agreement signed with

China in 1727. Müller recommended that the trade monopoly granted
the Russian government by the treaty be opened up to private
Russian merchants. He also insisted that private fur auctions be
allowed, that greater care be taken to avoid the extermination of
rare sables which frequentd the Amur region, and that a
colonization programme be initiated.

Other Müller essays carried a wealth of information on the
various peoples of Siberia, on the first Russian travellers to
China (from 1608): on three "heathen" tribes of the Kazan region
(Chermises, Chuvash, Votiaks); on the whale fisheries of
Kamchatka; and on gold mining in Bukhara. Müller also described
items found in grave sites, usually by mercenary grave robbers, in
Siberia and new Russia. Another exhaustive series in which he
depicted Russian voyages in the Arctic and Pacific from 1636 to
1745 appeared in ten parts, 1757-58. This last work was in part a
Russian rendering of Müller's 1753 response to Delisle, and also
an explanation of changes which were then being undertaken on maps
printed earlier by the Academy. It had an English (London, 1761
and 1764) and a French translation (Paris, 1766). In 1761,
Monthly Compositions carried the first bibliographical lists of
all maps and atlases of Russia. It was prepared by Müller, who
noted all foreign and known Russian works and commented upon many
of them.

A short essay by Müller on the background to the Nerchinsk
Treaty of 1689, which was supposed to delineate the border between
Russia and China, appeared in April 1757.[94] Müller was doubtless
aware of the fact that the Manchus were then faced with a major
rebellion by Dzungar Mongols in Central Asia and that several
Mongolian groups had sought to transfer their allegiance from the
Manchu dynasty to the Romanovs. Discussion between Mongolians and
Russians had begun already at Selenginsk in 1756, and the next
year St. Petersburg demanded that Peking agree to a revision of
the Nerchinsk Treaty. Müller's article explained the Russian case
and urged that the easternmost boundary line, then vaguely set
somewhere between the Tugur and the Ud, be moved south to the
Amur. He very carefully described the river system of the region
and sharply criticized the former Russian ambassador to China,
Sava Vladislavich, for allowing the Chinese to prevail thirty
years earlier at Kiakhta. At the time even the Ud was left in
doubt in spite of the fact that the Russians already had a fort
and an established trade practice there. The Chinese, however,
having crushed the rebellions, were not impressed by Russia's
attempts at intimidation.

The long account of the Amur region which Müller had been
commissioned to write in 1740 was spread over four issues of
Monthly Compositions in 1757. It was expanded to include more
criticism of the Kiakhta Treaty for giving the Chinese an even
firmer grip on the Amur than the Nerchinsk Treaty had done. The
article was published later in French (Amsterdam 1766) and in
German by A.F. Büsching (Halle, 1769) and Ulrich Weiss
(Offenbach-am-Main, 1777). We have seen that in 1740-41 Müller
went well beyond his terms of reference to urge a revision of the

Treaty of Nerchinsk. He repeated his position in <u>Monthly</u> <u>Compositions</u> and again in two secret memoranda commissioned by Catherine II in 1763 and 1764. The Amur essay opened with notes on the origins of the existing China-Russian boundary, with a Müller claim that the "cunning" Chinese had duped the Russians at Nerchinsk. He went so far as to insist that control of the Amur was vital enough to Russian interests that force should be applied if China would not co-operate.

The memorandum of 1763 was an actual battle plan for the conquest of the Amur region. Among other things he urged Catherine to settle Siberia from the Irtysh to the Argun with volunteer Russian peasant colonists. These peasants could be serfs whom the state would force the landed gentry to release. In that way Siberia could be opened up to economic development, and if war occurred with China than newly acquired territories might be settled immediately by peasants already living in Siberia.[95] The next year he reminded Catherine of the report he had sent to the government in 1741, and advised her to assign an envoy who demonstrated "manly firmness, dignity, wisdom, calmness, virtue and honesty", to deal with the Chinese. They respect such qualities, said Müller, even though they are "liable to many vices themselves." His concern for the development of Siberia was so great that he later wrote an essay in which he recommended that serfdom be abolished - so as to allow for mass emigration to that area of the Russian Empire. Not surprisingly, this paper was not printed until a year after his death, and then only in Hamburg.

Some of the essays on Kazan, Siberia, and Central Asia which Müller placed in <u>Monthly Compositions</u> had been readied in the early 1730s, when he prepared to address the Academy Conference on the Kalmyks. The paper on the peoples of the Kazan area was written in 1733 but was augmented in <u>Monthly Compositions</u> with corrections of mistakes made by Adam Olearius in his seventeenth century reports. More of Müller's contributions had been assembled between 1744 and 1747, while he was being thwarted in his attempt to complete the history of Siberia. Now that he could publish relatively freely, however, materials over which the Historical Assembly had bickered rapidly came to light. The complete Siberian history was printed in the <u>Sammlung</u> over the years 1762-63; and the six books which had not been included in the Russian language publication of 1750 appeared in <u>Monthly</u> <u>Compositions</u> in 1764.[96]

A spring issue of 1760 contained the first major study in Russian on the origin and history of the cossacks.[97] Gottsched already had printed parts of it in Leipzig in 1756, and told Müller that they had proven very popular. Müller wrote that the "language and law" of the cossacks "were one with the Russians." Their earliest settlements in "Little Russia" were formed by groups of refugees who fled the Polish conquerors at Volhynia in the 1340s. Müller outlined cossack history as that of border guards for the Polish kings and their turbulent relations with Polish aristocracy, Muscovy, and the Ottoman Empire. He included information on Ermak, who was driven into Siberia by Ivan IV, and

Gerhard-Friedrich Müller (in Russian: Fedor Ivanovich Miller), from a silhouette in the State Historical Museum, Moscow, the only known likeness. According to D.A. Rovinskii, in <u>Podrobnyi slovar' russkikh gravirovannykh portretov</u> (Detailed dictionary of Russian engraved portraits), St. Petersburg, 1889, Müller was described in 1761, when he was 56, as "a handsome man, very tall of sturdy build, with small eyes. He was very clever and resourceful, his thoughts were sublime, and he stood through thick and thin for the honor of Russia."

mentioned with no qualifying judgements the rebellion by Stenka
Razin. In this way, Müller brought to light more of the scattered
materials on which he had been labouring in the 1740s, but which
had been eliminated from his history of Siberia.

Besides his own contribution and extracts from works on the
Urals by V.N. Tatishchev, and on the Caspian Sea by J.-G. Gerber,
Müller published studies by three contemporary geographer-
historians - Fischer, F.I. Soimonov and P.I. Rychkov. Fischer
contributed three essays to Monthly Compositions: a piece on the
Tatars and the origin of their name; and another on the peoples of
the North in the February and May issues of 1755; and an
historical discussion of the Khans and the names for various
Chinese dynasties in October of the next year.[98] Soimonov's
description of the area around the Caspian Sea and parts of its
history appeared in all but one issue in 1763 and in book form,
edited by Müller, in that same year. The articles contained
information about the Petrine expeditions throughout the Caspian
region and a Persian tour in which Soimonov was involved in 1722,
and outlined the history of caravan trade in the area. Müller was
the first to give Soimonov written credit for his contribution to
the map-making expedition of the Caspian in 1719-21. As well, in
1764 he reprinted an atlas of the Caspian Sea which Soimonov had
published some thirty years earlier. After Soimonov was appointed
governor of Siberia in 1757, he provided Müller with valuable
geographical and natural historical information. Soimonov printed
so many reports on Siberia that later writers mistakenly named him
the author of Müller's own long essay of 1755 on Siberian trade.[99]

In introducing Rychkov's work to his readers, Müller
accomplished more than simply making historical information
available. It seems that without Müller's encouragement, Rychkov
might never have published his important studies on Orenburg
province, where he served the central government. Having
published a few minor essays in the 1740s, Rychkov asked
Tatishchev for assistance in his efforts to become a member of the
Academy. Tatishchev's recommendation in 1749 that Rychkov be
appointed an honorary member was turned down.[100] An article on
the history of commerce which Rychkov sent to the Academy in 1751
was ignored until Müller printed it unsigned in two issues of
Monthly Compositions. In a conclusion, Müller noted that its
author should be encouraged to continue his work. Rychkov
immediately notified the Academy Conference of his authorship,
thanked Müller, and sent him two more pieces, which were duly
printed. In 1758 and 1759 Müller nominated Rychkov to the
Academy, a proposition which once again embroiled him with
Lomonosov. Lomonosov opposed Rychkov on the grounds that he had
not yet proven himself a scholar, did not read Latin, and was not
versed in the "literary sciences". Müller won a partial victory
in this battle - in 1759 Rychkov settled for a position as the
Academy's first Russian "corresponding member".[101]

Rychkov regularly sent Müller information on Orenburg,
Astrakhan, and parts of Siberia; he also translated material for
Monthly Compositions, and was the only person to send in answers

to a "tasks" ("Zadacha") section which Müller added to the journal
in 1763. These "problems", which Müller said were to be "mainly
on the history and antiquity of Russia, and the natural history of
the Russian Empire", added to the historical dimension of the
journal. Probably the most important of Rychkov's contributions
to Monthly Compositions was his "History of Orenburg", which
appeared in 1759. This work had been completed in a slightly
different form and title in 1744 and had impressed Tatishchev, but
it was left to Müller to give Rychkov the exposure he wanted.
When Rychkov's Topography of Orenburg, which had been serialized
in Monthly Compositions in 1762, was printed as a two-volume book,
Müller reviewed it and said it should serve as a model for
topographical studies of other Russian provinces.

                                IV

Four months after the final issue of Monthly Compositions appeared
in December 1764, Müller took up residence in Moscow. Officially,
he went there to serve as director of Catherine's new Foundling
Home;[102] but A.F. Büsching, who helped persuade Müller to take the
post, reported that his main incentive was a desire to be "free
from the Academic Chancellory, from Lomonosov and people like him
..."[103] Two years later, Müller was appointed archivist for the
College of Foreign Affairs, a post which he retained for the
remainder of his career and where he helped train the next
generation of imperial archivists. Although he never again
attempted to write a general history of Russia, Müller finished
essays himself on the peoples of the Kazan' region, a history of
the Russian nobility, Peter I's youth, and on a variety of other
subjects.

        During his Moscow years, Müller's reputation as a geographer
and ethnographer began to outstrip his renown as an historian.
Even the Russian military took advantage of his expertise,
requesting and receiving new maps of Moldavia and Wallachia in
which special care was taken to delineate the Russian position on
the borders of Poland and the Ottoman Empire. Müller also made
meticulous charts of the Russo-Persian boundaries. The wide
exposure given to many of his earlier reports on Siberia, the
Caucasus, the Cossacks, and the peoples of Siberia and the Amur
region in journals edited by A.F. Büsching, A.L. Schlözer, and
Gottsched made Müller's name better known in Europe than that of
any other member of the Russian Academy. Consequently, he was
besieged by requests for information and copies of papers, and
invitations to review books and manuscripts.

        Even though he never returned to St. Petersburg, Müller kept
his Academy affiliation, acted as its delegate to Catherine's
famous Legislative Commission in 1767-68, and was named its
official agent in Moscow. He kept in constant touch with Johann-
Albrecht Euler, Leonhard's son who was appointed Conference
secretary in February 1769. Among Müller's many assignments he
was to serve as corresponding geographer and advisor to Academy-
sponsored expeditions. These included voyages by P.S. Pallas and

I.P. Falk to Orenburg;   Samuel Gmelin (J.G. Gmelin's nephew), K.I.
Hablitz (whom Müller recommended to the Academy in 1760) and J.A.
Guldenstadt to Astrakhan;   and I.I. Georgi to the Lake Baikal
region.[104]   As middleman for the Academy, Müller often took
possession of collections sent by expeditionary scientists,
including a large botanical collection forwarded to Moscow by
Guldenstadt from Tambov in 1769, and a detailed map of the
Caucasus from the same explorer in 1773.   In January 1771, Pallas
sent Müller fifteen boxes of material from one of his expeditions.
In turn, Müller forwarded scientific equipment, charts, and
general information to the travellers, and relayed whatever he
learned from them to the Academy.

This information included reports of the dangers to which
Gmelin and Guldenstadt were exposed from rebellious tribesmen.
Indeed, an entire series of letters to J.-A. Euler in 1773 display
worry and then a growing horror about the fate of Gmelin, who had
been imprisoned by a rebel Turkmen Khan and died of dysentery
after a long internment and seemingly bungled negotiations by the
Russian government.   The very next year Müller had to inform the
Academy of the death of G.-M. Lowitz at the hands of Pugachev's
rebels in the area of Astrakhan.   That Müller's knowledge and
experience proved valuable was illustrated in a letter from the
most famous of the expeditionary leaders, Pallas, to J.-A. Euler
in 1769, in which he noted the "unusual accuracy" of Müller's
correspondence with the Academy about the affairs of his
troupe.[105]

In 1770 Müller was visited in Moscow by T.I. Shmalev, a
captain in service at Okhotsk and Kamchatka who had accompanied
several Aleuts to St. Petersburg for presentation to Catherine.
Their lengthy discussions persuaded Müller once again to gather
documentation for a history of all Russian ocean voyages after
1743.   The association with T.I. Shmalev and his brother Vasilii
proved very fruitful.   They continued to send Müller up-to-date
accounts from Okhotsk, one of which he edited in 1774 for
publication in the Trudy of the Free Russian Assembly.[106]   In that
same year, and without his prior consent, the notes which Müller
had prepared on Kamchatka in 1737, for Krasheninnikov, appeared in
the first printing of Steller's Beschreibung von dem Lande
Kamtschatka (Frankfort/Leipzig, 1774).

Müller undertook many other important tasks in Moscow.   He
was commissioned to write a history of the Academy, edited for
publication in three volumes a history of Russia which Tatishchev
had completed in 1739 (1768-74), edited and printed such important
historical documents as the Stepennaia kniga (2 Vols., 1775)   and
Ivan IV's Sudebnik 1550 (1768), and assisted other historians in
their work by providing them with documents and advice.   In 1773,
Müller published a book, About the Peoples who Lived in Russia
from Ancient Times, in which he revived all his earlier arguments
against Lomonosov's theories about Russia's antiquity.[107]   He was
still publishing during the last two years of his life, when
extracts from notes he compiled in 1778-79 for a topographical
study of the Moscow regions were printed in Neues St. - Peters-

burgisches Zeitung, 1782-83.

Meanwhile, Catherine pressed Müller to complete his description of Russian sea voyages to the Arctic and Kamchatka. Although he began to compile new information and sift through materials which he had not used in 1758, this project was still unfinished by the time of Müllers death. Ten years later Pallas edited and published Müller's compilation separately and in several issues of Neue Nordische Beiträge.

Müller seems to have had his fill of Far Eastern geography anyway. The arguments of the 1750s over the Delisle map had been enervating at the time and had continued to plague him intermittently during the sixties. But they came back with a vengeance in the next decade when he was swept unwillingly into a bitter dispute with an eminent Swiss geographer, Samuel Engel. In 1765, Engel published in French a detailed geographical description of the Pacific and contradicted some of Müller's earlier conclusions. A few years later he wrote Müller a letter asking for some response. Müller ignored the request. But when Engel's book appeared in German translation in 1772, Büsching persuaded Müller to take some action. The Swiss writer had criticized him for making Siberia appear much larger than Engel believed it to be. He implied that Müller was merely trying to curry favour with the Russian government by increasing the size of its empire. Müller's answer to Engel's charges appeared in Büsching's Wochentliche Nachrichten von neuen Landkarten in 1773; Engel retaliated in 1777 with a biting personal attack on Müller and a general denigration of all discoveries claimed by Russian explorers. Once again Müller used Büsching's good offices to reply, albeit quite cautiously and with no invective. According to L. Breitfuss, who described this argument, the dimensions which Müller attributed to Siberia were much closer to reality than were Engel's; but Müller was unsure of his facts and preferred that the controversy be laid to rest. Busching was aggressive in Müller's defense, however, and wrote several very harsh reviews of Engel's work. Pallas also enthusiastically endorsed Müller's position.[108]

More of Müller's material appeared posthumously as entries in the Geographical Dictionary of the Russian State, edited by A. Shchakatov and L. Maksimovich in 1788-89. Besides helping H.L. Ch. Bachmeister in the publication of the Russische Bibliothek, Müller also assisted J.-G. Stritter in the compilation of the important Memoriae populorum. The tenth volume of the Sammlung, edited by Gustav Ewers and M. Engelhardt and published in 1816, contained many Müller documents; The Archeographical Commission of Moscow printed more of his reports and documents in the 1830s; and documents on the diplomatic relations between Muscovy and Austria (1486-1519), Muscovy and Prussia (1517-1700), and Muscovy and Denmark (1493-1562), which he and N.N. Bantysh-Kamenskii gathered for Catherine II in the early 1780s, were printed in various collections during the nineteenth century.

The second edition of Novikov's Ancient Russian Library included many more items from Müller's vast collection. In fact,

he entire Part VII (1789) and most of part XVII (1791) were taken
rom Müller's edited papers.   The <u>New Monthly Essays</u> (<u>Novyia</u>
<u>zhemesiachnyia sochineniia</u>, 1786-96) published more than twenty
apers from Müller's files.   A special series of documents and
orks from the era of Peter the Great, edited by Fedor Tumanskii
n 1787-88, included four of Müller's essays on Peter's youth.   In
793 Pallas edited for publication the long manuscript describing
ussian expeditions to the North and to Kamchatka between 1742 and
775 which Müller had started to compile in the 1770s.

Müller died on 11 October 1783 (O.S.).   He had won many
onours during his long and often stormy career in Russia.
irector of the Archives at the Moscow College of Foreign Affairs,
ctual State Councillor as of August 1783, and Cavalier of the
rder of St. Vladimir, 3rd Class.   He was honoured abroad by the
oyal Society in London, the Swedish Academy in Stockholm, the
cademie des Sciences in Paris, and the Göttingen Learned Society.
t home he was decorated by the Free Russian Assembly and by the
ree Economic Society.   Catherine II noted his passing with regret
n a letter to Baron Melchior von Grimm, and the government
ranted his widow a pension of 3000 rubles.

As a collector of documents on geography, ethnography,
tatistics, linguistics, the natural sciences and, above all,
istory, Müller was unsurpassed.   Even his critics acknowledge
hat he was the first in Russia to emphasize the importance of
ffical documentation for historical studies.   His reliance upon
uch documents and his insistence upon historical accuracy
ecessitated further large-scale archival research. Furthermore,
is exposition of a myriad of topics hitherto unknown to his
ussian readers contributed enormously to the growth of an
istorical consciousness in Russia.

In 1778 the famous British scholar, traveller, and minister,
ev. William Coxe, visited Müller in Moscow and later wrote what
an be taken as a fitting epitaph to the young German student who
dopted Russia as his homeland: "[Müller] will always be
onsidered as the great father of Russian history, as well from
he excellent specimens he bequeaths to future historians."[109]

Müller's research on Siberia demonstrates the prophetic
ature of Coxe's praise, for his work benefitted historians,
eographers, ethnographers, merchants, state officials, and
cholars, and stimulated Russian national consciousness.

ОПИСАНІЕ
СИБИРСКАГО ЦАРСТВА

и всѣхъ

ПРОИЗШЕДШИХЪ ВЪ НЕМЪ ДѢЛЪ,

отъ начáла

А ОСОБЛИВО ОТЪ ПОКОРЕНІЯ ЕГО

РОССІЙСКОЙ ДЕРЖАВѢ

ПО СІИ ВРЕМЕ́НА;

сочинено

ГЕРАРДОМЪ ФРИДЕРИКОМЪ МИЛЛЕРОМЪ,

Исторіографомъ и Профессоромъ Университета
Академіи Наукъ и Соціетета
Аглинскаго Членомъ.

КНИГА ПЕРВАЯ.

ВЪ САНКТПЕТЕРБУРГѢ
при Императорской Академіи Наукъ 1750. года.

Title page of Müller's Description of the Siberian Kingdom
and all occurrences there, from the beginning and particularly
from its conquest by the Russian State. St. Petersburg, 1750.
First edition.

ENDNOTES TO G.-F. Müller (1705-83) and Siberia

. For general biographical material on Müller, see A.F. üsching, Beyträge zu der Lebensgeschichte denkwürdiger Personen, nsonderheit Gelehrter Männer, III (Halle, 1785), 3-160; and P.P. ekarsky, Istoriia imperatorskoi Akademii nauk v Peterburge, I St. Petersburg, 1870), 308-430.

. See Svodynyi katalog russkoi knigi grazhdanskoi pechati XVIII eka, 1725-1800, IV (Moscow, 1966), 170-72; Materialy dlia istorii mperatorskoi Akademii Nauk, II (1886), 206 (hereafter, aterialy); and Müller, "Avtobiografiia," in Istoriia Sibiri, I Moscow, 1937), 147-8.

. Materialy, II, 3-4 (1885), 595, 600.

. Ibid., VI (1890), 250-52.

. Ibid., II, 326-7; Protokoly zasedanii konferentsii mperatorskoi Akademii nauk s 1725 po 1803 goda, I (St. etersburg, 1897), 65 (hereafter, Protokoly).

. For Müller's account, see below; Document 5.

. V. Ger'e, Sbornik pisem i memorialov Leibnitsa tnosiashchikhsia k Rossii i Petry Velikom (St. Petersburg, 1873), 60.

. "Propozitsii Fedora Saltykova." In Pamiatniki drevnei is'mennosti i iskusstva, 83, no. 5, series 4 (St. Petersburg, 891), 22, 24.

. Leo Bagrow, A History of Russian Cartography up to 1800 (Wolfe sland, Ontario, 1975), 111-12.

0. On Delisle, see Pekarsky, Istoriia, 124-49.

1. Raymond, H. Fisher, Bering's Voyages. Whither and Why. eattle, 1977, 34.

2. PSZR, V, no. 3266 (2 January 1719), 607; Sokolov, "Severnaia kspeditsiia, 1733-43 goda." Zapiski gidrograficheskago epartmenta morskago ministerstva, IX (SPb. 1851), 199-200.

3. On Strahlenberg and Messerschmidt, see E.P. Zinner, Sibir' v zvestiiakh zapadnoevropeiskikh puteshestvennikov i uchenykh XVIII eka (Vostochno-sibirskoe izd. 1968). For a general account of ie exploration of Russia's frontier see G.V. Lantzeff and Richard . Pierce, Eastward to Empire. Exploration and Conquest on the issian Open Frontier to 1750 (Montreal-London, 1973).

14. PSZR, VI, no. 3534 (29 February 1720), 141-50; no. 3788 (2 May 1721), 394-95.

15. On Bering, see Fisher, Bering's Voyages; P. Lauridsen, Vitu Bering: The Discoverer of Bering Straits (New York, 1969); F.A Golder, Bering's Voyages, I-II (New York, 1922-23); and L.S. Berg Otkrytie Kamchatki i ekspeditsii Beringa, 1725-1742 (Moscow Leningrad, 1946).

16. The notice is reprinted in Fisher, Bering's Voyages, 12-13.

17. PSZR, VIII, no. 6023 (17 April 1732), 749; no. 6041 (2 Ma 1732), 770-74.

18. Sammlung russicher Geschichte, I, no. 3 (1733), 195-221.

19. Materialy, VI, 253; Müller, A Letter from a Russian Sea Officer to a Person of Distinction at the Court of St. Petersbur (London, 1754), 11-12.

20. Materialy, 270; Müller, in Ezhemesiachnyia sochineniia, I (January, 1758), 11-12. [Hereafter, ES.] Lydia T. Black [se article in bibliography p. 30] says that Louis and Nichola Delisle were, in fact, full siblings, but that Louis used hi mother's maiden name.

21. Protokoly, I (3 July 1733), 69; Materialy, II (16 Apri 1733), 326-27.

22. Gmelin, Reise durch Sibirien von dem Jahr 1733-1743, (Göttingen, 1751), x; Müller, Istoriia Sibiri, 460-61. (see below.

23. See M.O. Kosven in Sibiriskii etnograficheskii Sbornik, II (1961) 120; Berg, Otkrytie, 129.

24. Materialy, II, 446; VI, 272-73; Gmelin, Reise, I, 3-4. Muc of the following material about Müller's travels has bee distilled from the various memoirs, including Müller's own, an official reports listed in the bibliography accompanying thi book. Specific references will be included only where they refe to incidents mentioned in only one source.

25. Gmelin, Reise, I, 18-22.

26. See especially Materialy, II (21 September 1733), 383-90.

27. Müller report to Senate, 7 August 1746, Materialy, VIII, 195

28. There was considerable fury in St. Petersburg when Gmeli printed his memoir of the voyage without Russian permission Their information had, by agreement, been the property of th Russian government. On the controversy, see the article by Lotha Maier in Jahrbücher für Geschichte Osteuropas, XXVIII, no. (1979), 353-73.

9. Materialy, VI, 285.

0. Ibid., II, 394-95; Protokoly, II, 130-31.

1. Lauridsen, Vitus Bering, 72.

2. See S.V. Bashkatova in Istoriia gorodov Sibiri dosovetskogo erioda (1977), 30-33.

3. Gmelin, Voyage en Sibérie, I (Paris, 1767), 46-50.

4. Müller, Istoriia Sibiri, I, 331-36.

5. Gmelin, Voyages, I, 53-4, 56-7, 70-77.

6. These are outlined in detail in a report submitted to the enate by Müller, 7 August 1746, Materialy, VIII, 196-97.

7. Gmelin, Voyage en Sibérie, I, 95-98.

8. Materialy, VI, 404.

9. Gmelin, Voyage en Sibérie, I, 244-45, 256, 283-85, 290-91.

0. Müller in ES, IV (July 1758), 14-15.

1. See S.P. Krasheninnikov v Sibiri. Neopublikovannye materialy Moscow-Leningrad, 1966).

2. Gmelin, Voyage en Sibérie, I, 381-82.

3. See S.P. Krashennikov, 175-93.

4. See Müller in ES, (January, 1758), 8-9, 22-22; B.P. Polevoi, Nakhodka podlinnykh dokumentov S.I. Dezhneva o ego istoricheskom okhode 1648 g." Vestnik Leningradskogo universiteta, no. 6 1962), 145-52. Raymond H. Fisher's, The Voyage of Semen Dezhnev n 1648: Bering's Precursor (London, 1981), includes copies of ocuments and an analysis of Müller's role in their discovery.

5. On Lindenau, see esp. Kosven, 201-05; on Fischer, Materialy, II, 272-3, 477, 478.

6. Ibid., 793-94; IV (16 April 1739), 95-97.

7. Ibid., IV, 317-18, 477-78.

8. Müller in ES, (August 1758), 116-17; Lauridsen, 117-26.

9. Protokoly, I (7 February 1738), 457.

0. Golder, Bering's Voyages, I (1922), 33-34.

1. Gmelin, Voyage en Sibérie, II, 55-56, 70-71.

52.   Ibid., 101-2, 126.

53.   See B. Gur'ev, "Istoriograf Miller v Tomsk," Russkii vestnik no. 11 (1881), 65.

54.   See Pekarsky, Istoriiia, I, 328-39.

55.   Ibid., 618-20.   Fischer was accompanied to Siberia by hi wife and three children.

56.   Parts of Müller's very detailed guide can be found in Radlov Materialy po arkheologii Rossii (1894), 106-14.   For Tatishchev' questionnaire, see Tatishchev, Izbrannye Trudy po geografii Rossi (Moscow, 1950), 77-95.

57.   Müller to Euler, 21 June 1740, in Die Berliner und di Petersburger Akademie der Wissenschafter im Briefwechsel Leonhar Eulers. I. Der Briefwechsel L. Eulers mit G. F. Müller 1735-176 (Berlin, 1959), 43.   Müller's letter from Tobol'sk is cited i Pekarsky, Istoriia, I, 329.

58.   Gmelin, Voyage en Sibérie, II, 186-88.

59.   Pekarsky, Istoriia, I, 330.

60.   Gmelin, Voyage en Sibérie, II, 254.

61.   Müller, Primechaniia k Vedomostiam, pts. 50-60 (1742), 197 228; Protokoly, I (31 October 1740), 305-6.

62.   Materialy, VI, 450.

63.   Ibid., VIII, 211-12.

64.   Müller, ES (October 1758), 333-34; Pekarsky, Istoriia, I 453; Golder, Bering's Voyages, II (1925), 37-51, 155-57 (fro Steller's log).

65.   The crisis is fully documented in Materialy, IV (passim) See also F. N. Zagorsky, Andrei Konstantinovich Nartov (Leningrad 1969).

66.   Materialy, V, 697-701; Pekarsky, Dopolnitel'nyia izvestii dlia biografii Lomonosova (St. Petersburg, 1865), 20.

67.   Materialy, VIII, 182-94.

68.   Ibid., 211-13.

69.   Ibid., 384-85.

70.   Commentarii, X (1747), 420-68.

71.   Materialy, IX (24 March 1748), 125-26.

2. The Academy Charter can be found in Istoriia Akademii nauk
SSR, I. (1724-1803) (Moscow-Leningrad, 1958), 436-53.

3. See "Akademik Miller i Fisher i opisanie Sibiri."   Chtenie
1866), 16-21.

4. Materialy, IX (14 April 1748), 150-51.

5. Lomonosov, Polnoe sobranie sochinenii, IX (Moscow-Leningrad,
952), 620. [Hereafter, PSS.]

6. Materialy, IV (10, 14 October 1748), 460, 480.

7. Bibliograficheskie zapiski, III, no. 17 (1861) 515-18.

8. Ibid., 517; P.S. Biliarsky, Materialy dlia biografii
omonosova (St. Petersburg, 1875), 105-6.

9. Müller, Istoriia Sibiri, I (1937), 462-63; Materialy, X, (13
une 1749), 17-18.

0. Lomonosov, PSS, VI, 85.

1. Ibid., X, 287; Trediakovskii's remark was cited by S.M.
olov'ev in Istoriia Rossii, XIII (Moscow, 1965), 542.

2. Materialy, IX, 427-32; Die Berliner, II, 1961, 202-3.

3. Materialy, IX, 273-76, 556-57.

4. For an English-language survey, see Dmitri Obolensky, "The
arangian-Russian Controversy: The First Round," in History and
magination: Essays in Honour of H.R. Trevor-Roper (ed.) H.
loyd-Jones (London, 1981), 322-42.

5. Protokoly, II (28 September 1750), 243.

6. Lomonosov, PSS, VI, 17-80.

7. Schumacher to Euler, 12 December 1750, in Die Berliner, II,
27.

8. Materialy, X, 614-65, 636.

9. Pekarsky, Istoriia, I, 365.

0. Fischer, Sibirischen Geschichte von der Entdeckung Sibiriens
is auf die Eroberung dieses Lands durch die russiche Waffen, Pts.
-IV (St. Petersburg, 1768).   A Russian translation appeared in
775.

1. Nouvelle Biblioteque Germanique, XIII (1753), 46-87.   See
lso Breitfuss article in Imago Mundi, III (1939), 87-99. See also
ydia T. Black, "The Question of Maps: Exploration of the Bering

Sea in the Eighteenth Century." Unpublished paper read at
Maritime History Conference, Anchorage, Alaska (September, 1979).

92. For a general description of the journal's content, see V.A
Miliutin, "Ocherki russkoi zhurnalistiki preimushchestvenn
staroi: 'Ezhemesiachnye sochineniia (1755-1764)'," Sovremennik
no. 1, section II (1851), 1-51; no. 2, section II, 151-82; no. 3
section II, 1-48.

93. Müller, "Izvestie i torgakh Sibirskikh," ES, II (Septembe
1755), 195-250; (December, 525-37; III (February 1756), 180-91
(March), 195-226; (April), 339-60; (May), 387-421. "Nachrichte
von den Handlung Sibirien," Sammlung, III (1760), 413-618.

94. Müller, "Istoriia o stranakh, pri reke Amure lezhashchikh
kogda onyia pod Rossiiskim vladeniem," ES, VI, 1 (July 1757), 3
39; (August), 99-130; (September), 195-227; (October), 291-328.

95. Müller, "Razsuzhdenie o predpriiatii voiny s Kitaitsami,
(1753), in N.N. Bantysh-Kamenskii, Diplomaticheskoe sobranie de
mezhdu Rossiiskom i kitaiskim gosudarstvami s 1619 p 1792-09 go
(Kazan, 1882), 378-93.

96. Müller, "Razsuzhdenie o posol'stve v Kitai," (1764) i
Bantysh-Kamenskii, 396-98.

97. Müller, "O nachale i proizkhozhdenii kozakov," ES, XI (Apri
1760), 303-48; Sammlung, IV (1760), 365-472.

98. Fisher, ES, I (May 1755), 421-50; (February 1755), 123-38; I
(October 1756), 311-27.

99. On Soimonov's relationship with Müller, see L.A. Gol'denberg
Fedor Ivanovich Soimonov (1692-1780) (Moscow, 1966).

100. See "Perepiska V.N. Tatishcheva za 1746-1750 gg.
Istoricheskii arkhiv, VI (1951), 290.

101. See generally, "Zapiski P.I. Rychkov," Russkii arkhiv, Bl
3, no. 11 (1905); Protokoly, II (29 January 1859), 420; Lomonoso
PSS, X, 76-77.

102. Protokoly, II (7 January 1765), 530; Müller
"Avtobiograiia," Istoriia Sibiri, I, 153.

103. Büsching, Beyträge, III (1785), 67-68.

104. Uchenaia korrespondentsiia Akademii Nauk XVIII veka
Nauchnoe opisanie. 1766-1782 gg. (Moscow-Leningrad, 1937), 12
124, 136-37, 144, 152, 233.

105. Ibid., 145.

106. Opyt trudov Vol'nago Rossiiskago Sobranie, pt. 1, no. VI
(1774), 195-212.

07. Müller, O narodakh izdrevle v Rossii obitavshikh (St. Petersburg, 1773), esp. 107-8, 21-22 (in second edition, 1788).

08. The Engel/Müller argument is outlined in Andreev, "Trudy G.F. Millera o vtoroi Kamchatskoi ekspeditsii," Izvestiia: vsesoiuznoe geograficheskoe obshchestvo, 91, no. 1 (Jan./Feb., 1959), 3-16. See also Fisher, The Voyage of Semen Dezhnev, p. 7.

09. Coxe, Travels through Poland, Russia, Sweden and Denmark (London, 1802), 5th edition, 294-95.

Tiumen. A page from the Remezov Chronicle of the Conquest of Siberia, discovered by Müller.

V O Y A G E S

F R O M

A S I A to A M E R I C A,

For Completing the DISCOVERIES of the

North West Coast of *America*.

To which is prefixed,

A SUMMARY of the V O Y A G E S

Made by the *R U S S I A N S* on the

F R O Z E N S E A,

In SEARCH of a NORTH EAST Paſſage.

Serving as an Explanation of a Map of the Ruſſian *Diſcoveries, publiſhed by the Academy of Sciences at* Peterſburgh.

Tranſlated from the *High Dutch* of
S. MULLER, of the Royal Academy of *Peterſburgh.*

WITH THE ADDITION OF THREE NEW MAPS;

1. A Copy of Part of the *Japaneſe* Map of the World.
2. A Copy of *De Liſle's* and *Buache's* fictitious Map. And
3. A large Map of *Canada*, extending to the *Pacific Ocean, containing the New Diſcoveries made by the* RUSSIANS *and* FRENCH.

By THOMAS JEFFERYS Geographer to his Majeſty.

L O N D O N:

Printed for T. JEFFERYS, the Corner of *St. Martin's-Lane, Charing Croſs,* 1761.

Title page of Müller's Voyages from Asia to America, London, 1761

ЕЖЕМѢСЯЧНЫЯ

СОЧИНЕНІЯ

КЪ ПОЛЬЗѢ И УВЕСЕЛЕНІЮ

служащія.

Генварь, 1755 года.

ВЪ САНКТПЕТЕРБУРГѢ

при Императорской Академіи Наукъ.

itle page of first issue of Monthly Compositions for Profit
nd Entertainment, edited by Müller, 1755-1764.

О П И С А Н І Е

живущихъ въ Казанской губерніи язы-
ческихъ народовъ,

яко то

ЧЕРЕМИСЪ, ЧУВАШЪ и ВОТЯКОВЪ,

Съ показаніемъ ихъ жительства, полѝтиче-
скаго учрежденія, тѣлесныхъ и душевныхъ
дарованій, какое платье носятъ, отъ чего и
чѣмъ питаются, о ихъ торгахъ и промыслахъ,
какимъ языкомъ говорятъ, о художествахъ
и наукахъ, о естественномъ и вымышленномъ
ихъ языческомъ законѣ, такожъ о всѣхъ у-
потребительныхъ у нихъ обрядахъ, нравахъ
и обычаяхъ ; съ приложеніемъ многочислен-
ныхъ словъ на семи разныхъ языкахъ, какъ то
на Казанско-Татарскомъ, Черемисскомъ, Чувашскомъ, Вотяцкомъ, Мордовскомъ, Перм-
скомъ и Зырянскомъ, и приобщеннымъ пере-
водомъ Господней молитвы *Отче Нашъ* на
Черемисскомъ и Чувашскомъ языкахъ.

сочиненное

Герардомъ Фридрихомъ Миллеромъ , Императорской
Академіи Наукъ Профессоромъ, по возвращеніи его
въ 1743 году изъ Камчатской Экспедиціи.

ВЪ САНКТПЕТЕРБУРГѢ.

Изданіемъ Императорской Академіи Наукъ.
1791 года.

Title page of G.-F. Müller, Description of the heathen peoples inhabiting Kazan gubernia, such as the Cheremis, Chuvash and Votiaks, indicating where they live, their political institutions, corporeal and spiritual talents, clothing, diet, trade and industries, languages, arts and sciences, the natural and heathen laws they have devised, as well as their rituals, mores and customs, supplemented by many words from seven of their languages, including Kazan-Tatar, Cheremis, Chuvash, Votiak, Mordvinian, Permian and Zyrianian, with translations of the Lord's Prayer into the Cheremis and Chuvash languages, compiled by Gerhard-Friedrich Miller, professor at the Imperial Academy of Sciences, on his return in 1743 from the Kamchatka Expedition. Published in St. Petersburg, by the Imperial Academy of Sciences, 1791.

Instructions given to Academician G.-F. Müller to guide him in his Siberian travels.[1]

ABOUT THE HISTORY OF PEOPLES

1. In order to augment historical understanding about the peoples through which the leader of the expedition, Bering, will travel on the way to Kamchatka - to observe in detail where each people is settled, the boundaries between them, and to what degree the different tribes are inter-related.

2. What are the principle origins of each people according to their own accounts, the essence of their ancient dwellings, settlements, and so on.

3. What is the faith of each people and whether they have some kind of naturalist religion? What notions do they observe in their religion.

4. The customs and rituals of each people, their homelife, marriage regulations, and so on, should be noted.

5. The commerce, agriculture, art, military skills and political direction of each people should be noted.

6. Provide several examples of the language of each people, for example: the translation of its main prayers, numbers, nouns, and most commonly-used names.

7. One must write as well the names of every people, country, river, town, and so on: of every people and its neighbour, adding wherever possible the origin and pronunciation of the name.

8. To describe the history of each people in detail, whence and how they emerged and, if they are under the rule of others, under what circumstances and by whom they were conquered - to the present.

9. All relics of various kinds, ancient monuments, ancient and modern vessels, idols and prospects of the more important towns are to be in part sketched, in part brought to St. Petersburg.

10. Several individuals of both sexes from each people and tribe who exemplify the characteristics of that people in their eyes and figure are to be accurately painted together with the clothes they wear, and several examples of clothing of each kind are to be brought to St. Petersburg.

11. Especially to observe in detail the origin, morals, customs and so on of those people who live on the north side of the Amur River, because it is rumoured that a Russian nation lived there in ancient times.

DOCUMENT 2

Account sheet for the Academy of Sciences professors and other servitors who are participating in the Kamchatka Expedition, and their annual salaries.[2]

Rank and Name	rubles	kopecks
To Professor Müller	1260	
to Professor Gmelin	1260	
to Professor Delisle de la Croyère	1260	
to Artist [Johann] Berkan	500	
to Drawing master [J.-W.] Lursenius	400	
to Geodesist Andrei Krasil'nikov	220	46 1/4
to Geodesist Nikofor Chekin	220	46 1/4
to Geodesist Moisei Ushakov	220	46 1/4
to Geodesist Aleksander Ivanov	220	46 1/4
to Student and translator Il'ia Iakhontov	120	
to Student Stepan Krasheninnikov	100	
to Student Feodor Popov	100	
to Student Vasilii Tret'iakov	100	
to Student Aleksei Gorlanov	100	
to Instrumental apprentice Stepan Avsianikov	72	
Total	6252	85

Victuals: meal, barley, oil, salt, etc., for the professors and their retinue annually in Kamchatka.

Rank	puds
For three professors, each 40 puds, total	120
For twelve men under them, each 24 puds, total	288
For two artists, each 30 puds, total	60
For four men under them, each 24 puds, total	96
For two geodesists, each 30 puds, total	60
For four men under them, each 24 puds, total	96
For six students, each 30 puds, total	180
For three men under them, each 24 puds, total	72
For instrumental apprentice	24
For one Corporal, twelve soldiers, one drummer, according to Ukaz	--
Total, besides soldiers	996

Bering, 15 February 1734

DOCUMENT 3

Anton Friedrich Büsching (1724-93) was a professor of theology from Göttingen who served as a pastor of a Lutheran church in St. Petersburg from 1761 to 1765. He was a close friend of Daniel Schumacher, and also of Müller, to whom he was related by marriage. In 1764, I.I. Betskoi, Catherine's adviser on education, offered Büsching a post as director of a foundling home in Moscow. He refused it in order to accept a position as head of a gymnasium in Berlin, and recommended Müller in his stead.

Aside from theology, Büsching's main interest was geography, to which he committed eleven volumes of Neue Erdbeschreibung (New Description of the Earth) before his death. This exhaustive series is generally regarded as the founding work in modern statistical geography. Büsching also edited historical and geographical journals. The most important of these for Russia was the Magazin für die Neue Historie and Geographie (Journal for New History and Geography), which carried a number of Müller's papers. The following piece on Müller's "Great, Long Siberian Journey," is taken from the first biography of Müller, part of Büsching's famous Beyträge zu der Lebensgeschichte denkwürdiger Personen, insonderheit Gelehrter Männer (Contributions to Biographies of Remarkable People, especially Scholars), I-VI (Halle, 1783-89). Büsching's study on Müller took up half of Volume III (1785), pp. 1-160. Büsching gleaned the section on Müller's journey through Siberia, pp.23-46, from Gmelin's Reise (Journey), from which he lifted passages regularly and without acknowledgment, and from conversations and correspondence with Müller himself. Translated by Victoria Joan Moessner.

ÜLLER'S GREAT, LONG SIBERIAN JOURNEY

The most arduous part of Müller's life was his ten-year ojourn through Siberia, as part of the academic expedition, hich he started on 8 August 1733 in the company of Professors ohann Georg Gmelin and Louis Delisle de la Croyère and which nded on 14 February 1743. They were supposed to go to Kamchatka ut Müller and Gmelin went only as far as Iakutsk and returned rom there to St. Petersburg.

Müller originally had not been designated for the expedition, ut the troubles which he had at the Academy, especially with chumacher, convinced him to participate. He was assigned to tudy and investigate geography and antiquities of the area, and he history of its peoples. How diligently and carefully he arried out this task is shown in his reports to the Senate and

49

the Academy, as well as in his published and unpublishe
writings. He prepared an exact description of his entir
journey, outlining all travel routes himself or having them dra
up by students assigned to him. He compiled geographic
historical and political descriptions of all towns an
surrounding regions, researched the archives in all of the towns
and had the most significant and useful information in the
copied, thus producing some fifty folio volumes. Archeologica
remains were sketched and described, as were the customs
practices, languages and religion of native peoples. Müller mad
a variety of new maps, and had others prepared by th
accompanying surveyors. He undertook all executive an
secretarial work of the Academic party and helped Doctor Gmeli
collect specimens. He himself did not have a description of th
trip published but Gmelin did in four octavo volumes which
however, only contain what he thought he could publish withou
reservation. I must refer my readers to those volumes since
can only provide the most general and shortest account of th
expedition here.

The Journey During 1733

They left St. Petersburg on 8 August 1733. After man
unpleasant experiences on the Volga, they arrived a
Kos'modem'iansk on 14 October. They made their first contac
with the Chuvash living in the area.

On 18 October they arrived nearly frozen at Kazan. Plato
Ivanovich Musin-Pushkin was the town's administrator. He ha
studied at German universities, but showed little liking fo
them.

Here they attended the religious services of the Mohammeda
Tatars. The co-operative Major la Mothe also allowed them t
witness Tatars and Votiaks taking oaths as soldiers, at whic
time the men kissed the Koran and received a cube of salted brea
laid on two crossed daggers. The bread is supposed to kill the
if they do not keep their oath.

The Mohammedan Tatars whom they encountered in the regio
after leaving Kazan were affable and obliging people. They wer
very satisfied with their meeting with them. The gift a Tata
had given for his wife to her parents had been 18 rubles.

On the way to Osa, they met Votiaks. Müller sent for a don
(sorcerer) and had him perform his tricks in two feigned cases o
theft and sickness because the man's cunning behavior amused him.

In a Cheremis village, a father had a rather good-lookin
fifteen-year-old daughter whom he wanted to sell as a wife for 1
rubles but only 5 had been offered to him. They jokingly offere
him the 10 rubles which he wanted but he did not respond to them
They saw women who wore small bells around their ankles. On th

ther side of Osa they saw a Kungur Tatar woman for whom her
usband had paid her parents 50 rubles.

On 26 December they crossed the Ural Mountains, which was
onsidered the dividing line between Russia proper and Siberia
nd between Europe and Asia.   On 27 December, they arrived in
katerinburg, a town built in German style, its commandant
eneral-Lieutenant von Hennin, President of the Regional Mining
ffice, helped them spend a few weeks satisfactorily and
sefully.   They acquired a good knowledge of mining and smelting
rocesses.

n the Year 1734

Müller arrived in Tobol'sk, the capital of Siberia, before
melin, who only reached there on 30 January 1734.   On 17
ebruary, at the beginning of the last week before Lent, they
atched an astonishing spectacle.   Nothing but revelling and
runkenness could be seen in the whole Russian Empire.   People
at on snow heaps singing and drinking without heeding the cold.
n 3 March they visited the Cathedral and listened as all
eceased tsars, patriarchs and many other persons (including
rmak, the robber chief who had discovered and conquered Siberia
or Russia) were praised as holy, while all unbelievers and
eretics, the Lutherans, Reformed and Catholics were put under
he great ban of the church.

At a Tatar wedding two Tatar musicians played, among other
ieces, one ballad which they called Ermak because it had been
omposed during the time when this adventurer was bringing their
orefathers under Russian control.   They themselves were moved by
he ballad.   They surmised that it was a lament about their
isfortune.   There are many conquered nations which hundreds of
ears later still bemoan their fates.

In Tobol'sk, Müller observed a Tatar wedding ceremony.   He
ould not get permission to watch the rituals for the bride on
he day before the wedding (since only the closest relatives and
rusted friends were allowed to participate).   But several years
ater in the Tobol'sk area he had the satisfaction of seeing
hese rituals in exchange for a few pounds of raisins and also of
bserving the bride who sat behind a curtain, ringed by girls
idding her farewell.

On 14 April he saw another festivity.   A house, standing on
ne of the hills near Tobol'sk, contained a lot of coffins with
he bodies of people who had been executed or died without
ommunion and for this reason could not be buried with the dead
n consecrated ground.   On this day many of their relatives and
ther people visited there to take leave of them and earn their
ntercession since they believed that such deceased persons would
ot be excluded even for a year from salvation if, on the
ollowing Thursday before Pentecost, the archbishop and the

priest led a solemn procession to this house of the dead an
absolved the dead of their sins.

In this town not only the feast days of the Russian court bu
also the birthdays and name-days in families are celebrated wit
dinner parties. A lover of eating and drinking can thus find n
better place in the world than here. He must, however, just lik
the numerous local merchants, leave a gift of a ruble or at leas
half a ruble on parting.

Müller also observed the circumcision of Mohammedan Tata
boys. He said that it was not treated like a religious or hol
ceremony but rather like an ordinary event and game. The bloo
was immediately stopped by the application of burned cotton.

Tea is the Tatar's revered beverage for all holidays.   I
their opinion tea, brewed together with milk and butter in
kettle, is the most delicious drink of all.

On 26 May they left Tobol'sk and continued their journey b
ship up the River Irtysh. Along the way they bought a sturgeo
two ells long for about three groschen and their companions abou
200 carp for a groschen. The town of Tara had 700 inhabitants i
1723 but since they did not want to take the oath of loyalt
which Peter I had decreed in 1722 regarding the royal succession
most had been executed. That was an extremely irrational act o
brutality in a region so devoid of people.

Some 9 to 10 miles from the fort Iamyshevskaia on the Irtys
River they saw large wild pigs living exclusively on grass an
roots.

From Iamyshevskaia they went by land to Semipalatinsk for
and from there to Semipalat in order to see the abandoned Kalmy
building, which Müller described in volume ten of the Commentari
(Acad. Petrop.) along with the Tangut manuscript found there
They travelled via the fort Ust'-Kamenogorsk to Kolyvan', a plac
famous for its silver-rich ores. Thus, they travelled farthe
and farther from the frontier of the region where the Kazak
horde and the Kalmyk roam.

In the Tatar village of Kaltirak on the way to Kuznetsk
Müller had a Teleut Tatar women brought to their rooms in orde
to have a sketch of her made. She was uncommonly beautiful. Sh
had black hair, a white, pleasant face and was friendly and wel
built. Her husband who came with her was blind in one eye
therefore they asked her if she were satisfied with this man o
whether she would like a better one. She answered that it woul
be nice if he were in better condition, but since God had wille
it she was satisfied.

On 15 September they arrived at the town of Kuznetsk. In
nearby village lived Teleut Tatars, who were not Mohammedans
Men and women, young and old, smoked tobacco and inhaled.   I

his region, as in others, Müller had some members of the various
atars groups come to see him, including their priests, whom he
ad perform their tricks, on their magic drums.

In Tomsk lived 3 men, Russian Old Believers. Ever since
eter I had ordered all men to shave off their beards each one
ad been voluntarily paying 50 rubles a year in order to obtain
ermission to keep his beard.

On 6 December they reached Eniseisk. At mid-month they
xperienced such intense cold that the air seemed frozen and
esembled a fog that the sun could not disperse. The sparrows
nd jays fell from the sky as though dead and froze immediately
nless they were taken into a warm room. If a house door was
pen, the escaping warm vapor froze immediately and looked like
og.

The <u>voevoda</u> there had a dwarf approximately one Russian ell
all, over fifty years old, with a second wife and five living
hildren.

n the Year 1735

From Krasnoiarsk they went to Irkutsk, where they arrived on
 March. They then continued their trip to Lake Baikal, via
elenginsk to Kiakhta on the border of China.

Among the Buriats, who speak Mongolian and live in these
reas, Müller collected information about the religion headed by
he Dalai Lama. He even went over the border into the nearby
hinese area in order to get to know the Chinese.

Then they returned to Selenginsk, where Brigadier Buchholz
ffered them his hospitality. From there they travelled to
erchinsk to visit the area's famous silver mines, then to the
order town of Tsurukhaitu, the town of Udinsk, and back to
rkutsk. Since Tungus live in this area, Müller was able to
amiliarize himself with their way of life and religion.

They arrived in Irkutsk on 20 September. Merchants from
owns all over Russia bring their wares here in order to trade
ith the Chinese. Many a merchant, coming here from Moscow and
hen travelling on to Kiakhta and finally to Irkutsk with his
emaining trade goods, only returns to Moscow again four and one-
alf years later. If he has been prudent and lucky, he will have
ade a 300% profit. At least that is how it was at that time.

n the Year 1736

On 26 January 1736 they left Irkutsk, going north towards
limsk. Along the way Müller had Tungus shamans (sorcerers)
emonstrate their conjuring arts for him. In the town of Ilimsk,
here they arrived on 4 March, they stayed for a while because
üller found a lot of information in the local archives which

took him a great deal of time to examine. Many of the Tungus i
the area have blue stripes and figures on the faces.   Specia
artists, using a needle and thread blackened with soot, sew the
on adults between the ages of 12-20 as well as on children.

On 24 March they left for Iakutsk by way of Kirenga. Of th
25 carters they used, only 5 had unmutilated noses. The rest ha
had theirs slit open as punishment.

All over Siberia they found the highest possible level o
alcohol consumption, especially during holidays and before time
of fasting.

Even in Siberia it does not suffice to forbid something b
threat of capital punishment, for, if it is to mean anything, i
also has to be carried out. Everyone, however, breaks the law
because he knows if he is caught it will not cost him his hea
since he knows he can buy off the commandants.

Kindness, leniency, and friendly persuasion are of no hel
with Siberians. One has to be extremely severe with them to mak
them behave well. And these people are called Christians. It i
easy to imagine how very offensive heathen peoples find them
When Müller and his travelling companions met nomadic Iakuts, a
was his habit, he asked about their idolatrous religion and thei
way of life.

Toward the end of August, Müller began to find the cold s
unpleasant that he returned to Iakutsk earlier than hi
travelling companions. He arrived there on 31 August. The whol
party only got together again there on 11 September. By 2
September the Lena River was already frozen over. A few day
later it was possible to chop pieces of ice one and one-half ell
thick from it. Instead of windows the people put blocks of pur
ice into the window openings from the outside. They let throug
light but not the cold wind no matter how stormy it might be
Wealthy people put windows on the inside of the window opening
to prevent the ice from giving off steam. The cold was so fierc
once that a voevoda who wanted to go from his house to his offic
about 20-25 klafter away, although he was covered from head t
foot in fur, froze his hands, feet and nose, and they coul
barely be restored to use.

In the local archives Müller found important informatio
indicating that at the end of the 17th century sea voyages ha
been undertaken almost every year from the mouth of the Lena o
the Arctic Ocean to Kolyma. In fact, he found that a man using
little boat not much longer than a skiff had gone from Kolym
around the Chukotka Peninsula to Kamchatka.

Since Iakutsk lies at $62^{\circ}2'$ latitude it is barely light b
9:00 a.m. in the winter. During storms and snow flurries it i
necessary to burn lights all day. In good weather it is possibl
to see the stars again at 2:30 in the afternoon. The inhabitant

rrange their lives according to time and conditions. They not
nly sleep the whole night but barely take the time to eat before
oing back to sleep. In fact, on dark days they do not even wake
r get up. But the scurvy which is commonplace here makes it
ery unhealthy to sleep a lot. That is why Müller and his
ompanions avoided sleeping for long periods as much as possible.

On 8 November they went to a dinner they had been invited to
t 7 o'clock in the evening. At 9 o'clock Gmelin's house, where
ller kept his cash, went up in flames. Three days after it had
urned to the ground, they searched through the ashes and
ecovered over half of their money. Some of it was undamaged and
ome of it was melted.

n the Year 1737

By the middle of April, the travellers could already enjoy
oring air. With the breakup of the river on 11 May, winter
uddenly disappeared. Müller observed and described the Iakuts'
iolatrous religious customs and magic acts.

From Iakutsk Müller and his companions were supposed to
ravel to Okhotsk and from there to Kamchatka, even though he had
egun ailing the previous winter, but neither the sea expedition
ed by the renowned Captain Bering, which was to go there, nor
ne Iakutsk voevoda chancellery wanted to provide them with the
ecessary provisions. The sea expedition, indeed, gave them no
ope for their being able to cross from Okhotsk to Kamchatka, so
hey had to postpone their trip. Professor Delisle de la Croyère
ecided to go down the Lena to the quite northern regions in
rder to undertake astronomical observations, while Müller and
nelin sent their adjunct (and later professor) Krasheninnikov
nead to Kamchatka with the necessary instructions. They then
repared for the return trip in order to spend the next winter on
ne upper Lena in a somewhat warmer region.

On the journey thus far they had covered:

rom St. Petersburg to Kiakhta	10,355 versts
rom Kiakhta back to Selenginsk	91 versts
rom Selenginsk to Iakutsk	6,525 versts
otaling	16,871 versts

hich is over 2,410 German miles.

On 9 July 1737 they started their return trip up the Lena,
nd arrived on 3 September at Kirenga or Kirenskii ostrog, which
ney had chosen as their fall and winter quarters. Here they
ere disturbed neither by visits nor by correspondence with the
nancellories as they worked up their collected observations and
eports. Here they could gather information from St. Petersburg,
obol'sk, Irkutsk, Iakutsk and Okhotsk. Couriers constantly
oved between these places and the Kamchatka Sea Command and

could not go through the Kirenskii ostrog without their knowin
about it.

Here they were also satisfied with their situation an
generally healthy with the exception of Müller. He had alread
become aware of a decline in his strength during the previou
winter in Iakutsk. This included depression, frequent bloatinc
anxiety, pressure in his chest, and unusually cold fee
(especially his soles) even in rooms where no one else had
similar experience. Frequently he was spared these symptoms an
it seemed as if the summer journey had brought considerabl
relief from all those symptoms. But they started again eight t
fourteen days after his arrival in Kirenskii ostrog.   I
addition, he suffered from violent palpitations of the hea:
combined with indescribable anxiety which often woke him from h:
sleep, bothered him for hours and occasionally forced him t
weep.

Dr. Gmelin, who ascribed Müller's illness to the difficultie
which he had encountered during the trip as well as to his grea
sensitivity, often found it necessary to let Müller's bloo
Since they had left their surgeon with Professor Delisle de 1
Croyère in Iakutsk but knew that the Chinese caravan in Irkuts
had a surgeon, they decided that Müller, fortified with Gmelin'
counsel and medicines, should travel to Irkutsk. On 6 Novembe
he set out for there even though the roads were not a
comfortable for a sick man as he might have wished.   F
frequently sent Gmelin, in Kirenskii ostrog, reports on the sta1
of his health. So-called nerve-strengthening medicines, mac
from all sorts of resins mixed with aromatic spirits, which ha
been prepared with a touch of wine residue, and seventeen bloo(
lettings, each about five to six ounces, over a period of tv
months, restored his rather wasted condition. He made urgent a:
repeated requests to the chancellery asking it to have t
provisions needed by him and his companions sent to Ochotsk a:
Kamchatka. Finally it promised to do what it could.

In the Year 1738

An ill Gmelin arrived at Irkutsk on 12 March 1738. Mülle:
however, who had come several versts to meet him, looked mu(
better than he had upon his departure from Kirenga. But Müller
illness was not over, merely milder.

Since the hopes for provisions were uncertain and t
expedition was in its fifth year with no end in sight, ev(
though upon their departure from St. Petersburg they had be(
led to think that they would be back in five years, they wrote 1
the Senate and asked permission to return to St. Petersbur(
Their petitions were sent in May.

During June they undertook a short trip to watch a religio'
festival among the Buriats. They had several good Buriat ridi:
horses selected for their use. Müller had barely mounted h

hen it reared because it was not used to a cannon bit and fell
ver backwards with him.   At first he appeared to have no
njuries except for some pain in his back and the small of his
ack.   But since the pain continued and some swelling appeared in
he small of his back and Gmelin had no medicines with him,
melin prescribed a sweatbath for Müller.   This healed him.

Upon return from this trip they were informed by the
ssistant town administrator that there was no way that he could
et the desired provisions for their trip to Kamchatka by year's
nd.   It might well be two years before they could be dispatched.
n the meantime they could examine other regions of Siberia in
nich they had not yet been.

Among these were areas along the Angara and Tunguska rivers
elow Irkutsk, where Buriats and Tungus lived.   They decided to
isit these areas.   On 2 August 1738 they set out down the Angara
nich empties into Lake Baikal below Irkutsk.   A few weeks later
ney arrived at Eniseisk, a town they had left nearly four years
arlier and in which they spent the following winter.

n the Year 1739

In January 1739 Adjunct Georg Wilhelm Steller arrived.   He
ad been sent by the Academy of Sciences to help Gmelin with
atural history.   This young man was readied for the difficult
rip to Kamchatka, where Krasheninnikov had already arrived.   In
ne summer they themselves travelled down the Enisei River to
angazeia despite bad relapses of Müller's illness in the winter
nich should have made him avoid this cold region.

By 6 June they reached the city of Mangazeia which lies north
f the 65th parallel.   At their departure from Eniseisk 10 days
arlier the fields had been green and blooming, but at Mangazeia
ne fields were still covered in snow since it had snowed on
0/21 June.*

By 14/25 June all the snow was gone.   The grass was growing
isibly and the next day yellow violets, which in other places
nly grow at high altitudes, were in full bloom.   Beginning 11/22
ine there was no noticeable difference between night and day.
ney could read small print at midnight just as well as in
outhern climes at midday with overcast skies.   They saw the sun
ne whole night, especially from the low church tower from which
ney could see the whole disc of the sun.   They could simply look
ito the sun without being blinded since there were no rays.   But
oward 12:30 the rays could be seen clearly.   Since they had
ever seen this sight before and had no hope of experiencing it
jain, they dedicated a whole night to it.   They sat down on the

* These double dates are references to both the Julian and
regorian calendars.   [ed.]

street at a table, turned their faces toward the north and fixed
their eyes on the sun and followed its course.

At this place they also saw a huge number of birds
especially wild geese and ducks, coots, gulls, sandpipers
snipes, curlews, cranes, black storks, divers and many others
Their calls were so diverse, sometimes harmonious, sometimes not
that they considered them pleasant music in the area.

In June members of a lot of different peoples, for example
Ostiaks, Samoyeds, etc., came to a market held here.   Mülle
examined and inquired about their customs and languages.

When they returned to Eniseisk on 26 July they found severa
packages from St. Petersburg.   Their contents made Müller happ
but Gmelin sad.   Müller had permission to return to St
Petersburg but Gmelin was ordered to stay in Siberia and to go t
Kamchatka as soon as possible.   Gmelin once again wrote St
Petersburg to request his recall; Müller, however, was so cheere
by the fact that he could decide on his own when he wanted t
return, that he stayed in Siberia longer than he had previousl
wished.

They left Eniseisk on 5 August and went upstream t
Krasnoiarsk, where they arrived on the 19th.   From here they roc
Tatar horses for almost 5 months southward to Abakansk, wher
among other things, Müller inspected old Tatar graves, some c
which were still magnificent.   The researchers removed belts
earrings, bracelets and gold and silver in containers from then
No Tatar would plunder his ancestors' graves for they are muc
too sacred.   The Tatars living in the areas around the grave
allude to their ancestors' wealth.   Since their religion serve
them so well, this is the reason they reject the Christian ar
Mohammedan religions and Mongolian idolatry.   After endurir
great hardships, Müller and Gmelin arrived back in Krasnoiarsk c
7 October.   There they rested while organizing and evaluating th
materials they had collected.

In December a common woman, who had already spent 12 years i
prison for killing her husband, was buried alive, i.e., accordir
to Russian law, standing and up to her breasts and neck.   A guar
was stationed by her to prevent anyone from giving her anythir
to eat or drink.   This was probably done to lengthen her agony
She gradually lost strength.   A couple days before her death sh
became apathetic.   Fourteen days after being buried alive sh
passed away.

The next summer in Krasnoiarsk Gmelin saw another woman,
25-year-old baptized Tatar buried alive.   In a fit of jealous
she had cut off her husband's head.   She died 5 days later.   I
is uncertain if she died from starvation or from plague she migh
have caught from insects.

Here too as at other places in Siberia, they heard of women who had drunk so much alcohol that they died on the spot.

On the second feastday after Christmas they saw a great number of midwives in festive costume leave the churches. They heard that they were not only from the city but also from the many neighboring villages. After church services on this day the midwives made merry since they believed that this holiday, because of their predecessors' help at the Lord's birth, belonged to them more than all others. Probably they had been given permission to enjoy themselves the day after His birth. That evening they were rather drunk when they took leave of each other.

In the Year 1740

On 2 February 1740, Müller travelled to Tomsk to get somewhat closer to St. Petersburg and, at the same time, to examine the archives there as well as to get to know the Ostiaks better. Gmelin, however, stayed in Krasnoiarsk and the region around it until he received final word from St. Petersburg about his fate. In the summer Adjunct Fischer, who was to take over and continue Müller's study of ethnic history, joined him in the area around the town of Narym, and Adjunct Martini joined Gmelin in order to help him. That summer Müller went as far as Berezov and in the winter to Tobol'sk and Tiumen.

In the Year 1741

In June Gmelin received the news he wanted to hear from the Academy that the Senate also had agreed to his return. He hurried to join Müller, who had gone to Ekaterinburg and Isetskii Province that summer and found himself in better health than during previous years. They met on 17 September at the Iset River and arrived in Tobol'sk on 26 October. The ever alert Müller took advantage of the opportunity to observe precisely the funeral of a Bukharan Mohammedan Tatar, who had been a member of the Kalmyk delegation to St. Petersburg. It was noteworthy for its diverse religious rituals. Gmelin relates Müller's observations on page 236 in part four of the description of his travels.

In the Year 1742

They left Tobol'sk on 18 January 1742 and travelled toward Verkhotur'e. On the way to Turinsk at Krasno-Slobodskoi ostrog on the Noza [Nitsa], they met a colonel, an exiled German named Weiding, who had become so accustomed to Siberia and this area that he turned down an imperial pardon allowing him to return to St. Petersburg. In Turinskaia Sloboda on the Tura they found a commander, a Swede, who had been a military preacher at the battle of Poltava [1709] where he had been taken prisoner. But after he converted to the Russian-Greek Church. He was, however, a bad human being.

Now and again in the Russian Empire one finds such people
from Germany and other nationals, and not infrequently there is
at least one such depraved former minister among them.

At Turinsk in March Müller's body, already weakened by a lot
of illnesses and arduous travel, was so violently attacked by a
serious illness that for 3 weeks Gmelin feared for his life.
Finally Müller overcame the peril and gradually recovered his
strength permitting him to travel to Verkhotur'e and spend the
summer there.

Here Müller found what he had neither sought nor expected to
find; namely, a wife, the German widow of a German surgeon. They
were wed by a Protestant minister who had been assigned from
Ekaterinburg. At the same time he received a helpmate perfectly
suited to him, who served to cheer him up as much as to care for
him, and to whom he was married for 41 years before leaving her a
widow.

Around Verkhotur'e one very frequently finds what the
Siberians call a cedar (<u>Pinus foliis quinis</u>, <u>cono erecto</u>, <u>nucleo</u>
<u>eduli</u>). In Siberia and Russia its nuts are considered good
tasting and eaten with the fingers. Oil is also pressed from
them. The well-to-do use it instead of butter to make baked
goods and to prepare fish during Lent. These nuts are a widely
available and popular food throughout Russia including St
Petersburg. Verkhotur'e is the first place from which they can
be shipped to Russia. They prefer to have them sent from the
closest spot rather than the farthest. Travellers from Siberia
to Russia purchase them in Verkhotur'e. On Müller's and Gmelin's
return trip a pud (40 Russian pounds) of them cost 15 kopeks
(about 4 1/2 groschen). Despite the low price collecting them
was preferable to working at the grain harvest, no doubt because
it was easier. In St. Petersburg I was not able to develop a
taste for them.

In December they crossed the Ural Mountains on the way to
Solikamsk in a fairly high region and tried to determine the
height of the area by taking barometric readings. They paid no
attention to the penetrating cold in the mountains because they
were heading for St. Petersburg and they arrived safely in
Solikamsk. 15 December was the beginning of the fast period that
ended the day before Christmas; so it was difficult for them to
obtain meat. But a certain respectable German exile who had put
up provisions so that he would have meat during the fast period
occasionally sent them something from his store.

The place is famous for its salt wells, from which salt is
refined. Like all salt from Perm it is considered the best in
Russia. The children of the Demidov family, who lived there and
owned some salt wells, were generally well brought up. They were
five to eight years old, but judging by their manners and
behavior might have been considered much older. They had also
been taught in languages and sciences.

In the Year 1743

They left Solikamsk toward 11:00 on the night of 1 January 1743. In the city of Vologda, where many Germans lived, they found a German surgeon whom the medical chancellory in St. Petersburg had sent as city surgeon in 1742. The inhabitants, however, had not yet become accustomed to him but rather, because he was paid by city hall, they looked upon him as more of a burden than a blessing. Perhaps he was the same man, a Prussian born subject, who in 1762 had given my great friend, the then Secretary of the Danish delegation at St. Petersburg and present Councillor and Knight of the Danebrogorden (Order of the Danish Flag), Mr. von Schumacher, 20 rubles. He asked him to distribute them among the Prussian prisoners of war. I took them and used them for ill Prussian prisoners of war being released from the hospital.

Müller and Gmelin wanted to have new clothes made to replace the ones that had become old fashioned on the long trip. They could get the necessary cloth there, but the tailors knew as little about the new styles as the ones in Siberia.

Müller finally arrived again in St. Petersburg on 14 February and Gmelin on 16 February, but the former continued to be plagued for several years by the serious hypochondriac illness which he had picked up on the Siberian journey. The complete, nearly ten-year, journey had covered some 31,362 versts, i.e., 4,480 German miles. The only other remark I wish to make is that Müller, at Empress Anna's personal command on 1 February and the Senate's on 8 February, drew up reports for State Councillor Lange, who was being sent to Irkutsk as Vice-Governor, and who requested them for his negotiations with the Chinese. What Müller believed he could publicly report, he presented in his history of the Amur River, in the second volume of his collection of Russian history.

Müller is not Paid for the Trip

Readers of this short history of that long, difficult and dangerous journey will ask how Müller was rewarded. In 1732 when the Senate decided to create the Kamchatka Expedition and send along several professors to explore the natural attributes, geography and history of Siberia, it asked the same question of the Academy, which answered that the professors worked on contract. Indeed, they were duty bound to work for the Academy, but need not allow themselves to be sent on expeditions. At this Empress Anna decreed that those professors deciding to undertake the trip would receive double pay and promised that on their return they would be well rewarded.

At that time the youngest professors received, aside from 60 rubles subsistence allowance, only 600 rubles income. Müller, who belonged to that group, received twice that when the expedition started. He returned with a lot of useful and significant information as well as a very weakened constitution,

only to discover that during his and his travelling companions'
absence, every professor had received a 200 ruble supplement in
1738.

Müller and Gmelin sent the Senate a petition requesting
payment for services rendered, payment not only of the double
salary enjoyed during the trip but also of the supplement given
the other professors. With housing and lighting allowances their
request came to 1,660 rubles. The Senate acknowledged their
request as being just, but, since the Court had gone to Moscow,
consoled them with hopes upon its return. The Academy had no
president at the time and Director Schumacher did what he
pleased. After Müller's and Gmelin's return he put them back on
the income of 600 rubles which they had before the trip. They
thus received no payment, but rather 200 rubles less than the
youngest professors. The Court did, indeed, return to St.
Petersburg. Count Kiril Grigor'evich Razumovskii was made
President of the Academy. He passed Müller's and Gmelin's matter
over to the Senate. There it again came to the chancellory and
Schumacher, who set it aside.

Gmelin did not stand this flagrant injustice for long. He
returned to his fatherland to become a professor of chemistry and
botany in Tübingen. Müller, for a long time, lived in distress
and poverty because no one came to his aid.

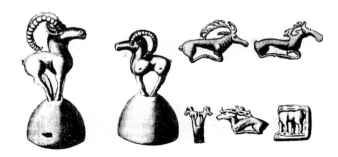

Gold objects from Enisei burials, obtained by Müller's expedition.

DOCUMENT 4

G.-F. Müller, Travels in Siberia, 1733-1740, from "Istoriia Akademii Nauk G.-F. Millera, 1725-1743, "(Materialy dlia istorii imperatorskoi Akademii Nauk, VI [St. Petersburg, 1890]), pp. 252-54, 269, 71, 279-87, 340-66, 383-422). Translated by Victoria Joan Moessner.

Anno 1732: [pp. 252-54]

The Academy's participation in the Second Kamchatka Expedition is the most noteworthy event of this period. It is all the more necessary to write about this in a history of the Academy because incomplete information has reached the public, even from myself, since I was not given official permission to inform the world about it. Captain Bering's first voyage had not answered the questions which the great Tsar Peter I had ordered the Expedition to answer. The second voyage was to continue research in the Kamchatka Sea and along the American mainland as well as to determine the geographic relationship of Japan to Kamchatka. In addition, voyages to the Arctic were to be initiated to determine whether the long overland route through Siberia might be replaced by an easier route to the Kamchatka Sea, to help to foster trade. The Senate's head secretary, Ivan Kirillovich Kirilov, a very patriotic man who was fond of geography and statistics, was the main driving force behind the second expedition. He contacted Captain Bering who, like his two lieutenants, Martin Spangenberg and A.I. Chirikov, declared himself prepared to undertake a second voyage. Kirilov prepared a treatise on the project's advantages for Russia and combined it with other proposals for expanding Russian trade towards ·Bokhara and even to India. As a result of this treatise, the famous Orenburg Expedition which Kirilov himself initiated was later undertaken. He died on it in 1737. Kirilov's treatise had to be translated into German so that he could give it to Chamberlain Ernst-Johann Count von Biron, whose support he hoped above all to obtain. Because he chose a poor translator, Captain Bering counselled him to have the translation improved by me. That is how I came to become acquainted with Kirilov - something which would not be without consequences.

On 17 April [1732] the Tsarina commanded the Imperial Senate to have Captain Bering, who in the meantime had been given the rank of Captain Commander (chef d'escadre), prepare a second expedition to Kamchatka. Both the Senate and the Admiralty College told him what he was to observe and undertake there. At the time the authorities stated that, above all, they needed as much correct information as possible about the area to be explored on the other side of Kamchatka - an area not found on most maps. They wanted to know how far Spanish ships were sailing along the coast of North America and the extent of colonization in the direction of Kamchatka. They wanted to determine the distance between the two parts of the world and make preliminary estimates about the course mariners would have

63

to take for future exploration. Mr. Joseph-Nicholas Delisle
glued together an eight page map of the northern half of the
South Seas or Pacific Ocean as described by the European mariners
he knew. To this he added a written report on the sources he had
used in which he emphasized those phenomena, which, in his
opinion, should be most closely investigated.

Mr. [Louis Delisle de] La Croyère possessed a superb
collection of geographical reports from all empires and
countries, which he had probably inherited from his brother, the
famous geographer, Guillaume Delisle. It is hard to understand
why he failed to exploit these materials fully on this occasion
and why he let himself be misled by old, incorrect relationships.
His map hindered explorations beyond Kamchatka more than it aided
them.

Anno 1733: [pp. 269-71]

The reader should remember from the previous year's history
that two of the Academy's professors, J.G. Gmelin and L. La
Croyère had volunteered to participate in the Kamchatka
expedition. Their names were then proposed to the Supreme
Governing Senate and approved by it. Throughout the winter
preparations were made for the expedition. They nearly came to
naught because of a dangerous turn in Mr. Gmelin's health. What
began as a slight pain around his liver grew worse with each
passing day despite all of the medicines he took to heal it. His
ruddy appearance disappeared; he lost weight in his face and on
his whole body. If a sympathetic friend told him that he looked
poorly, he became upset like a consumptive. Gmelin, a competent
doctor himself, recognized that his life was in danger and that
he would have to forego the expedition to Siberia, so he withdrew
his previous offer to the Academy. This was not held against him
since for several months no one had thought that he was healthy
enough to undertake the trip.

At the time the Academy was hoping that Dr. Ammann would come
from London to take a position as Professor of Botany and Natural
History, but the date of his arrival was uncertain. If the
Academy did not want to have Mr. La Croyère travel alone, then
Mr. Gmelin had to be replaced quickly. I shall not discuss the
reservations people had, or should have had, about Mr. La
Croyère. Later experience demonstrated that the scientific
intent of the expedition would have met with failure if he alone
had been entrusted with such an important task.

Because no one at the Academy could take Mr. Gmelin's place
as a natural historian, we thought that it would be just as
useful to let an interested professor from another scientific
field participate in the expedition. The Academy, despite our
contracts binding us to Petersburg, had always honored our right
to volunteer for an expedition.

Even before there was any discussion about my joining the expedition, Captain Commander Bering, with whom I had had frequent contact, had excited my interest in it. Kirilov, the Senate's head secretary whom Bering had told about my interest, knew me and asked me to offer myself as Gmelin's replacement on the expedition. No one opposed me at the Academy. The matter was presented in writing to the Senate on 26 February 1733 and approved on 22 March. I was happy to be able to escape from the chaotic conditions at the Academy for a long period of time. Far away from the hatred and hostilities, I could create and enjoy my own peace and quiet. Not once have I regretted my decision to go, even in view of the serious illness I suffered in Siberia. Indeed, the expedition seems to me to have been an act of providence which made me truly useful to the Russian Empire. Had I not gone on the expedition, I could only have acquired the information and materials I did with great difficulty.

In terms of human experience Mr. Gmelin's was even more remarkable. Mr. La Croyère and I were preparing to leave when Gmelin, contrary to all expectations, and I almost want to say, by a medical miracle, regained his health and his urgent desire to participate in the trip. I do not know if he did it because he was convinced for medical reasons that it could bring about a great change in a dangerously ill person's condition, or because of lust, as occasionally violently befalls some ill people as well as some women, or if it was due to impatience caused by his long illness and ever increasing pain, or perhaps, because of a hidden presentiment of unknown origin, but one evening when Gmelin was all alone he made friends with a bottle of the best Rhine wine, or perhaps two, until he had completely quenched his thirst. No one saw him in this condition but he did not keep it secret from his friends. In a few days Gmelin had recovered. When he informed the Senate of this and his continuing wish to participate in the Kamchatka expedition, on 11 June the Senate commanded the Academy to send Gmelin with us on the same terms we had.

Thus, instead of one, three professors went on the Kamchatka expedition, one from each of the three classes at the Academy; we were a group worthy of Russia and one which was to get to know all aspects of Russia's vast empire better than ever before.

To our great pleasure Her Majesty, Empress Elizabeth and both royal princesses personally bade us farewell and granted us their most charitable, highest blessings for our expedition. Since we did not have enough draft horses, most of our group together with our baggage left on 3 August and travelled by barque down the Neva, the Ladoga Canal, and the Volkhov River to Novgorod and Bronnitsy. On 8 August, we set out by wagon for Novaia Pristan and from there by water to Novgorod, where we waited from the 14th to the 18th for our Petersburg barque, which arrived in Bronnitsy on the 25th. Currents and waterfalls on the Neva and Volkhov had delayed it.

Readers should not expect me to convey observations made on our trip here since they are of the kind you would expect from novices just beginning to learn how to describe unknown places. We first needed personal experiences to stimulate and nourish our powers of observation. Both Mr. Gmelin and I kept diaries. I, of course, let him have mine to use, since my observations otherwise might have been lost to him. His journal was published later in Göttingen. I did not like some of his supposed humorous remarks, which are not excused by his claim that they were not written for publication (since they were indeed published). We both decided to keep our scientific observations in a number of different books depending upon the subject matter so that they could be written up systematically for the benefit of their future readers. We both only wanted to use the diaries for superficial descriptions of the expedition, i.e., for a general description of our activities as well as the resources and obstacles we encountered.

At Bronnitsy we encountered difficulties when we tried to examine a hill near the post station that State Councilor and later Privy Councilor Tatishchev had suggested we should inspect. Since it stood isolated by itself, we wanted to determine if it were natural or man-made. The two small burial mounds at the foot of the hill whetted my desire to see if they contained any artifacts. This was an opportune activity for us since we had nothing else more important to do while waiting for the barque. We had set out ahead of the barque for Bronnitsy so that we could be finished with our inspection before its arrival. The area commander did not support our work. First there were no workers and then no shovels. Because we were pressed for time, we did not stay there long. We only established that the small hills were burial mounds of recent origin.

We decided the isolated hill, because of the large rocks and a constantly flowing spring on its summit was not man-made but natural. We later learned that the commander's and inhabitants' antipathy to our work stemmed from their belief that the hill was considered holy because of its unusual spring. That is why a chapel had been built on it. Every year on St. John the Baptist's Day, processions go there from the village.

On 27 August our whole group left Bronnitsy by wagon. Continual rain and very bad roads often prevented us from covering more than 12 to 15 versts a day. On 7 September we arrived at Vyshnii Volochek, where we hired a wagon to Tver. We arrived there on the 14th. If possible, I have always preferred the comforts of travelling by water to land because I can use my travelling time fruitfully.

In Tver, Captain Commander Bering, who had established his spring camp there, provided us with a large covered barque at my request so that we could travel as far as Kazan that summer. He also provided us with a warrant officer, a boatswain and three sailors whose efforts in preparing and maintaining the barque,

specially during various incidents on our voyage we gratefully
acknowledge. The barque had various cabins or compartments with
stoves and the one in the middle even had a kitchen stove.   We
had every needed comfort. We could sail or row. We had hired
the workers to go as far as Kazan. We charged everything to our
postal costs we would have had to spend if we had gone by land,
the remaining balance was returned to the Crown.

On 21 September, while preparations were being made for us to
travel by water, we completed our first report to the Governing
Senate. It included our observations and descriptive remarks up
to that point.   The report itself was in Russian, but the
observations were left in the language [German] in which we had
written them. That is also how we continued to do things in the
future. The Senate always forwarded everything to the Academy.

In Petersburg we had not thought about taking along a surgeon
who could let blood or perform other surgical operations and
cures in emergencies. We informed the Senate of our need and
also requested that the surgeon be supplied with a field
dispensary. The Senate ordered Captain Commander Bering to send
us one of his surgeons and a field dispensary. But because he
was already so far ahead of us, our request could only be
fulfilled upon our arrival in Tobol'sk. He gave us a surgeon
named Brauner, a capable Swede with whom we were very satisfied.

Our departure on 27 September from Tver was accompanied by
some apprehension. Given the late season of the year, low
waters, which would cause unknown sandbars to appear, contrary
winds which could prevent travel, we wondered whether we would be
able to reach Kazan. We hurried as fast as we could.   I,
nevertheless, still tried to compile a directory of all the
cities, market towns, villages and places with names along the
Volga as well as the rivers and streams we passed. I was helped
by the inhabitants serving us as guides or pilots whom we picked
up in one city and dropped off in the next along the way.
Several times I had the boat stop for a few hours at noteworthy
cities to observe them, especially at Uglich, Iaroslavl,
Kostroma, Nizhnii-Novgorod and the cloister of Makar'ev. One of
the soldiers accompanying us, a Cheremis, thought that it would
be possible for us to visit Cheremises and Chuvash in their
homes, so Mr. Gmelin and I used a shallop to go between
Koz'modem'iansk and Cheboksary. The barque was supposed to give
a signal when passing Cheboksary. It was held up by contrary
winds. Since we thought we must have missed the signal, we
sailed the open shallop the rest of the way to Kazan without
stopping along the way. The trip was very uncomfortable for us
because we had neither a kitchen nor supplies nor warm clothes
even though it was already fairly cold.

We arrived in Kazan on 18 October. Two days later our barque
arrived. A couple of days later it could have been trapped in
ice on the Volga since on the 21st the Kazanka froze over. Here
we waited for a supply train of sleds and had time to collect a

lot of useful observations in this noteworthy town as well as t
make clean copies of the ones we had collected since leavin
Novgorod.

Francesco Locatelli, the Italian, finally decided to burde
us no longer with his company. He had met Major La Mothe an
told him about his circumstances, that he wanted to travel t
Persia to join Prince von Hessen-Homburg. When asked if he had
passport, he admitted that he did not have one for Persia excep
for one issued in the name of a merchant for Moscow. Therefore
La Mothe took Locatelli to the governor and he sent him to St
Petersburg under guard. He himself recounts his late
experiences in <u>Lettres Moscovites</u>, a book filled with lies an
slander, which appeared in German titled <u>Moscovitische Brief</u>
(1738) and includes explanatory notes refuting him. Our part
did not totally escape his criticism in this book, but he did no
write anything negative about us personally. I have to confes
that I would have expected him to want to revenge himself mor
than he did for our recalcitrance.

Without a doubt Kazan is one of the largest and best Russia
towns and has a superabundance of all kinds of goods. Part o
its inhabitants are Tatars. I was able to establish contact wit
them. Aleksei Tevkelev, a Kazanian murza (religious leader) who
I had known in Petersburg, had just returned from a diplomati
trip during which he had bound the Kirgiz-Kaisaks [Kazakhs] o
the Little Horde by oath [to the Russian Empire] and conducte
high ranking men as hostages to St. Petersburg. Tevkelev ha
traits which distinguished him from his fellow countrymen. Ther
was no one who surpassed his loyalty and diligence in providin
useful services to the Empire. He had heard Peter the Grea
express the desire to expand Russian trade as far as India an
hoped he could see this encouraged and realized. He remained
steadfast Mohammedan and raised his children in that religion
This, however, did not prevent him from rising in the ranks o
the service until he died as a major-general still believing i
the Koran.

I would have liked to have taken a trip to the ruins of th
old city of Bulgar if the season of the year had been favorable
I could not carry out my goal of describing it and having i
sketched because snow covered the country. I was satisfied to a
extent with copies of gravestone inscriptions which Peter th
Great had had made there. On the Tsar's trip to Persia in 172
he went to Bulgar, and viewed the ruins. He considered th
inscriptions -- some of which were in Armenian but most of whic
were in Tatar -- important enough to have them copied by men wh
knew the languages completely. He sent these copies fro
Astrakhan to the commander at Kazan. At the same time he ordere
him to have the brickwork of the old buildings repaired wher
necessary to prevent their total decay. I had no troubl
obtaining permission to copy the inscriptions and the Tsar'
command.

A large Tatar settlement on the outskirts of Kazan where
trading flourishes contributes a great deal to the population of
the city.   There we had our first opportunity to observe a
Mohammedan religious service.   The Russian clergy has often tried
to spread Christianity among the Tatars and other non-Christians
peoples, but how great must be the barriers arising from the
differences in languages.   For this reason these peoples'
children were being taught Russian and Christianity so that this
knowledge would be of use some day in the conversion process.
This was done especially in Silantov Monastery near Kazan where a
seminary for church servants had been founded.   The pupils were
mainly Tatar, Cheremis and Chuvash boys.   Its influence appeared
promising.

Mr. Gmelin and I enjoyed inspecting the monastery and
seminary.   It is difficult to like his almost incomprehensible
description of our visit in his diary.   This could easily have
been corrected when it was printed.   I shall not discuss whether
conversion from the Mohammedan to Christian religion is a rarity
all over.   Their clergy are no less zealous in converting other
non-Christian and non-Mohammedan peoples than ours and often have
converted heathens before the Russians could -- this is a remark
which I heard during my time in Siberia -- this despite the fact
that proselytizing by Mohammedans among heathen peoples in Russia
has always been severely forbidden.

Mr. Gmelin described the Tatars' religious services rather
exactly, but almost too strangely.   Here I would like to refer to
the Russian translation of Ricaut's book and to Cantemir's
Systema.*

I would have liked to have observed circumcision, wedding
and burial ceremonies.   Either none took place or no one told us
about them.

In Kazan we became interested in the way in which the
Russians as well as the Tatars dye sheepskins black, red and
yellow -- better than in other Russian cities but not as well as
Georgians and Armenians in Astrakhan.   I have to admit, however,
that, on the one hand, we in part did not have enough knowledge
to ask the kinds of questions we should have in order to get
information and, on the other hand, the tanners might not have
been willing to disclose their methods and the advantage of
Astrakhan tanning -- which resembles the preparation of Turkish
Safians -- even if they knew that it was different.   That is why
we are unable to provide much information.   This area seems to be
the source of all tanning in Russia, even of Russian leather

---

*   Sir Paul Ricaut, <u>The Present State of the Ottoman Empire</u>
(1688); Demetrius Cantemir's <u>Systema</u>, a description of the
Mohammedan religion, was published in St. Petersburg in 1722,
[ed.].

which is distinguished from other European leathers by bein
tanned with birch oil. The Bulgars living along the Volga an
Kama are the Russians' closest neighbors. They traded over
wide area. In fact, even today Russian leather in the Bukhara
region is called <u>bulgar</u>. Tanners thought that they could mak
the leather more supple and durable by using seal fat instead o
birch oil. They discovered, however, that another quality of th
leather -- its pleasant smell which is so important in the trad
-- would be lost. That is why Peter the Great's decrees aimed a
improving leather have not been carried out all over.

A textile factory established by Peter the Great in Kaza
whose ownership was later transferred to a merchant named Miklae
-- as was done with several factories -- was flourishing. W
more than enjoyed visiting such a good factory with it
magnificent buildings several times. The first owner, who ha
run a flourishing business as well as given a great deal fo
building some new churches, had died. His heir was no
considered capable of continuing his work. Possibly in th
following years the factory went into decline. At the presen
time it is in good hands and has 96 looms for weaving ordinar
cloth for soldiers' uniforms since that has the most certai
market, and 20 looms for weaving other kinds of wool clot
(<u>karazeia</u>). At present the factory employs 1128 men and women.

I found it a pleasant duty -- since I had the most ampl
opportunities to fulfill it during my stay in Kazan -- to mee
the non-Russian peoples, the Chuvash, Cheremis, Votiaks, and t
some extent, the Mordvins living in Kazan province and t
describe in detail their way of life, religion, customs an
habits as well as collect vocabulary lists and other examples o
their languages. In the beginning I thought I could imitat
those learned men who had gathered translations of the Lord'
Prayer in all of the known languages and printed them. But th
people found the ideas contained in the Lord's Praye
incomprehensible. This soon taught me that this was not the wa
to examine languages thoroughly and compare their origins, so
made a list of single words for simple, physical objects whic
could not be misunderstood by anyone. I requested each person t
pronounce them in his own language and tried, as well as I could
to write them in the Latin alphabet. I used this list as a guid
on my whole Siberian trip in similar situations. Mr. V.N
Tatishchev, after taking over Siberian matters, had another lis
sent to all of the towns and ordered translations which th
voevoda in these towns had done, as proven by several example
brought back by Professor Fischer and given the Göttinge
Historical Institute. I later included the description of thes
peoples completed in Kazan in the third part of my <u>Sammlun
russischer Geschichte</u> (Collection of Russian History).

I will only say of Mr. La Croyère's observations that the
were rarely propitious, as he was wont to excuse himself. Mr
Delisle, however, claimed to know how to use them to calculat
the longitude of Kazan quite accurately. Fortunately, Mr. I

Croyère had a surveyor, Krasil'nikov, with him who had learned how to calculate longitude. He, Krasil'nikov, could compensate for what Mr. La Croyère failed to observe, etc. The other surveyors were also skilled enough to calculate latitudes.

It was actually Mr. La Croyère's duty to make meteorological observations all over and commission capable people at the most important places to continue them (we had been given an adequate supply of barometers and thermometers for this purpose). Mr. Gmelin preferred to do this himself since he was especially skilled at filling and graduating the tubes. In Kazan this task was turned over to a teacher at Silantov Monastery with the knowledge of the governor and archimandrite.

On 8 December we sent our second report from Kazan to the Senate. Then, since enough snow had fallen, we continued our trip to Siberia on the 9th and 12th. Mr. La Croyère went on ahead with four surveyors, two students and the journeyman instrument maker. Mr. Gmelin and I followed with the rest of the group.

The shortest route from Kazan to Siberia is by way of Osa, Kungur and Ekaterinburg. This route is easier than the one over the Verkhotur'e mountains. We hardly noticed where we passed through the mountains on our way. Since the choice of a travelling route was completely up to us we chose this one.

We arrived at Kungur on 22 December where we viewed the alabaster caves described by Strahlenberg. We had a more accurate drawing made of them than he had been able to do. We passed two copper mines, Soksunskoi and Irgenskoi zavods. State councilor Demidov owned the first and a Balakhnishch merchant Sokin the other. Because of the holidays we saw nothing of importance. At that time there was nothing but a solitary house or customs station called Klenovskaia zastava to mark where Siberia's jurisdiction or rather Ekaterinburg's began. A few years later, because of Bashkir unrest a small fort called Klenovskoe krepost was erected. On the way from Klenovskoe to Ekaterinburg we saw 2 more iron works, Bilimbaevskii, owned by Baron Stroganov and Shaitanskie, owned by Vasilii Demidov.

On 29 December we arrived at Ekaterinburg where we found Mr. La Croyère and his group. He continued his journey on 8 January toward Tobol'sk. But Mr. Gmelin and I remained awhile in Ekaterinburg in order to get to know better this noteworthy town and the mining and smelting works dependent upon it.

Siberian trip: Anno 1734 [pp. 340-366]

We met the commander of Ekaterinburg, General-Lieutenant von Hennin who was very supportive of our work. He was a very friendly man who had served Tsar Peter I as an experienced artilleryman ever since the conquest of Azov (1696). Even before

that he had overseen mining operations at Olonets with
distinction.

Mr. von Hennin helped in every way possible to expand my
geographical knowledge of the region and also to give Gmelin the
opportunity to take advantage of von Hennin's expertise, because
he wanted to become better acquainted with the region's
mineralogy. Other countries' experiences are by far inadequate
for judging the advantage of Siberian ores, mines and smelting
methods since they have their own properties which have to be
taken into account. From Petersburg we were dependent upon
mining experts whom we were supposed to meet in Ekaterinburg. An
assayer named Herdebol had already been sent ahead to Kamchatka.
A tunneler, Michael Kutuzov, was to meet us at the Lena near the
Orlenga River where signs of silver ore had been discovered,
which he had been employed to trace. The general assigned
another miner to Mr. Gmelin at his request because the man knew
how to use a mining drill, which the head mining office had
issued him along with accompanying equipment. In addition Mr.
Gmelin had several physical instruments made which he had not
been able to get in Petersburg.

We had to take advantage of Ekaterinburg's many skilled
workers and artisans all the more because we could not expect to
find the same services on our long journey.

Ekaterinburg had been established in 1723. Together with its
mines and smelters and the villages and hamlets in the district
belonging to them it appears to be completely developed. New
ores were being discovered almost every year and new smelters
erected. The general assisted me in every way possible to draw
up from written reports a quite complete description of mining
conditions in the Ekaterinburg and Perm areas.

Polevskoi zavod, a copper works where silver had also been
found, was under construction. The general accompanied us there
even though it is 52 versts from Ekaterinburg. The trip took one
day -- the 8th of January. We left very early in the morning and
returned late in the evening.

We were also supposed to visit Sisertskoi zavod an iron works
which had been established at the same time as Polevskoi zavod,
in the general's pleasant company. He prized this place more
than all the other iron works because of its great abundance of
the best, rich iron ore. That is why he had named it Tsarina
Anna. Something, however, happened which prevented me from going
along so only Mr. Gmelin could accompany the general there and
even farther.

We were already used to Mr. La Croyère's wanting to work
without us so that there would be no witnesses to his
astronomical observations and the difficulties he liked to
complain about. On 9 January he set out ahead of us for Tobol'sk
with the surveyors and two students. Up to then Gmelin and I had

ever been separated as now happened for a time. This did not happen again on the expedition except in the later years when it was necessary in order to speed up the completion of our work. We did not let that prevent us from doing each other's work. Gmelin collected geographical descriptions and I plants and various natural history specimens as well as other information about natural history.

On 14 January I received Captain-Commander Bering's letter from Tobol'sk asking us to speed up our journey as much as possible. He had various things he wanted to discuss with us. He would be continuing his own trip from Tobol'sk shortly, etc., etc. Gmelin and I immediately reached a decision that we could satisfy Bering's request without our work in Ekaterinburg suffering. That is, we separated. I left Ekaterinburg on the same day with all the baggage. Gmelin remained behind in Ekaterinburg for a few days to finish a meteorological observation with the help of Andrei Tatishchev, a mine surveyor the general had assigned to him. He also did not want to miss the opportunity of accompanying the general to the rest of the mines and therefore remained several additional days in Ekaterinburg.

On the evening of the 19th I arrived in Tobol'sk where Mr. La royère had been since the 15th. After leaving Ekaterinburg on he 19th with the general, Gmelin arrived on the 30th. He had not only visited and described Sisertskoi but also Kamenskii zavod, the oldest iron works in Siberia, and the annual fair at rbit which was being held at the time.

Captain-Commander Bering wanted to let us know in writing that the Governing Senate had instructed him to consult us in important matters needing quick decisions. This seemed a questionable practice to us since it assumed we would always accompany the commander, even at sea where Gmelin and I would be of no use. Mr. La Croyère, however, could make astronomical observations. At this time we were only asked to appoint and instruct surveyors for the ships which were setting out at the same time as the Kamchatka expedition to discover a passage through the Arctic Ocean. This was no problem. We turned over two surveyors, Ushakov and Shchekin, to the commander. He was satisfied to find any others he needed among the ones already working in Irkutsk Province. Together with the commander we drew up their instructions and signed them.

A few facts about the voyages through the Arctic: ships were built and provisioned at four places: Arkhangel'sk, Tobol'sk, Eniseisk and Irkutsk. The Arkhangel'sk ships were only to sail as far as the Ob'. It took them 3 summers to reach their goal. They had to winter twice on the way and overcome innumerable obstacles. The Tobol'sk-built double sloop named the Tobol'sk, whose launch we watched, had a closer destination. It was to go only as far as the Enisei. In 1734 Lieutenant Ovtsyn, the ship's commander, was forced to turn back at 70° latitude. On his

second attempt in 1736 he reached 72°50' latitude before turning
back again for a second time. Using a new ship in 1738,
Koshelev, the fleet's commander, who had been appointed by the
Admiralty College to take Ovtsyn's place, succeeded in sailing
around the eastern tip of the Ob Gulf at 75°15' latitude as far
as the Enisei. I will relate more about these events when I
describe our arrival in Iakutsk, where we were able to learn more
about the voyage of discovery.

The governor of Tobol'sk, Aleksei L'vovich Pleshcheev, an
Imperial privy councilor, was a man of the highest character who
appeared to have made it a rule to encourage our scholarly
activities in every way possible. He most willingly provided me
any information about the situation in the city and surrounding
area I requested from the Provincial Chancellery. I confess,
however, that I did not yet know by far at that time what I
should request or inquire about. I needed practical knowledge
which is only acquired through experience -- that is, unless one
has previously had that kind of instruction, which I had not had.

I began here to research Siberian archives and order copies
of documents explaining the area's history and geography.
Tobol'sk's archives do not go back to the time of its conquest.
That period is only known from the chronicles, which vary
greatly, thus raising important questions about their validity.
I was very happy to obtain an old Siberian illustrated chronicle
in Tobol'sk [the Remezov Chronicle - Ed.] which answered all my
questions and cannot be disputed. This valuable treasure I gave
to the Academy Library upon my return. There is no other copy in
existence except for the one I had made for my own use. I used
it as the basis for my history of the conquest in Part I of my
Siberian history.

I had complete access to all of the information about
previous periods in the archives. The materials were mostly well
preserved, except for some damaged by fire. They were not well
organized, something that was easily corrected. My first task
was to organize each locality's old records [stolpy] (volumina)
and books chronologically. Then I perused each for information I
wanted to have copied. For convenience I was allowed to take
anything home I wished. I only needed to note on the margins
what I wanted. There was no shortage of copyists provided by the
Provincial Chancellery as well as by all other chancelleries. I
could always be certain everything I requested would be copied.
In most places the chancelleries also reorganized their archives
according to my guidelines.

I took advantage of every opportunity to collect geographical
information whenever I stayed for a period of time, especially
from people who had travelled widely.

I do not have anything important to say about Messrs.
Gmelin's and La Croyère's efforts. During the winter a natural
scientist has almost no opportunity, while travelling or spending

time in a town, to expand his knowledge of what a region has to
offer in all areas of nature other than through oral inquiries.
An astronomer, however, who has not yet provided enough evidence
of his skills or assiduity, should be glad to show witnesses his
observations. That was not the case here, even though there was
not the slightest disunity between the observer and the people
who offered to be witnesses.

At the governor's we saw 4 Kalmyk cows -- actually from Tibet
-- and 2 live sables which were sent to Petersburg. Mr. Gmelin
had them sketched.

An unexpected incident took Mr. Gmelin back to Ekaterinburg.
Letters from General-Lieutenant von Hennin arrived for Governor
Pleshcheev and Mr. Gmelin, in which von Hennin asked Gmelin to
treat him for a serious illness that had befallen him. Gmelin
discussed the matter with the Governor. He advised him to go
since he would not be missing out on the continuation of the
expedition. Thus, he left Tobol'sk on 1 March, reached Tiumen on
the evening of the 2nd and arrived in Ekaterinburg around noon of
the 4th. Fortunately for the patient, his illness was no longer
dangerous. Gmelin was able to set out again on the 9th and
arrived back in Tobol'sk at noon on the 13th.

In Kazan I had already begun to describe the customs and
practices of the heathen peoples living there. My opportunities
for this were even better among the Mohammedan Bukharans in
Tobol'sk. Since ancient times they have lived in the lower part
of the city as well as in the villages. Bukharans also live in
Tiumen, Tara and Tomsk. They live from trade and agriculture. I
met some of the most eminent of them. One was an old achun who
spoke Russian well. He had made a translation of Abul Ghazi's
history book for Swedish prisoners. He had translated the Tatar
text into Russian for them and they had then translated into
German. From this emerged the French translation printed in
1726. The achun and abiss are the most respected religious men
among the Siberian Tatars and Bukharans. They, as well,
administer the laws in unimportant matters just as the
kadileskier do among the Turks. The achun was to marry a couple.
He invited me to his village 12 versts from the town. Mr. Gmelin
accompanied me. It was the 15th of May. To me the wedding
ceremony seemed far less a religious ceremony than a legal or
civil act.

A couple days later in the town I watched two boys being
circumcised amidst the din of hand drums and shawms so that the
boys screams could not be heard. I found it informative to
listen to the knowledgeable people give their opinions about the
purposes and age of circumcision -- which is very different from
the Jewish practice. We postponed observing a burial because we
wished to observe one for a somewhat eminent person and no such
death occurred when we were in Tobol'sk.

We left meteorological instruments in Tobol'sk with Jacob
Mirovich, whom we considered qualified to do the work. He was a
former pupil at the Petersburg Academy gymnasium and a syn
boiarskii [minor noble] in Tobol'sk. Gmelin took over the task
of instructing him thoroughly in their use.

According to an agreement with Captain Commander Bering we
did not need to hurry to Iakutsk. Easily two years could be
required for the preparations for the journey to Kamchatka. We
therefore had to plan to use this time profitably for other side
trips. At the end of February Bering went ahead by land.
Captain Chirikov, the other naval officers and Mr. La Croyère
took the heavy baggage by boat on the rivers Irtysh, Ob, Ket,
etc. The governor advised Mr. Gmelin and me to use boats to
travel up the Irtysh. That would permit us to use the first
summer adequately and sufficiently. We already knew it was
better to go by water since we did not have to sit idle during
the trip. During the last 10 years of Peter the Great's reign,
forts had been built in the upper reaches of the Irtysh, as
documented in the Tobol'sk archives.

Akinfii Demidov had already surveyed the Kolyvan copper and
silver works in the Altai Mountains between the Irtysh and Ob
but their actual worth had not yet been made public. That is
probably the reason for the patriotic governor advising us to
undertake the trip. Mr. Gmelin prepared to study mining and the
southern areas promised to offer him a rich harvest of new
observations and discoveries so that all of the reasons together
lead us to follow the governor's advice rather than staying
together with Mr. La Croyère in one group.

Before leaving, Mr. Gmelin and I talked with Mr. La Croyère.
We promised each other in writing that we would help each other
wherever we could and wanted to in each other's area of study to
foster the general knowledge of Siberia. Using my format Mr. La
Croyère was to make a list of all the towns, market towns,
villages, rivers, etc., he saw on his journey as well as to
describe the customs and practices of the peoples he met and to
collect all kinds of natural objects. Gmelin pledged to collect
all of the physical observations as he had been doing. I
promised to supervise a surveyor's calculations of the latitude
based on the height of the sun at noon as well as other geodetic
observations; especially the preparation of an exact map of the
river Irtysh in as far as we got to know it.

As a precautionary measure to aid our work the governor gave
us a general order addressed to all the commanders of the places
we were to visit. He had three copies prepared for us. The
order repeated and reaffirmed the Governing Senate's mandate to
us. In addition, it evidenced the governor's special respect for
us by stating that they all were to honor us and carry out our
requests without objection. In those distant regions the
governor must have thought it necessary to protect us, since we
possessed no appointed position or rank, from inexperienced

ubordinates' prejudicial behavior.   The provincial chancellery
ent ahead special orders on our behalf to the vice-governor in
rkutsk and the provincial voevoda in Eniseisk.

Since we had to report all of our activities and observations
ince our stay in Kazan up to May first to the Governing Senate,
e took the opportunity to include with the report a request
hich would influence the rest of our trip and thus has to be
entioned.

Our present instructions and orders from the Senate stated
hat Mr. La Croyère was to go to sea with Captain-Commander
ering to make astronomical observations.   We knew that if the
ommander requested it we all had to offer him aid and advice in
mportant matters.   Was this duty for Mr. Gmelin and also [for
e?] to include the sea voyage?   We asked for clarification.

We suggested that we would be of no use at sea because the
hip probably would not stop as long on foreign shores as we
eeded for our research.   During the sea voyage we could be more
sefully employed in Kamchatka completing our projects there
ooner, thus making it possible to undertake observations in
ther parts of Siberia.   The Governing Senate approved our
uggestions.

After completing this dispatch, Mr. Gmelin and I on 15 May
rove the 18 versts to the ruins of the Tatar ruler's former
esidence before the Russian conquest.   No one had lived there
ince Kuchum's times.   No one could probably live there now
ccording to our present style of life.   The place is called
ibir'--the origin of the whole province's name.   It lies
pstream from Tobol'sk on the high, steep eastern shore of the
rtysh River and is surrounded on the landward side by three not
ery large earthen walls.   We saw no remains of stone buildings.
uchum must have lived in wooden huts or in tents.   The trip
here and back took one day.

Siberian rivers are not immediately navigable after breakup,
especially upstream when they rise and flood over their low
shores.

Captain Chirikov, along with Mr. La Croyère, left Tobol'sk on
0 May.   Gmelin and I gave him all of the baggage we thought we
id not need on our trip to take to Eniseisk.   He was accompanied
y the surveyor Krasil'nikov, capable of making latitudinal
bservations, and 2 students, N. Popov and L. Ivanov, who had
een chosen by lot.   The two artists Johann Berkhan and J.W.
ussenius, a surveyor and the rest of the students remained with
melin and me.   We divided them between us.   Krasheninnikov and
ret'iakov were to help him.   I was to have Garlamov and
akhontov, who could also help translate German.   First I wish to
ention briefly Mr. La Croyère's journey from Tobol'sk to Irkutsk
s contained in his written reports.

At Samarovskii iam, where the Irtysh joins the Ob, they wer
to take the Ob upstream, but they had to make other trave
arrangements, which caused a delay for several days. He arrive
in Surgut on 11 June, in Narym on 3 July, in Ketskoi ostrog on 1
July and in Makovskoi ostrog on 3 August. There everything wa
loaded on wagons. He arrived in Eniseisk on 9 August. On 2
August he took the Enisei and Tunguska upstream and arrived on 1
September at the mouth of the Ilim River. Captain Chirikov se
out up the Ilim. Mr. La Croyère, however, continued on th
Angara.   After passing the Shamanskoi, Dolgoi and Padu
waterfalls, he arrived in Bratskoi ostrog on 29 September, i
Balagansk on 10 October and in Irkutsk on 18 October in the mids
of a lot of drift ice. We met him there again the followin
winter.

Gmelin and I intended to leave Tobol'sk on 22 May. We had
boats called doshchaniki in Siberia, one for us and the other fo
our artists and the other members of our party. We were on boar
the one when the other began to sink before our eyes. We worke
hard to get our things quickly back on land, but we stil
suffered losses and damage. Repairing the vessel would hav
taken time. The helpful governor had a better suggestion for us
A merchant's doshchanik, recently built in Verkhotur'e, ha
arrived that same day. It was to be loaded in Tobol'sk wit
goods for remote Siberian areas. The governor bought it from it
owner. The necessary partitions were installed the next day, s
we could continue our journey toward evening on 24 May withou
any further problems.

We went up the Irtysh River since men on shore could pull th
boats. Where this was not possible we used other methods. W
could not use sails as on the Ob since the Irtysh is not the sam
size. In addition, the Irtysh is filled with incredible twist
and bends between Tobol'sk and Tara. Sometimes we arrived agai
in the evening near the same place we had been in the morning
No wonder we made slow progress, but this helped our work a lot
Gmelin had more time to do botanical work along the shores, an
I, using a sea compass I always had on me, could prepare a mor
exact map of the Irtysh's course than had previously existed. I
helped that I knew the distances between places which had bee
measured a long time ago. From time to time I also measured th
speed of the river. I had never read anywhere that it flow
exceedingly fast. I used little hour glasses like the one
sailors use to measure the speed of their ship or sea currents
I also tied bright pieces of cloth to a string to show a quarter
half and full arshin and then attached the string to a small
flat ship-like piece of wood. I anchored a boat in the middle o
the stream. At the same time as I threw out the little ship
turned the hour glass over and counted the number of cloth
carried overboard until the hour glass ran out. At Tobol'sk th
Irtysh flows very slowly, but the farther upstream one goes, th
faster it flows. It flows fastest where it emerges from th
Altai Mountains. I continued my usual practice of making a lis

f all the inhabited as well as noteworthy uninhabited places we
assed.

On 13 June we arrived in Tara, where we stayed for a few
ays, obtaining twenty cossacks to take along to protect us if
arauding Kirgiz-Kazakhs tried to attack us.   The governor had
ut two cannons with ammunition and two artillerymen on board
ach boat in Tobol'sk to scare away any rabble along the way.

The town archives were quite complete, dating from the town's
eginnings.   I was unable to use them as much as I should have,
ut I gained another benefit.   I had discovered that I could
rder straight from the chancellery of each city trustworthy
nformation about the actual situation and statistical
omposition of a city.   Here I began to formulate specific
uestions which I turned over to the city chancellery, from whom
 received quite satisfactory answers.   Any missing information I
ould ascribe to the shortcomings of my questions.   With
xperience my questions gradually became more comprehensive and
hus produced more information from the towns.

On 20 June we departed from Tara and arrived in the fort of
msk.   At that time the area had a far smaller population than
ow.   Only Tatars, who suffered a great deal from marauding
irgiz-Kazakhs, lived on the Barabinsk Steppe.   Only later were
orts and villages built in the region between the Irtysh and
obol.   Omsk itself has only a few inhabitants.   That unique area
howed what could be achieved there with time.

Beyond Omsk we found little forts about 200 versts apart
here we were able to obtain fresh provisions.   The rest of the
egion was barren.   Peter the Great had ordered these "upper
rtysh forts" built in order to make it possible for him and his
uccessors to get to the Kalmyks, Bukhara and India and take
ossession of the rich gold sands found in many of the rivers
here.   I have already written a special treatise based on
rchival information and oral research about the Tsar's important
lans and their successes.   My oral research could not have been
ostponed for very long, because at that time several officers
ere still alive who had been part of the undertaking from its
eginnings.

Even though we also travelled through barren regions, I
ruthfully can say that the areas along the Irtysh are among the
ost pleasant in Siberia.   Later, we travelled through areas near
he Chinese border which were just as beautiful.   Here, however,
verything was new for us.   Because no discomforts, wants or
angers dampened our spirits we were enraptured.   We entered a
aradise filled mainly with unidentified flowering plants, a
oological garden with rare Asian animals gathered before us, an
ntique museum of old heathen graves which preserved all kinds of
uriosities -- in a word, regions not yet visited for the benefit
f science.   So many opportunities for new research and
iscoveries encouraged us to work extremely hard.

Because in Omsk we had nothing else to do but to replace ou
Tatar cossacks with soldiers, we could leave the next day. On
July we arrived in Zhelezinskaia where we did not need to stop a
all but could go on farther the same day. From there, however
for my mapping purposes, I had to have the distances measure
from one place to the next with a measuring chain along th
shore, because no one could give me the distances more exactl
than from fort to fort. We encountered no more big twists in th
river, but the water did become shallower, thus, slowing ou
progress. We were afraid that this might delay our planne
overland trip through the Kolyvan mines. We were not equippe
for winter travel and still had to visit three forts along th
Irtysh -- Iamyshevskaia, Semipalatinsk and Ust'-Kamenogorsk -- a
well as various buildings erected by the Kalmyks, the forme
owners of those areas. Impatience to take care of our work ther
led us to order horses from Iamyshevskaia so that a small grou
of us could ride the last 60 versts overland. Meanwhile, th
boats with the rest of our party would follow us.

In this way we arrived in Iamyshevskaia on 14 July in th
midst of amazing heat. The boats arrived on 16 July. The othe
forts are dependent upon Iamyshevskaia. We had to make
decision there regarding how we could get the most out of ou
trip. We did not want to fight the current any longer. In orde
to complete our map we sent a boat ahead as far as possible an
continued overland with the protection of forty soldiers unde
the command of a lieutenant.

Often on those dry steppes travellers or hunters start gras
fires which spread over large areas if rain does not fortunatel
fall to prevent dreaded damage. By day we could see smoke in th
distance. At night we could see the reflection of fire on th
clouds. For several days and nights before we arrived i
Iamyshevskaia we could see these signs to our left.   I
Iamyshevskaia the fire came so close that it threatened the fort
The commander and part of his garrison stopped it by tramplin
and shoveling away the unburned grass. There are indeed example
in Siberia of uninhabited wooden forts and buildings bein
consumed by such fires.

The most noteworthy site at Iamyshevskaia is the salt lake o
the same name (actually Iamysh), which provides the entir
Tobol'sk province with very good salt at no cost other than fo
transportation. The salt crystallizes to a thick crust on th
flat bottom of the lake on hot summer days, especially if
little rain has just fallen. In no case should we let uninforme
writers convince us that the salt swims like ice on the surfac
of the water. This would be contrary to nature since sal
settles to the bottom from its own weight. There is, to be sure
not much water or salt brine above the salt, because, as the sal
crystallizes and sinks to the bottom, the pure watery part
evaporate. There is, however, always enough water or brin
present so that a skeptic, who has to see for himself, can li
down on the shore of the lake and observe the process with hi

wn eyes and be convinced.   That is what Mr. Gmelin and I did, by
riving out to the lake on 15 July, a very hot day.   The lake is
ix versts 304 faden east of the fort in a wide, almost egg-
haped plain.   From west-northwest to east-southeast it is three
ersts 300 faden long and two versts 350 faden wide.   I obtained
he shape and size by having the entire circumference of the lake
easured with a compass and sketched.   Before arriving there we
aw a purple-red color, quite high above the lake, in the air.
t is perhaps caused by the reflection of the salt water.   I
hall leave it up to others to guess the source of an
nmistakable odor of violets we smelled as we approached the lake
nd by the lake itself.   The salt is of the best quality and will
lways be plentiful.   Not too far away is a much smaller fresh
ater lake from which a small stream flows to the Irtysh.   I
anted to describe it in quite some detail because I would not
ave such a convenient opportunity anywhere else.

An ensign in the artillery, Vassili Halberg, an ex-Swedish
risoner of war, appeared capable of making the meteorological
bservations at Iamyshevskaia.   Therefore, he was assigned these
asks.   Mr. Gmelin instructed him thoroughly and also gave him
he usual written directions and instruments.

In Iamyshevskaia I was told about an old Kalmyk building the
ussians call the "<u>Kalbasunskaia bashnia</u>", located on the west
ide of the Irtysh.   I could not go there since Mr. Gmelin and I
ad agreed that our trip could be speeded along if I took the
ustomary path along the east bank of the river to Semipalatinsk.
herefore, I instructed Lursenius, our artist, to sketch and
escribe this abandoned building if he were to come across it on
is river trip.   Later, I included his well-executed sketch of
his building as well as information about other similar
uildings in an academic treatise about Tungus manuscripts found
n Siberia.

On 19 July the boat for Semipalatinsk left Iamyshevskaia.   On
he 21st, we followed by land.   We had to leave one of our first
oats in Iamyshevskaia because it had been damaged.   We arrived
n Semipalatinsk on 26 July.   We sent 20 men from the fort to
eet and help the boats when they arrived on 5 August.

Fort Semipalatinsk is named after seven stone buildings or
ather their ruins, on the right bank of the Irtysh River which
ere built by Kalmyks when they lived in the area.   The existence
f the buildings had been known for a long time.   Tungus
anuscripts had been found in them.   Peter the Great had some of
hem sent to France in 1722 in order to find out what they were.
hen Mr. Gmelin, Berkhan the artist, and I visited the ruins on
7 July, all of the roofs were gone and the buildings, made of
nbaked brick and in one case shale, looked like they would not
ast very long either.   I had a sketch made of them.   My treatise
entioned above about Tungus manuscripts found in Siberia
ontains everything worth mentioning about them.   They are about
5 versts upstream from the fort.   Except for Mr. Gmelin's daily

natural history observations we had nothing else to do here
Once our entire party was together again we thought of nothin
else but continuing our journey.

We were very tempted to shorten the trip by going straight t
the Kolyvan mines. Instead, we made a detour by way o
Ust'Kamenogorsk, the last Russian fort in the region, in order t
extend the map of the Irtysh as far as possible by land. Abov
all, we wanted to visit Ablakit, a remarkable place 100 verst
beyond the fort, a former Kalmyk heathenish temple where
quantity of Tungus, Mongolian and Kalmyk texts had bee
abandoned. Because the road there was said to be mountainous an
difficult for wagons, we sent the wagons with the baggage on t
Kolyvan and rode on horseback along the Irtysh. We also divide
the escort which had been accompanying us since Iamyshevskaia
An officer and 20 men remained with us and the other 20 me
accompanied our baggage. On 7 August we left Semipalatinsk.

The next day, 37 versts beyond the fort, we came upon th
ruins of houses on flat steppes. They had been built of unbake
bricks, but now were almost level to the ground. We also sa
traces of irrigation systems like the Bukharans use fo
irrigating their fields. This led us to conclude that Bukharar
had built the houses. The Kalmyks had sent them there t
cultivate the land. The Bukharans left after the Kalmyk
departed because the dry, sandy steppe soil is not ver
productive.

By not stopping along the way we arrived in Ust'-Kamenogors
on 11 August. The fort gets its name from its location. It lie
at the foot of the high Altai Mountains where the Irtysh emerge
(actually at the mouth or opening in the rocky mountains). A
that time the fort was the only place inhabited in that area c
the Irtysh. The forts Dolonskaia and Ubinskaia had ceased to b
used. Mr. Demidov had not yet built Shulbinskoi zavod, a coppe
smelter.

I was most interested in information I received that ther
were wagon loads of manuscripts at Ablakit. There was, however
danger of attack from the marauding Kirgiz-Kazakhs who wer
warring against the neighboring Kalmyks. We were told that
garrison soldier recently trying to cross the Irtysh (Ablaki
lies on the western side of the river) had been killed by th
marauding rabble. This danger frightened us. Because it was no
our job to face danger unless absolutely necessary, we sent
corporal from our Tobol'sk escort along with 30 garrison soldier
and a scribe to describe and measure Ablakit. All of them wer
well-mounted and well-armed. They also took six pack horses c
which to load manuscripts. That is how, in my above mentione
treatise, I was later able to give quite detailed informatic
about Ablakit and the Tungus manuscripts found in Siberia.
surveyor, whom Privy Councilor Tatishchev sent out two year
later, was able to do more. His sketches of the floor plans an
side views of Ablakit houses I also used in my descriptions.

I gave the six horse loads of manuscripts to the Imperial art gallery. All of the members of the party that went to Ablakit said it would have been possible to take three times as many manuscripts if they had wanted to weigh themselves down even more. They saw no sign of the enemy. Our people had worked hastily. They had left the evening of 12 August and returned with their imposing booty early on the morning of 15 August.

While crossing the steppe I often had seen old graves, mostly open, because grave robbers had searched for and found in them objects made of gold, silver and copper. During our stay in Ust'-Kamenogorsk, I had some apparently untouched graves opened. I was present to examine their contents and prevent anything of significance from being stolen. My efforts were in vain. The people living there said I would not find anything. The earlier grave robbers could tell the rich graves from the poor ones and left them untouched. I never learned what signs to look for -- something proved at various graves where we found absolutely nothing of value. Only in Kolyvan did I have an opportunity to purchase a few beautiful gold artifacts from graves. After my return I turned them over to the Imperial Art Gallery. Her Imperial Majesty, Catherine the Great most graciously requested me to write a special treatise explaining the various gold objects found in the graves. Since this has been published, I do not need to go into detail here.

On the evening of the 16th we headed for the Kolyvan copper mines. By travelling at night we arrived there on 19 August. We spent ten days there inspecting the excavations, inquiring about the advantages of their smelting process and going over the mine's accounts in order to better judge the productivity. At that time there was no talk of silver being present in Kolyvan. A year before our trip Mining Councilor Reiser had visited there on orders from the Senate. He also had not discovered any silver. Mr. Demidov had the luck of enriching his coffers for 10 to 12 years after we were there before a German master miner whom he had insulted decided to inform the mining authority about the real contents of the Kolyvan ores and their value which had been being kept secret.

Be that as it may, Akinfei Demidov is to be thanked for having laid the basis for the present prosperity in the Barnaul area and for helping to begin to settle a previously totally uninhabited area. There was still some doubt about whether the Kalmyks would surrender the area around the mines in the mountains without resistance. It therefore helped a great deal that Demidov had prepared the Kalmyks for accepting Russian possession of the area. It was a case of whoever took or used something that did not belong to anyone had the most right to it. Even the Kalmyks seemed to acknowledge this, for very frequently some of them came to the mines to trade with the Russians, primarily to buy flour. They behaved very peacefully and appeared to want nothing more than friendship. Such people were

in Kolyvan when we were there.   At various times they entertaine
us with their skill at archery.

Even though there was nothing to fear from the Kalmyks
Demidov had requested 100 cossacks from Kuznetsk to protect th
works. We took 20 of them along with us on our next trip instea
of the soldiers commanded by a lieutenant that we sent back t
Semipalatinsk.   Demidov's mining superintendant was so polit
that he offered us free of charge as many of his master's horse
working at the mines as we needed for the continuation of ou
trip. We accepted. Thus outfitted, on 29 August we set out fro
Kolyvan.

Only a few people know the origin of the name Kolyvan. I ha
to ask a lot of people before I found out.   There is a lake o
this name on the road going from Iamyshevskaia to the Kalmy
region of Kankaragai taken by Russian traders wanting to trad
cheaply for beautiful sables.   There was no place with a nam
closer which could be used for naming the new mines.   They
however, were given an additional designation: Voskresni
(Kolyvano-voskresenskie zavody) because the mountain where th
initial diggings were undertaken was called Resurrection Mountai
(Voskresenskaia gora). We did not go past the lake because th
road was no longer used when we were there.

We could have been much closer to the Ob but we were tol
about a more comfortable detour which would permit us to chang
horses more easily. We went to the mouth of the Barnaul Rive
where a small Demidov village had recently been established
Afterwards it became the main place for mining and smelting work
in the area. Not too far there, the Chumysh River with Russia
villages built along it, flows into the other side of the Ob
This was the normal crossing point. There the roads fork towar
Tomsk and Kuznetsk. We chose the latter so that we could cover
larger area and arrived in Kuznetsk on 11 September, where w
stayed until the 27th.

The town lies at the conjuncture of the Kondoma River and th
Tom. It takes its name from the wrought iron produced by som
neighboring Tatars who use little clay hand ovens -- smaller tha
anywhere else -- for smelting iron to make their househol
articles.   They were doing this before they became Russia
subjects. Mainly Tatars live upstream from the town on the To
just as mostly Russians live downstream where they cultivate th
land.   The land is very fertile.   The Kuznetsk sable are a
valuable as the Kankarai.   I soon learned that the Abints
(Abalar), mentioned by Strahlenberg, living very close to th
town are not a special people. They are only a special group, a
is the case with all of the Tatars who are still heathens. Thei
separation may be ever so old, they still consider themselve
related if they are descended from one ancestor and, therefore
do not intermarry.   They cannot be differentiated from the res
of their people by customs, language and religion.

Another kind of Tatar, the Teleuts or Telengits, living in the Tomsk and Kuznetsk regions in their own villages or mixed in with the Russians, might be considered a separate group or descendants of the Kalmyks, judging by the name, "White Kalmyks," used by the Russian chancelleries. Earlier, they were dependent upon the Kalmyks. That is why the Russians consider them Kalmyks, even though they have separated from them and placed themselves under the Russian government. Because their complete make-up, especially their facial skin color was quite different from the Kalmyks, the Russians called them "White Kalmyks." Everything about them is Tatar, nothing Kalmyk, except for the few remaining words in their language taken on during their earlier association with the Kalmyks. On 16 September, Mr. Gmelin and I visited the closest Teleuts by going only 14 versts down the Tom.

The next day we made a small excursion 15 versts up the Tom to the mouth of a small river, the Abasheva, to see a mountain we were told had smoke continually pouring out of it. We did not find anything remarkable. The mountain has never erupted. There is a spot half way up where smoke continually rises, but it is otherwise not like a volcano. People can go very close to it without thought of danger. The fire may have been burning for a long time. It might have been set and peat and tree roots continue to feed it without its spreading. A heavy rain will undoubtedly put it out.

On 19 August we made another excursion 40 versts up the Kondoma River to the Barsak Tatars to see how they smelt their iron and to observe a sorcery or shamanistic ceremony, as it is called in Siberia. The Tatars and Teleuts there are still shamanistic heathens. They call their shamans "kam," a word used by the first Christian travellers writing about the Tatars. They, however, confused it with the word for prince, "chan." We heard a lot about the astonishing deeds one such shaman could perform. We at least wanted to know if any of it were true. We found no other shamans among the people than the ones mentioned here. They may actually be scarce or else they were concealed from us.

Mr. Gmelin has taken pains to describe in detail all of the shamanistic ceremonies I saw (for he also witnessed them). It suffices for me to say that all of them are basically similar. Nothing miraculous happens. The shaman emits an unpleasant howling, while jumping about senselessly and beating a flat drum which has iron bells attached inside to intensify the din. He now and then falls to the ground as if in a faint and then imparts oracular decrees about the things people had asked him about. Some of the shamans resort to the help of sleight-of-hand tricks like our magicians, though by far less adept, but still enough as not to be caught in the act by their ignorant public. Someone seeing this jugglery for the first time will feel a sense of horror if he has the shaman's words translated in the midst of the noise and hears that it is done to call forth evil spirits to

appear to the shaman and answer his questions. It does not take
long, however, to be convinced of the futility of the farce, o
the deceit by those earning their living in this way
Shamanistic ceremonies are like a trade passed from parents t
children. In this way they have an assured, secure livelihoo
and status among their people that is almost the same as lega
power, since a shaman is asked for advice in all importan
matters and his advice is followed. He does not, however
counsel on his own but rather at the orders of spirits he call
forth to help him. He also acts as a doctor, not by usin
medicines but rather by shamanistically invoking spirits the
believe have set goals for people which they then can extend whe
the shaman intercedes. They admit that a good god bestows th
good that man enjoys, but that is already such a part of th
order of things that no service or superior persons for suc
service is necessary. An evil spirit, on the other hand, i
terrible, is the source of all misfortune which the shaman ca
ward off and mitigate. If we wanted to consider it in terms o
the Manes school, we would also have to conclude that no othe
teaching has spread out as far in the world as this one or els
that it is the most natural one for unenlightened huma
intelligence. In addition, it is far more heavily suppressed b
Christianity than by the teachings of Mohammed and the Dalai
Lama.   The Barabinsk Tatars had their shamans before th
Mohammedan proselytizers began converting them and the Mongolia
peoples still have their shamans who in certain ways oppose th
total spread of the Dalai-Lama religion. I hope my readers wil
excuse this digression, because such shamanistic ceremonies stil
occur, but this was the first time I saw them.

In Kuznetsk I drew up a statistical survey of the city an
its region.   In addition to my own observations I obtaine
necessary information from the city chancellery. I also worke
for several days on a dictionary of the Tatar and Teleut dialect
spoken there.

From here we were to travel to Tomsk, where we expected t
continue our journey by using convenient sleds. We divided ou
party into groups in order to be able to describe the are
better.   Mr. Gmelin and most of the party went by large covere
boats on the Tom River. I went by land with the interprete
[Il'ia] Iakhontov, and a Tatar interpreter assigned to me by th
city commander. We left Kuznetsk on 27 September, at the sam
time as the others. I arrived in Tomsk on 1 October, he on
October because shallows in the river had often delayed him. H
passed three ostrogs, Mungatskoi, Verkhotomskoi and Sosnovskoi o
the Tom River.

Before arriving at the last ostrog, Gmelin had a sketch mad
of figures scratched into a cliff. He then gave me this sketc
since it belonged to my area of expertise. On following journey
I have also seen similar figures and had them sketched
Strahlenberg had been our predecessor; in Gisbert Cuper's letter
(p. 108) are found the same things. I do not know what to mak

f them.   I will gladly leave it up to others, if they be so
ortunate as to know how to make use of them for history.

Since Tomsk is a trading city, where not infrequently Kalmyk
aravans as well as ones from both Bukharas arrive with their
egional products and leave with Siberian wares, we now met
umbers of those kinds of merchants and had an opportunity to
uestion them and receive all kinds of information about
onditions and the state of affairs in areas we, for the most
art, did not yet know.   I collected geographical and statistical
nformation that could be used for describing Tomsk and the areas
elonging to it.   I also began to examine the archives, something
ade difficult by the cold.   I consoled myself by saying that,
ecause Tomsk was a town in the middle of the region, we would
ave to pass through it upon our return.   In this area I spent my
ime making a dictionary of two Tatar dialects, of the Tomsk-
stiak language and the language of the Zyrians and Permians
iving in Perm.

We heard about a kind of iron ore which farmers in the
ussian village, Bogorodskoe selo on the Ob River, 51 versts from
he town, smelt in hand ovens.   On 31 October, Gmelin and I drove
ut there and found the ovens far better than the ones in
uznetsk.   Consequently, they obtained larger, good quality cakes
f iron, but not in large enough quantities for developing trade
xcept for local use.   On the following day we returned to Tomsk.

Immediately after our arrival, Mr. Gmelin, who had begun
eather observations, assigned Peter Salamatov, a cossack, to
ake charge of their continuation.   People who are able and
illing to comprehend something are more useful for some things
han the half-educated with too big opinions of their abilities.
n the other places where we wanted weather observations
ollected we almost always found and chose similar young, clear-
eaded cossacks, who could read and write.   Such a cossack then
as privileged over his fellow compatriots.   He was freed of all
wn duties and mostly took advantage of the opportunity.

Winter came earlier than usual that year.   The Tom and Ob
roze over in the first half of October.   The Chulym River, which
lows through wooded areas and was to be used for our continued
ourney to Eniseisk, allowed us to lengthen our stay in Tomsk,
ecause they said it would freeze over later than the rest of the
ivers.   The direct road to Krasnoiarsk across the steppe was
ittle used and mostly uninhabited at that time.

On 26 November we left Tomsk and arrived on 6 December in
niseisk, a town that is important in the summer when merchants
rom Tobol'sk and Irkutsk meet there and in the midst of
ransshipping their goods hold a kind of fair.   We neither could
or wanted to spend much time there, because we wished to be in
rkutsk before the end of winter if it would be necessary for us
o continue on to Iakutsk the following summer.   That is why I
eft the local archives, the most complete in all of Siberia,

untouched for the time being. Otherwise, our activities were r
different from other places. I was also rather satisfied for th
time being with the information the local provincial voevoda ar
commander   of   the   city,   Khrushchev,   provided   me   from   th
chancellery.   During his stay Mr. La Croyère had ordered a man t
make weather observations whom Mr. Gmelin found to be in no wa
qualified.   The city commander suggested that a cossack, Kozm
Charoshchnikov, do them.   Thereafter he collected them with god
results.

In   the   extraordinary   cold   something   happened   to   th
thermometers that no one had anticipated in Petersburg and ha
not happened before on the journey.   Mr. Delisle had prepared ar
graduated the thermometers according to his new method.   The
should have been able to record the most extreme cold, but abou
the middle of December in Eniseisk, it became so cold that th
scale   intended   for   recording   the   low   temperatures   did   no
suffice.   The mercury sank to the lower bulb which began at 20
degrees.   Not the slightest bit of mercury stayed in the tube
Thus, no degree of cold could be observed on the thermometer
When Mr. Gmelin saw this, he called me over (we were living i
the same house) to observe the remarkable phenomenon.   We waite
to see if toward noon in milder air temperatures the mercu
would   rise   in   the   tube   again.   That   was   the   case.   Th
thermometer did its duty as before.   The problem lay solely wit
the short length of the tube or scale.

Soon after this it became even colder.   The temperatures
however,   could   be   completely   and   exactly   observed   because   M
Gmelin had made new thermometers with scales down to 300 degrees
A cold of 281 delisle units, 125° Fahrenheit, or 70° Reaumu
excited us.   The reading was made early in the morning on
January.   Again I was called to be a witness.   The thermomete
was   in   no   way   defective.   Immediately   after   this   astonishin
experience, Mr. Gmelin put it in boiling water.   The mercury ro
to the height it was supposed to.   Moreover, we ourselves fe
and experienced the strongest effects of cold imaginable.   M
Gmelin has described most of them in his journal.   He did no
want to tell everything because he felt that such a new an
unexpected   experience   should   be   reserved   for   his   scientif
descriptions.   The weather observer in Tomsk reported that it wa
also so cold there that all of the mercury had sunk in the bul
thus   making   it   impossible   to   record   anything.   Furthe
information   is   contained   in   a   study   of   Siberian   weathe
observations presented by Professor [Joseph] Braun many year
later in the Neuen Commentarien (New Commentaries), (vol. VI, p
429).

It is necessary to state that at the end of 1734 we sent
report from Eniseisk containing descriptions and sketches we ha
finished to the Governing Senate.   The report was dated
December and sent on 2 January, thus showing the Senate as we
as the Academy that we were doing our best to carry out ou

ities.   It also showed that the more experience we had in our
undertakings the greater our success.

The list of items sent to the Senate could be included here.
Since it is already in the Senate archives, I will only include
it later if it is sought and not found there.

Let me use this opportunity to make a suggestion that seems
to be very important: the Senate archives as well as the
archives of the Academy's chancellery should be catalogued
according to subject matter as well as chronologically.   Only
then can we know what they contain and find whatever we are
looking for without wasting time.

Continuation of the Siberian Trip, 1735

On 13 January we left Eniseisk and took the road to
Krasnoiarsk, where we did not intend to spend much time.   We
wanted to reach Irkutsk before the sled route was gone.   That is
why on 3 January I sent a student ahead to Krasnoiarsk with a
written request for the commander there telling what we needed to
have ready for us to facilitate our work.   My request contained
the questions I wanted to have answered by the city chancellery
and asked him to retain in the city until my arrival the most
knowledgeable person from those there from each of the tribes
living in the Krasnoiarsk region that were in the city to pay
tribute, so that I could obtain information from them.   Beginning
in Eniseisk I had the student, Iakhontov, practice describing our
route and all of the spots along the way with names in Russian as
had been doing up until then in German.   We arrived in
Krasnoiarsk on January 17.

Not all of the requests I had sent ahead were fulfilled.
Nevertheless, we found so much to do there that we could have
spent the whole winter working.   We restricted ourselves to doing
the most necessary work in order to comply with the original
plans we had drawn up.   We also hoped that our route on our
return trip from Kamchatka would bring us into these blessed
regions once more.

Mr. Gmelin found musk deer here.   He described several
specimens in the greatest of detail.   He had the most remarkable
one sketched and a skeleton prepared from one of them.   This we
sent to the Academy along with some huge mammoth teeth found in
the vicinity.

Samples of copper ore and cakes of smelted copper were
brought from the Saian Mountains, which are part of the Altai.
They looked promising but also showed that the ores needed to be
worked better than Andrei Sokolovski, a poor, untrained
inhabitant of Eniseisk had been doing.   We also concluded that
the mountains had to have rich deposits of copper ore because of
the copper tools found in the old graves in the area that were

sold as old copper in Krasnoiarsk. I bought a lot of thes
objects and turned them over to the Imperial art gallery later.

We sent the Governing Senate a report on the newly-discovere
ores and proposed that the Crown should begin to mine the ore
regularly and build a smelter. As a result, miners sent fro
Ekaterinburg the following year built a smelter on the cree
Lugasa. They found rich ore all over, even on the level stepp
and in the mountains, but mainly in places where the previou
inhabitants had left traces of their mining activities, ol
shafts. This was exactly the case at the Kolyvan mines, onl
copper and silver were sought. The former inhabitants did no
seem to have known about iron or else they ignored it sinc
copper was so abundant. Among the artifacts found in graves wer
knives, daggers and other cutting tools made from copper.

Because I had a cold, Mr. Gmelin went without me to th
underground caves on the Enisei River and to the steep cliff
abutting on the river, which were covered with inexplicabl
figures just as on the Tom River. He described them and had the
sketched. He sent the student Krasheninnikov and thirty worker
ahead to break a trail through the deep snow. He followed the
on 4 February and returned to Krasnoiarsk on the evening of th
fifth.

Due to our haste I could not do much with the large number
of manuscripts in the Krasnoiarsk archives. Despite this,
received very good information from the chancellery as well a
orally that helped me with my statistical description of th
Krasnoiarsk area.

I compiled dictionaries of the local people's very divers
languages. Some of them even have indications of being of th
same origin as the Samoyed. One of them is undoubtedly th
language of the Arintsy, a small tribe with only one single ma
who was still able to understand the language, all the mor
remarkable because the language will probably die out completel
in my time. We sent messengers ahead to Kansk and Udinski
ostrogs, which we would be traveling through. Kotovtsy lived a
the former and Buriats at the latter. We wanted the commander
to have a few of the members of these peoples available to u
upon our arrival.

My research in the area on the Enisei River extended up t
and beyond the border between the Russian empire and China an
Chinese Mongolia. I am referring here to a cave with idols o
the Enisei and old buildings on the Tess River, where Tungu
manuscripts were found in Semipalatinsk and Ablakit, some o
which Dr. Messerschmidt brought back from Siberia. See m
treatise on Tungus manuscripts.

In order to speed up our trip to Irkutsk, on 2 February w
sent the student [Vasilii] Tret'iakov ahead with our heav
equipment. We followed on the 18th. On the 20th we arrived i

Kanskoi on the Kan River and on the 27th in Udinskoi on the Uda River, which is later called the Chuma [Chuna], and finally, the Tosseeva [Taseeva] when it flows into the Upper Tunguska.   I mention this in detail because there are two other places and rivers of this name which can easily be confused with this one: the Uda River, with the town of Udinsk at its mouth, flows into the Jelenga [sic; Selenga] River, and the Ud River, with Udskoi ostrog, flows into the Sea of Okhotsk.

We found travel very difficult because of the continuing very extreme cold and because no villages had yet been established where we might rest and warm up. We had to have our tea and food cooked in the open and then we ate it on our sleds. Everything was almost frozen before we could get it to our mouths. The best part was that we had become accustomed to spending the night in the sleds or wagons whether they were moving or not. When, on 25 February, we came to the Solonaia, a stream that was not frozen, Mr. Gmelin could not resist tasting the water. It was not salty but rather unpleasantly hard. When the area is settled in the future, it will probably be useful for medicinal purposes.

From Udinskoi, where only four Russian families were living, we had to travel 101 versts along an uninhabited road to the village of Tulun. From there travel was easier. We went by way of Barluzka sloboda to Balagansk in the region belonging to Irkutsk.

On 8 March we arrived in this regional capital, where the vice-governor told us to our chagrin that we had hurried for naught since the preparations for the trip from Iakutsk to Kamchatka were far from complete. In the meantime we would have to try to use our time profitably and well. Before our arrival we had thought that we might be told we had to go to Irkutsk the following summer in order to join Captain-Commander Bering.

Mr. La Croyère, who had learned of the difficulties awaiting us upon our arrival in Irkutsk, had not sent us word of them. He, however, provided us with a good example of how to put the time to good use. We did not find him in Irkutsk; he had left for the Chinese border. What better was there for us to do but to follow him into one of the most beautiful regions of the world, where we hoped to have one of the richest harvests on our journey. Mr. La Croyère gave me the following report about his trip.

He had asked the surveyor Ivan Svistunov who had been recommended to us from among the people who had spent many years in Siberia to join him. He was to help him in the same way as Krasil'nikov with astronomical observations on the trip. The three of them left Irkutsk on 21 January. First he went to Nerchinsk, where he arrived on 12 February. Here he was joined by two other surveyors Peter Skobel'tsyn and Vasilii Shetilov. Captain-Commander Bering had selected them on his trip through Irkutsk according to the Governing Senate's instructions and

according to an agreement reached with us in Tobol'sk. Their
task was to find, describe and map a shorter route through
Nerchinsk to the Kamchatka Sea. They showed Mr. La Croyère
Bering's and our common instructions with which they had been
sent from Irkutsk on 5 August 1734. They claimed to have run
into insurmountable obstacles, especially the lack of guide
posts, which prevented them from carrying out their tasks. Thus
they had returned to Nerchinsk. If they had not run into Mr. La
Croyère there, they were planning to travel to Iakutsk to await
further orders from Bering. Mr. La Croyère referred them to
Captain Chirikov in Ust'Kut on the Lena so that he could notify
Bering in Iakutsk.

After spending six days in Nerchinsk, Mr. La Croyère set out
alone for the Nerchinskii (also known as the Argunskii) silver
mines. On 3 March he returned to Nerchinsk by way of Argunski
ostrog. He set out again on the tenth, arrived in Udinsk on the
22nd, in Selenginsk on the 26th, and in Kiakhta on 23 April
Here he stayed until 6 May when he returned to Selenginsk. He
completed his journey by taking a convenient merchant's wagon
filled with goods on 25 May and arrived happily in Irkutsk on
June. He had no other complaints but about continual obstacles
of his astronomical observations.

Mr. Gmelin and I followed Mr. La Croyère's examples. Because
we wanted to spend our time profitably, we could not have chosen
any better regions than those along the Chinese border. The
month of March was drawing to a close. We crossed safely and
comfortably over the ice on Lake Baikal, which not only freezes
over after all of the rivers but also thaws later than they do.

We would already have set out again on 22 March if the vice
governor, an unfriendly man, had not caused difficulties with our
teams. Only on the 24th were we able to obtain horses. We left
Irkutsk and arrived the following morning in Nikolskaia zastava
Customs control, the purpose of this post, caused us no problems
On the same day we proceeded along the northwestern shore of Lake
Baikal to Golousnoc Sirnowie [sic. Goloustnoe Zimov'e]. We
arrived early in the morning of the 26th at the Posotsko
Monastery on the south side of the Lake and in Udinsk on the
evening of the 28th.

Here the roads forked. We did not want to take the one to
Nerchinsk as Mr. La Croyère had but rather hastened to
Selenginsk, where we found thirty colleagues whom we had not seen
since Tobol'sk. Here Brigadier Bucholz, who had founded
Iamyshcheva and Omsk in 1715, was the highest ranking commander
He was in charge of border matters as well as correspondence with
China. He also governed the town and the Selenginsk region and
commanded a regiment of infantry. A man of such experience could
be of great assistance to me, and he was.

I showed him [Bucholz] my description and history of the
forts on the upper Irtysh, and he gave me more detailed

nformation about some aspects of them. The town chancellery
also gave me all of the information I requested without
objecting.   In this way I was especially able to collect
nformation about the old as well as the new borders with China,
which I used afterwards in my history of the Amur River.

Mr. La Croyère told Gmelin and me about the work done by the
surveyors Skobel'tsyn and Shetilov. At the same time an Udinsk
cossack, Gerasim Trutnev, told me that he knew the regions along
the Amur and its tributaries because he had trapped sable there
in the winter for many years. He also knew which rivers began on
the other side of the mountains along the border and flowed into
the Lena, the Ud or the Amur. Finding such a man, who could
guide our surveyors to the Ud, would have perhaps been an arduous
task if he had not turned out to be what he claimed and I had not
got to know about him through my other research. He combined
knowledge of the regions with sound judgment and the willingness
to do what was asked of him. And I did not hold back any
promises if the goals of the journey were fulfilled. After
conferring with my colleague, we unanimously agreed to send out
surveyors once again under the cossack Trutnev's guidance. As a
result, we had to requisition Trutnev from the Selenginsk
chancellery, because it was responsible for Udinsk, and recall
the surveyors from Irkutsk. On 10 April Mr. La Croyère wrote
them. They were instructed to expect Mr. Gmelin and me in
Udinsk.   From there they were supposed to accompany us to
Nerchinsk, where we would prepare them for the rest of the trip.

After putting things in order, Gmelin and I traveled on 10
April some 70 versts from the town up the Chikoi River to meet a
Mongolian taisha or prince named Lopsan, who acknowledged Russian
sovereignty.   I wanted to learn about the way of life and
idolatry of the dominant Dalai-Lama religion practiced there.
Lopsan as well as the clergy lived in spacious, magnificent
tents.   There were no such large buildings as Mr. Pallas saw,
described and sketched on his journey. Lopsan had been a
religious leader of that sect. Now a Tungus gelün was the head
of the idolatry there. We had gone on horseback. The prince and
his head priest, the gelün, who had been informed of our trip,
had ridden on horseback to meet us some versts from his ulus with
a large following. It was a kind of gathering to honor the
taisha as well as us. He had a standard carried ahead of him
with the Russian words: "I yield to no one!" And, "Given to the
Mongolskii Family in 1727." Count Sava Vladislavich, commonly
known as Raguzinskii, because he had been born in Raguza, had
given the prince this standard as a token of his favor in 1727
when he concluded a peace and border pact with the Chinese.
Mongol was the name of the prince's family, for the Mongols, like
other oriental peoples pay exact attention to the differences
among the families to which they belong.

We arrived at the ulus at eleven a.m. on the 12th.   The
prince led us into his and the gelün's summer quarters which were
not very far apart. I do not intend to describe everything we

saw. I refer to Gmelin's travel descriptions. Unfortunately, we
had not thought of bringing beds with us so that we could spend
several days at that pleasant spot. Before nightfall we left,
accompanied by the same kind of escort as on our arrival, so that
we would not have to sleep on evil-smelling Mongolian bedding and
arrived back in Selenginsk at noon on the 13th. Some time after
we had been in Kiakhta that amicable gelün came to Selenginsk to
visit me. I will report about this later.

Mr. Gmelin, as everywhere else, was responsible for weather
observations in Selenginsk, but no permanent observer was
appointed. The student, Tret'iakov, was left behind for that
purpose as long as we were traveling to Kiakhta and Nerchinsk.
Our barometrical observations here and in Kiakhta showed how
extraordinarily high that region lies. It seemed to all of us as
if, as in high mountains, we could not breathe as easily as in
lower regions. The water is very pure and clear. A mountain
chain on the Chikoi divides the waters flowing into Lake Baikal
from those flowing through part of northern Mongolia into the
Amur. There are no traces of any previous great flooding, no
petrification, no stones with figures. Readers can read Gmelin's
thoughts about this in the introduction to his _Flora sibirica_.

We could not leave for Kiakhta until the 22nd of April
because the Chikoi down which we were to travel was not yet
completely free of ice. Mr. La Croyère had left a day ahead of
us. We caught up with him again in Kiakhta where we arrived
early on the morning of the 24th.

The Kiakhta, an insignificant creek with both Russian and
Chinese trading settlements, flows from the north into the little
Bura River to the south, which then flows to the west into the
Selenga. Keeping the old border along the Bura and establishing
the trading settlements there would have been better. Then there
would have been enough water flowing in the river instead of the
stream at the village of Kiakhta that is dried up in places.
Wells have been dug to help out the situation. The settlements
are within a musket shot of each other. Halfway between them are
two border stakes. The Russian one says: "Rossiiskoi krai
torgovoi slobody [Russian border trading settlement]." The
Chinese one has texts both in Chinese and Manchurian which Gmelin
has taken from a copy I made and included in his travel
description.

There have never been any fortifications beyond the initial
groundwork on either side of the border; thus, the Russian
settlement has an advantage over the Chinese. The Russians had
built a somewhat regular fortification called Troitskii with a
garrison of a captain and one hundred men about four versts this
side of the trading settlement on the creek Kiakhta. The Chinese
settlement consisted of little alleyways with wooden huts on each
side and wooden storehouses behind them, where the Chinese
merchants also lived. In the middle of the Russian trading
settlement is a square wooden bazaar (_gostinnoi dvor_) with little

shops as well as storage areas. Special houses had been built for commandants and other guests who only stayed for a few days. Some Russian merchants have also built their own houses.

Trade was flourishing and was extremely advantageous for the Russians. All of the Chinese goods were very cheap. A tjun of kitaika used to calculate and to determine the price of other goods cost no more than three rubles. The Chinese sold the finest raw silver for ten rubles per pound. They liked to buy flour, grits, cattle and horses for the Chinese army fighting the Kalmyks because transport to the front from Kiakhta was closer than from China. This was done illegally but was tolerated because it brought a lot of fine silver into the country.

My readers will not want me to describe this remarkable place in any more detail. Gmelin and Pallas have described it and its trade in great detail at various times. I have also written in a sketchy manner about it in my treatise on Siberian trade. Gmelin has noted the special traits of natural history in Kiakhta and Selenginsk in the preface to the first part of his _Flora sibirica_.

Two weeks in Kiakhta was enough time for us to obtain information we wanted and Chinese supplies we needed for our journey to Kamchatka. On 7 May we headed back towards Selenginsk where we arrived the following day.

The student Tret'iakov had done his job so very well in our absence that he could continue to collect meteorological observations. In addition, during our coming trip to Nerchinsk, he was to collect blossoms from all of the flowering plants, and in the fall, their seeds, to preserve the plants and to stuff unidentified birds (because we had no specially trained taxidermist). He was to join us, at the earliest, the following winter, when Mr. Gmelin wrote him.

Two empty doshchaniki sent from the Tutern area of the Selenga River to pick up supplies for the Selenginsk and Kiakhta garrisons permitted us the comfort of traveling to Udinsk by water. On 23 May we left Selenginsk and went ashore again the following day in Udinsk, where we only stayed long enough, that is, until the 27th, to make arrangements for our trip to Nerchinsk. Mr. La Croyère caught up with us there, but he only stayed for a few hours. He was in a great hurry to get to Irkutsk, where only idle hours awaited him in the short summer nights.

On the 30th, when we arrived at the little river Ona which flows into the Uda, it was so swollen that we had to have a raft built in order to cross it.

I could think of no better way of spending the time than going to visit an eighty-year old Buriat sorceress living in the vicinity, to whom Russians as well as heathens ascribe miracles.

Mr. Gmelin accompanied me. He has described in detail what we
saw, therefore, it is unnecessary to repeat anything here. Her
grandson, the taisha Erintsei, met us and took us first to his
yurt or kibitka and then to his grandmother. We found her
sitting on a raised upholstered seat. She did not move from the
spot but undoubtedly accepted and approved of our respects to
her. The whole region regarded her as an oracle. Because the
Buryats living on the Uda and Khilok were still believers in
shamanistic heathenism, this benefited her and her grandson very
much. Because of her great age she did not want to produce
illusions with her drums any more. She limited herself to
dispensing medicines, foretelling the future and distributing
idols made of felting, not for worship but as amulets.
Otherwise, both the grandson's and the grandmother's yurts were
filled with shamanistic frippery. An even larger store of these
things kept in a third, uninhabited yurt.

     In the following period, especially under the current
auspicious government, new Russian and Polish colonists have been
settled in the areas on the Uda and Khilok not settled enough by
the Buryats. Eravninskoi ostrog was the first place we visited
in the Nerchinsk region that was inhabited by Russians. We
arrived there on 1 June. It is an insignificant spot lying
between two lakes. Only in winter do the neighboring Tungus come
there to pay tribute.

     On 3 June we set out again and went past several large, fish-
filled lakes and then crossed low, rambling mountains which
divide Lake Baikal's watershed from the Amur's. They are called
Iablonovye Khrebet (the Apple Mountains), not because apples grow
there, but ironically, because they are covered with small fist-
sized stones which look like apples. In other spots, especially
toward the east, they are called Stanovoi Khrebet, the Main
Mountains, just as we have a cephalic vein (stanovaia zhila) in
our bodies. In the northeast they stretch as far as the region
inhabited by Chukchi, where in the region of the Amur River they
are recognized as the border between Russia and china. On this
side the ascent up the Apple Mountains does not appear to be as
steep as the descent. There is a pleasant view toward the Ingoda
River where the Amur begins.

     The Chita ostrog, also known as the Plotbishche, a place
where ferries or rafts are built, is located where the little
Chita flows into the Ingoda. Since the establishment of
Nerchinsk travellers have been taking rafts from Chita. We
preferred travelling by water to land. Thus, we had barely
arrived at Chita 6 May before immediately requesting rafts built
for our continued journey. We left on the 8th and arrived in
Nerchinsk on the 13th. Occasionally we were held up by shallow
places in the Ingoda, where the rafts had to be laboriously
lifted across. Travelling was easier after the Ingoda joined the
Onon to form the Shilka. The small river Nercha flows into the
Shilka on which the city of Nerchinsk is situated in a very
pleasant and fertile area.

Here we met Skobel'tsyn and Shetilov, who had arrived two days before us. My primary task was to prepare them for their journey to the Ud River. I had supplied them with a guide in Selenginsk, but they also brought along one from Irkutsk named Andrei Korolev. He claimed he had exact knowledge of the regions along the Zeia and Ud rivers. After hearing their accounts, I no longer could hope that the journey's goal could be accomplished, i.e., to find an easier and more direct way to the Kamchatka Sea than by way of Iakutsk and Okhotsk. In my opinion it should be done with or without Chinese permission along the Amur. Nevertheless, the opportunity to make an exact map of a large stretch of still completely unexplored and unsurveyed land could not be ignored. It was also necessary to become better acquainted with a region that in the Nerchinsk Peace Treaty of 1689 with the Chinese had been left with a very ill-defined border between both empires. The best sables in all of Siberia are found there. Because it is uninhabited, subjects of both empires frequently hunt there. It might become the source of future strife if Petersburg were to lay claim to the entire Amur region to improve navigation to the American and Kurile Islands, Japan and India. Thus, both patriotic duty and a desire to expand geographical knowledge caused me to strive energetically to complete the preparations for the undertaking.

In order to have common agreement about the undertaking Mr. Gmelin and I conferred with the surveyors and guides on 17 June and drew up a written plan for the expedition. We instructed the surveyors in accordance with newly received directives in which their duties were better formulated than in the ones we had drawn up with Captain-Commander Bering in Tobol'sk. In addition, they received two Russian guides who had volunteered for the expedition and six Tungus acquainted with the region, a Tungus translator, and an escort of twenty cossacks because they thought it unsafe to travel without them.

We requested all other necessities -- supplies, oxen, horses -- from the Nerchinsk chancellery at Crown expense. We also had to take care of the final preparations so our trip to the Argun silver mines would not be delayed. The surveyors left Nerchinsk on 3 August.

On 29 June Mr. Gmelin went ahead by the shortest route to the silver mines. It goes over the mountains and can only be taken on horseback. He had taken the student Gorlanov along to describe the route. On 2 July he arrived at the silver mines which as his travel descriptions indicate he has described in detail. My contributions stem from information obtained from documents in the Nerchinsk archives.

Until 5 July I was occupied with the archives and information from the town chancellery about conditions in the town and the entire Nerchinsk region. I also reaped a rich harvest of oral information. I heard of a Tungus shaman living not far from the town. I sent for him to parade his arts. Mr. Gmelin, who had

not yet departed, has described them. Little distinguishes one
kind of trickery and conjuring from another of this sort. Even
the Russian inhabitants in Siberia, even the commander of the
town, whom I often invited to accompany me, gradually became used
to watching unafraid all of the exorcising. This is undeniably a
means of reducing superstitious beliefs in witchcraft.

I made a half-circle across the steppes to reach the Argun
silver mines in order to better describe the Tungus living on
this steppe with their large herds of cattle. A straight road
leads to a salt lake which supplies the Nerchinsk region with
finished salt. But because the lake did not especially interest
me, I turned left and arrived at the silver works on 13 July.
From there Mr. Gmelin and I went to Argunskoi ostrog on the 16th
but returned to the mines on the 18th. We did not undertake the
trip to see that insignificant ostrog, which had decreased in
importance because of the Peace Treaty of 1689, and even more,
because the caravan route had been rerouted over Selenginsk. The
only thing we wanted to see, and did see, were the Chinese border
stakes opposite the ostrog, which were renewed every year by
people expressly sent from Naun for that purpose. On the stakes
is written when and by whom the accuracy of the border was
determined. The old stakes are left until they rot. They had not
yet put in new stakes that year.

A Swede Peter Dames, the manager of the silver mines, had
enough knowledge about making weather observations to persuade
Mr. Gmelin to have him supervise a chancellery clerk, Peter
Kovyrin, who was to continue the weather observations Mr. Gmelin
had begun. We were very critical of the mining and smelting
operations. Corrections were only made later when the general
mining board of directors in Petersburg sent Saxon miners.

We planned the continuation of our journey so that we would
not have to return to Nerchinsk in order to be spared the
difficult overland route from Nerchinsk to Chitinsk ostrog, since
travelling against the current on the shallow, swift rivers is
even less manageable. We decided only to return to the large
regional road in Chitinsk. Because we had noticed a lot of old
grave mounds at Gorodishche sloboda, below the mouth of the Onon
River, we sent our student Gorlanov there to have them excavated
for any artifacts which he would then turn over to me. He found
nothing worth all of the trouble, only bones. A similar
excavation in my presence of a couple of grave mounds between
Eravna and Udinsk on my return trip was just as fruitless.

Another excursion on which we sent the surveyor Ivanov and
the student Krasheninnikov came about because, while doing my
usual geographic research, I had heard about a hot spring on the
upper Onon River not too far from the Mongolian border. The
Mongols used it for treating both internal as well as external
maladies. Mr. Gmelin would have been delayed if he had gone
there himself. It also seemed unnecessary for him to go there
because we could rely upon the ability and diligence of our

tudent to describe anything he saw there. We ordered the
urveyor to help the student describe the route they took, to
ake the sun's altitude at noon -- his usual task anyway -- and
o make a map of the hot spring. Both completed the assignments
e had given them.

On 24 July we left the silver mines and arrived the same day
t the jasper mountains along the shores of the Argun River.
ften, beautiful green pieces have been sent to Russia from
here. Craftsmen complained that they were too small for making
mportant objects. We wanted to see for ourselves, so we climbed
p the mountain to the jasper quarry, even though dusk was
alling. We did not find any pieces bigger than three to four
oll wide or long, and among others also pale green ones of the
ame hardness. Several pieces broke easily into smaller ones,
erhaps because they were weathered from lying out in the open.
o one had tried to see if larger and better pieces could be
ound at a depth. But even if they were found, would not the
ransportation costs outweigh their worth?

Many thousands of pud of unmarketable lead are lying at the
ilver mines. They probably will only be used if war were to
reak out with China. The jasper has another drawback, i.e.,
very rock lies isolated by itself in rotting earth. There is
ittle hope that large masses of it, let alone veins, will ever
e found.

We still needed to visit the upper reaches of the Argun
iver, where Russians have only begun to live since the last
eace Treaty of 1727, when a decision was made to establish a
order trading settlement, like the one at Kiakhta, between the
wo empires where a former caravan route crossed the Naun. The
pot is called Tsurukhaitu. It cannot be compared with Kiakhta.
o one lives there permanently. The place is very unpleasant.
he entire region has absolutely no wood for building. Even thin
rush for fires has to be hauled a long distance. This brush has
een used to build several huts for the use of the Nerchinsk
ossacks standing guard there until they are relieved. In the
ummer, when Chinese border observers are there, some minor
rading takes place with the Russian border guards. Merchants
rom Siberia, let alone Russia, do not go there. That at least
as the situation when we were there. We arrived on 26 July and
tayed until the 28th.

About ten versts on the other side of the Argun were supposed
o be the ruins of an old destroyed city in a now uninhabited
rea that we could visit without the Chinese -- that people
nclined to complain about every trifle -- knowing about it. I
id not let the opportunity slip by, and my constant companion
r. Gmelin accompanied me. It would have been amusing if the
hinese had found us in their country without passports and taken
s to Peking as prisoners. When we arrived there, we found
othing more than the square earthworks similar to the ones often

found on the southern steppes of Siberia. We returned t
Tsurukhaitu on the same day.

On the morning of the 29th, after travelling the whole night
we reached the frontier between Siberia and China, at the foot o
a mountain Abagaitu, on whose peak both sides had put borde
markers. From here we could see the whole Argun River region an
that it flows from the Hailar River rather than from Dalaino
Lake as is commonly believed. Near the mouth of the Hailar i
splits into three branches, two of which become the Argun and th
third flows into Dalai Lake. This can be concluded from th
various currents of its branches. We decided not to follow ou
predecessor Messerschmidt's example and cross the border into th
region lying before us. In his travel accounts he describe
going as far as Dalai Lake where he spent several days. At tha
time there was no doubt that the lake did not belong to Russia.

One day was sufficient for us at Abagaitu Mountain. On th
morning of the 31st, we were once again in Tsurukhaitu. A
nightfall we were heading straight across the steppe to the Ono
River. Having to haul wood for cooking made travel difficult
but we did not want to use dried horse manure as most people did
We could not do without a wagon with wood and a barrel of fres
water.

These steppe Tungus were more docile and friendly tha
peoples we met anywhere else. Their way of life is unlike tha
of the forest Tungus but rather like that of the Mongols. The
live from raising cattle. They have a superabundance of horses
cattle and sheep. Some of them do not even know how much stoc
they own. They gave us horses for our wagons whenever and a
many as we wanted. They use nooses to capture horses out of th
herd. At every station they brought us a young bullock an
several sheep. We and our party took as much as we could eat
Several times all of the meat, especially from the bullocks -- n
piece excepted -- tasted strongly of garlic, probably becaus
they grazed in areas where wild garlic grows.

Tungus shamans are generally considered more adept tha
others, but they are not. I ordered various ones of them t
gather. One shamanka, who had formerly practiced her art amon
the Mongols, was more famous than the others. At that time th
Mongols were not all yet adherents of the Dalai-Lama religion
Otherwise, that religious clergy spares no effort in spreadin
their idolatry as far as possible. Some of them had trie
converting the Tungus but without success.

An unusual feature of this shaman ceremony, which Mr. Gmeli
has described, was that the shamanka had covered her leathe
shaman coat in front and back with round, cast pewter disks wit
loops on them. One side was smooth but the other with a loop ha
Chinese characters on it. She had obtained the disks from China
I gave some of them to the Imperial Art Gallery.

An old, haggard man was alleged to be able to pull an arrow through his body during his shamanistic exorcism. I demanded he should demonstrate his crafts honestly, if he really could do them. If, however, he were thinking about deceiving us, I assured him that we had sharp eyes and he would be punished for his deception. After a long discussion, he admitted that his craft was a deception. All he did was shove an arrow through one side of his coat past his pulled-in stomach and out through his coat on the other side. That is what he did when I had him perform for me. That would have been difficult for a stocky, fat man to do. I had the trick sketched. It can be found among the pictures of peoples for which Mr. Georgi wrote the accompanying descriptions. The engraver Roth obtained my drawing -- I do not know how -- from the Academy.

An animal called the chagatai, unique to the Mongolian steppe, is something between a horse and a donkey. Messerschmidt called it _mulum_ _foecundum_ _Aristotelis_. We spent a few days in the neighborhood of the Nerchinsk salt lake because Gmelin wanted to see and describe this quite unfamiliar animal. The Tungus said that it occasionally ranged into the area and could be caught by undertaking a large encircling hunt (_oblava_). We sent our fifty Tungus, vigorous, strong people, on such a chase. They chased energetically around fifty versts for a whole day without getting an animal. Later I obtained one for Mr. Gmelin, which will be described in due course.

The salt lake is nothing special. On 5 August we set out again. We sent our wagon straight to the Onon River. In the meantime Mr. Gmelin and I made a detour on horseback to inspect an underground cave we had heard marvelous things about. We were taken to the supposed cave north of the river Borsa which flows into the Onon. There are three other rivers of this name flowing toward the Argun. We also inspected another cave not far from it, but found nothing marvelous anywhere. We then had to hurry to get back to our wagon after having ridden eighty versts mostly at a gallop. We caught up with it late in the evening at a predetermined spot on the river Onon. The direct path from the salt lake to the Onon is fifty versts.

If we wanted to take the most direct route to Chita ostrog, we had to cross the Onon at that spot. It already is quite wide and deep in that area, also hazardous because of its swiftness. The Mongols and the Nerchinsk Tungus had no boats on the river because they do not like to fish and live solely from raising animals. If they want to cross the river, they stretch dried ox hides over poles to make boats, something the Russians also do when they want to cross the river. When merchants and imperial caravans were still travelling to Peking by way of Naun, this was their usual route. We had not foreseen a need for ox hides and obtaining them and then making boats from them seemed to us too time consuming. There was plenty of wood. We had sent orders ahead to build a raft. We used it to cross the river the following day.

While the large number of people, horses and wagons wer
gradually being transported across the river, we spent the tim
pleasantly enough with a Tangut lama living among the Tungus i
the region of the Onon not only to preach his idolatry but t
give them medical help for illnesses, for which he was pai
excessively. We had heard his skills praised. We had sent
message to him to come to that place that day. He arrived wit
all of his medical equipment and gave a good account o
everything. Mr. Gmelin has described everything he saw and hear
from him in his travel description. I had too little time t
talk to the lama about other matters. He gave me an Indian boo
and one covered with painted idols. He spoke Tungus well. Sinc
we could take along or find good translators everywhere we went
we had no problem communicating.

On 7 August we set out again and arrived on the followin
morning at a spot on the Aga River, which flows into the Ono
where not long before promising signs of copper ore had bee
discovered. There was nobody, however, who could show us th
diggings.   A few years later a smelter was built and name
Aginskii zavod, but it was not permanent because of insufficien
wood.   On 10 August we arrived at Chita ostrog, where shortl
before us the surveyor and student from our group, whom we ha
sent to the hot spring on the Onon and to grave mounds a
Gorodishche, had also arrived.

We had no reason to stay there. On the 11th we set out alon
the same route we had used on the trip from Udinsk.   On the 13t
we arrived in Eravninskoi ostrog, where we stayed for one day
while fresh teams of horses were being assembled. On the 17th w
arrived at Udinsk, where we had ordered two boats, doshchaniks
to be waiting to transport us over Lake Baikal back to Irkutsk.

We assumed the boats would be waiting for us because we ha
written the provincial chancellery at Irkutsk on 10 April fro
Selenginsk.   They, however, did not arrive until the 23rd an
were loaded with goods for the imperial caravan to China.   An
then only one of them was intended for us. There was not enoug
room on it for our whole party. We had to write the brigadier a
Selenginsk for a second boat, and it took until 13 Septembe
before we could load our party onto the two doshchaniks in Udins
in order to return to Irkutsk. We could not use all of the on
from Selenginsk because it was partially filled with goods seize
by customs at Kiakhta. We could only use the remaining space
It was, however, new and well built, which the other two wer
not.

While we were tied up in Udinsk, we spent our time wit
things we had not been able to observe and describe in enoug
detail on the journey. Some things had only been noted hastil
with three words and left for a better opportunity when we coul
get back to them. These we worked out in detail here.   Th
artists now had time to complete pictures sketched along th
journey only in primary colors. By winter we also had to prepar

report about our activities for the Senate. We could not begin that soon enough. I was especially concerned about finding an opportunity to do something I might never have another chance to do, i.e. to have Dalai-Lama clergy teach me the secrets of their religion. I therefore asked taisha Lopsan's Tangut gelün to send one of his subordinate clerics to me in Udinsk with whom I could talk about spiritual and scientific matters. In response the gelün sent me one of his Mongolian students who stayed with me as long as we were in Udinsk. Thus, the seemingly inopportune delay of our boats turned into an advantage for our undertaking.

As soon as our boats were ready we left Udinsk on 13 September. Two days later we arrived at the middle mouth of the Selenga River on Lake Baikal, from where most crossings are usually begun since the lake is narrowest there. Should I mention a superstition found throughout the region, i.e. that the lake is a sea, indeed a sacred sea, into which one should throw some money as an offering during the crossing. Above all one dare not ridicule it. No, I do not think I should! Gmelin has already done it. It is enough to say that some crosswinds at the mouth of the Selenga and along the northern coast held us up some before we could reach the mouth of the Angara. We arrived with both doshchaniks safe and sound in Irkutsk on 20 September.

Here in letters from Iakutsk we discovered that it was not necessary for us to hurry our preparations for the journey to Kamchatka since the preparations for the voyage were going slowly in Okhotsk and the ships intended for the sea voyage were not yet under construction. Four ships were to be built: two to explore in the direction of America and two to sail along the Kurile Islands to Japan. We could not expect to start our journey to Kamchatka the following summer. Iakutsk promised to be very boring if we stayed longer than one winter. How could we divide our time so that we had enough to do, did not stay too long in any one place and did not travel too far from the main Iakutsk road so that we could be in Iakutsk when notified? Unless we wanted to look farther into the future, we knew that we had at least the entire following year at our disposal during which our presence would not be required in Iakutsk. Therefore, Mr. Gmelin, Mr. La Croyère and I discussed what we should undertake.

Mr. Gmelin and I decided to remain in Irkutsk until January of the following year (1736), then travel to Ilimsk and toward spring to the Lena River and from there downstream to Iakutsk, which could take a few days compared to the weeks we thought of spending. Mr. La Croyère, however, who liked being away from us, who had married in Irkutsk during our journey to Nerchinsk, decided to travel to Selenginsk and Kiakhta again at the beginning of the year to see the results of the observations he had started on his first journey. The following spring he would travel to the Lena and proceed straight to Iakutsk by water without stopping anywhere.

If we did not count our daily tasks, which were the sam
everywhere, then I especially still had to get a lot o
information and documentary proof about the town and region o
Irkutsk, so it was necessary to keep the provincial chanceller
busy. There was less for me to do in the archives there since th
town had only grown in recent times through trade with China an
it initially had been an insignificant ostrog dependent upo
other cities and ostrogs. We were mostly occupied with writing
report for the Governing Senate about our trip and activitie
since Eniseisk. We were able to include an impressive number o
observations, descriptions, sketches, artifacts and other kind
of rarities. The importance and quantity of things was one reaso
for our sending them with a soldier from our escort t
Petersburg. Another reason was because we needed various dail
necessities from Petersburg. We could only be certain o
receiving them if we had them expressly picked up and brought t
us.

In the meantime in Petersburg Chamberlain von Korff had no
only become president of the Academy in name but also in fact.
had been personally acquainted with this superb man since th
arrival of the Court from Moscow. He gave our association
indeed the Academy, his utmost support. Gmelin and I had jus
returned to Irkutsk when we found the first effect of hi
willingness to help us. Various things were waiting for us eve
though we had requested them from friends in our private letters
At the same time we received a letter the Chamberlain ha
addressed to all of us in which he informed us of his appointmen
as Head of the Academy (he was in the habit of using the Frenc
term) and admonished us to work harmoniously together. Thi
letter deserves to be included here in the original. Imperia
Councilor Goldbach wrote it as could be concluded from it
beautiful Latin, even if the handwriting did not corroborat
this.

Gentlemen:

The Empress has recently imposed upon me the task of
governing the Academy, and in order to fulfill my duty in
accordance with my own views, I realize that I have need
not only of the united efforts of its present members,
but expecially of your unremitting labor, your vigilance
and, what is essential, your agreement. Therefore, on a
journey fraught with so many dangers and surrounded by so
many obstacles, put aside impartially any disagreements
existing among you, keeping in mind the human condition,
and give priority to the public good.

In the matter of your desires, Croyère, I painfully
perceived in your letter of last year that all the
mathematical equipment entrusted to your care had
seriously deteriorated because of rain and stormy
weather, but I surmise that through the effort of

yourself and of your associates this equipment has been repaired in such a way that it has been adequate for the subsequent calculations which in great numbers you have initiated. If, however, you have any need of equipment or any other supports, please accurately describe them in letters to me, and be completely assured that I will attend to this matter.

In as much as I greatly approve of the diligence which you have exhibited in investigating and describing various matters, for which I thank you in the name of the whole society, so also do I strongly urge you all to include in your correspondence with me a copy of any detailed reports you sent to the Governing Senate, so that it will be unnecessary for us to request your writings from another source, a situation which you yourself will adjudge both inappropriate and laborious and fatiguing. Because you have up to the present neglected to do so, no journal of the whole trip you have completed was delivered to the Academy. It will be your responsibility to make up this loss at the earliest opportunity.

In experiments of any significance, the experimenter will invite his colleagues to join him, if they are resident in the same city, not merely as witnesses but so they themselves may help the experimenter, familiarize themselves with the method of the experiment, and furthermore may amicably admonish him if any error or negligence seems to have occurred.

Since I am communicating with you at the command of her Imperial Majesty, I have no doubt that you will faithfully abide by these injunctions.

Given at St. Petersburg, 23 December, 1734, Korff

This letter's references to strife among us, strife that we ᵼould end for our own common good, refers to letters Mr. Gmelin ᵼd I had written President von Keyserlingk and several members ᵼ the Academy, our friends, from Kazan and Tobol'sk. We had ᵼpressed our opinions of Mr. La Croyère and his astronomical and ᵼher observations. They were not complaints like those of ᵼople living in strife but rather they came from loyal, well-ᵼunded concern that he could not fulfill the goals of such an ᵼportant expedition. In Petersburg we had suspected, based on ᵼe results of his trip to Lapland, that Mr. La Croyère was ᵼexperienced and careless. This was fully confirmed for us ᵼrsthand in Kazan and Tobol'sk. The matter, however, was taken ᵼry lightly in Petersburg. On the one hand, the Academy was not ᵼthout blame for accepting Mr. La Croyère solely on Mr. ᵼlisle's word that he was qualified for the expedition. On the ᵼher hand, Mr. Delisle, who had a good reputation, could

forcefully represent his brother during any deliberations abou
the matter.

The letter's conclusion seemed to suggest that an observe
should invite his colleagues to be present at his importan
observations. They could not only corroborate such observation
as witnesses but also become used to observing such observation
so that they could call the observer's attention to any error o
inaccuracy he might make. Does not this suggestion itself refut
the suspicion of strife and enmity? A witness from whom one i
supposed to accept reminders has certainly to be a friend o
surely one will always find enough excuses to avoid the witnes
and his reminders.

In fact, on the journey there was never any discord or strif
between Mr. La Croyère and us and none could have taken place
None of us were inclined to it. Mr. La Croyère, especially
willingly accepted or appeared to accept all of the reminders w
gave him in a friendly and polite manner. We, therefore, coul
refer to Mr. La Croyère himself in our answer to Mr. von Korff
He affirmed our vindication in writing after we stated in detai
everything that we had not liked about him and let him read i
before sending it so that he might immediately include an
justifications he wished in his letter. This proves that ther
was no enmity among us. Probably no legal matter has ever bee
dealt with more coolly and equitably. Thus, Gmelin and I avoide
any suspicion of slander. The Academy and Mr. von Korff coul
now make a decisive judgment if and how the complaints agains
Mr. La Croyère might be handled rather than why we, having don
our duty, had no further reason to be concerned.

To save space I am not including the letters here even thoug
they are interesting. If necessary, they can be obtained fro
the Academy archives. I cannot overlook the matter because o
its consequences. Our complaints did not cause Mr. La Croyère t
improve. He also was not recalled.

Our surveyor Krasil'nikov determined longitudes and latitude
whenever they were needed. The Academy wanted to include a
astronomer in our party and supplied us with Mr. [Johann
Christopher] Libertus from Berlin. This man did not have th
necessary abilities and had a contrary, egotistical nature. W
tried to obtain another astronomer but he did not want t
undertake such a long journey. In the meantime we had learned t
be satisfied with Krasil'nikov and afterwards, come what may, w
did not think about a better arrangement.

We were unable to comply with the decree requiring us to sen
copies of our observations and descriptions for the Senate als
to the Academy. We did not have scribes in the various language
we would have required and the students with us were kept bus
enough with the scientific work we assigned them. Not lon
afterwards the request became superfluous because the Governin

Senate in Petersburg sent everything we sent to the Academy and
continued to do this as long as the expedition lasted.

The soldiers were dispatched on 9 December. The following
day we received an order from the regional Mining Chancellery in
Ekaterinburg, dated 14 October, announcing that Councilor [V.N.]
Tatishchev had been appointed commander-in-chief that year to
replace General-Lieutenant von Hennin.

We were surprised to receive an order from a Chancellery with
no jurisdiction of any kind over us. Up to then all of the
Siberian chancelleries had corresponded with us through
memoranda, a practice they also continued to follow afterwards.
We thought we were working directly under the Academy. The order
was directed to all of us. The content actually only concerned
Mr. Gmelin. I replied in his name in the form of a private
letter he signed. To justify our reaction to this unexpected
order, I am including here our answer which closed the matter.

To State Councilor Tatishchev in answer to the Ukaz sent us
by the Regional Mining Chancellery:

> Your Excellency's agreeable letter of 14 October this
> year has been received by all of us here in Irkutsk on
> the 10th. We obediently thank Your Excellency for
> graciously promising to help us with our work as much as
> possible. At the same time we received an ukaz from the
> Siberian Mining Chancellery addressed to my colleagues
> and me, also dated 14 October. In it Your Excellency
> desires to know about traces of silver ore I had the
> honor of reporting on 22 May from Selenginsk and
> suggested improvements advantageous to imperial interests
> at the Argun silver mines. It also states in answer to
> my request for a crucible that a man capable of making
> such a crucible had been dispatched to us with the
> necessary materials by the Siberian government on 27
> March. I have, indeed, weighted the contents of this
> ukaz with my colleagues. May Your Excellency graciously
> allow me, however, to inform you what we deem to be our
> duty.

> We were surprised to have the Siberian Mining
> Chancellery send us an ukaz instead of using the usual
> manner of memoranda between us and the Siberian regional
> mining office and demanding that we report to the
> Chancellery whatever we would find in our investigations
> of the traces of silver ore discovered at Selenginsk and
> at the Argun silver mines. Even though we have always
> taken the greatest pleasure in carrying out all of the
> specific requests Your Excellency has made upon us and
> wish nothing more than that our work in the name of the
> Empire meets with your gracious approval, our privileges
> were granted by the Academy of Sciences in the most
> glorious memory of His Imperial Majesty Peter I and

reconfirmed by Her Most Gracious reigning Imperial
Majesty. The ukazes and instructions given us at our
departure by the Governing Senate and the Academy of
Sciences upon the orders of Her Imperial Majesty provide
no directive for us to accept ukazes from the Siberian
Mining Chancellery. The Academy of Sciences in St.
Petersburg only corresponds with its colleagues in the
empire through memoranda. Until the above date, we, as
members of the Academy, have received no ukazes from any
Chancellery, only those from the Governing Senate. We
can provide samples of memoranda sent us by the
government chancelleries in Tobol'sk and Kazan and also
by the previous Siberian regional mining office.

Furthermore, we had to certify in writing at the time
of our departure that we would give no one reports of our
work except the Governing Senate. And even though we
know very well that Siberian mining has been solely and
completely entrusted to Your Excellency by Her Imperial
Majesty and that this means that any discoveries we have
made or will make should rightfully be sent to Your
Excellency. But we are not permitted to do this unless
ordered to by higher authority.

We suggest that Your Excellency consider that the
work required of us in our instructions was well as the
circumstances surrounding our entire expedition do not
permit us to accept such commissions from the Siberian
Mining Chancellery other than those given us concerning
the Argun silver mines. We have only been sent out to
make discoveries and do research in the sciences. We
have not been ordered to do anything regarding the
economy of the empire. We do not understand it anyway,
have never served at a mine and are totally inexperienced
in Chancellery rules. If we were supposed to learn all
of this on our trip and be employed later in such areas,
then we would need a lot of time for this which would
interfere a great deal with the work we have actually
been ordered to do. Moreover, we cannot arrange our stay
at a given place and our special excursions according to
our own desires but always have to consider the interests
of the entire expedition and especially of the voyage
planned by Captain Commander Bering. For this reason the
Governing Senate has specified no specific tasks for us
to do but instead has given us in all cases the freedom
to decide what we should do and, depending upon
developments along the journey, to arrange our special
side trips.

As Your Excellency will recognize from the above, we
have the most important reasons for most obediently
informing him of them. Thus, we also hope that our
statements will not be misinterpreted, that, in view of
the high imperial privileges most graciously granted and

conferred to the Academy of Sciences, and the ukazes and instructions specifically given us as well as our own personal circumstances on the present journey, high goodwill will be shown us, so that we will be exempt in the future from ukazes from the Siberian chancellery as well as similar orders which are in no way part of our mission.

In regard to the three points contained in the ukaz, I most obligingly answer that I only guessed about possibilities when I found traces of silver ore in Selenginsk. I did not report this to Your Excellency before having enough proof in front of me for it to be made public. Because I do not have a good crucible I have not been able to ascertain the true content of the ore. I, therefore, cannot report anything more than in my letter from Irkutsk on 8 December of this year. Together with the letter I sent a little sack with some small samples addressed to the Siberian provincal chancellery.

We have received Your Excellency's letter of 4 April regarding our request for a crucible, stating that one had been sent. We obediently wrote on 15 November that we had not received it and requested information about how it had been sent so that we might make inquiries here and in Ilimsk all the more energetically. We also have heard nothing of three men mentioned in the ukaz capable of making the crucibles.

And finally in regard to the Argun silver mines, about which Your Excellency has requested information: On 8 December we sent a full description of them by courier to the Governing Senate. We returned here on 20 September from our trip to Selenginsk and Nerchinsk. Thus Your Excellency can see that it would be impossible for us to carry out the instructions even if we had the necessary qualifications.

Once again we are repeating our request in a memorandum of . . . April from Selenginsk to the Siberian Regional Mining Office to forward us a copy of the meteorological observations made thus far in Ekaterinburg and in the future to continue to do this quarterly as well as also to inform us if the instruments have been damaged after our departure.

Just as I have the honor to report all of the above, I also have been charged by my colleagues to assure Your

Excellency of their continued, most obedient respect.   I
especially remain in humble submission,

Your Excellency's most obedient servant

        J.G.G.

We initiated two missions from Irkutsk: one to establish the
geographic location of Tunkinskii ostrog and the other the hot
spring near Barguzin. I suspect from oral reports and the
distances to surrounding places that Tunkinsk must lie more than
a degree farther south than shown on the maps. Either the
surveyors had not been there at all or else they had not compared
the position obtained from geodetic descriptions with the sun's
altitude at noon. Our surveyor Ivanov set out on 22 December to
do this and returned to Irkutsk on 2 January. Tunkinsk lies
exactly where I had suspected. One reason more for me to
continue my oral investigations most carefully and to expand
them. The better I spoke the local language the easier
everything became for me.

The second mission belongs to the following year 1736 just after
our departure from Irkutsk, so I will wait until then to relate
it.

        Müller did not finish the account of his decade in
Siberia. His assistant J.-G. Stritter, who covered the
Academy years 1725-1743, completed the history of the
Academy. He, however, paid little further attention to
the Academy contingent of the Kamchatka expedition. Only
the following fragments provide additional information
related to Müller's long stay in Siberia.

(1740)

        In a personal ukaz, dated 1 February 1740, the Tsarina
assigned Müller the task of drafting a description of the Amur
River. On 20 February the Senate sent an ukaz to the Academy
stating that Müller, at the Tsarina's personal request, was to
provide the Vice-Governor of Irkutsk, State Councilor Lorentz
Lange, the description. It was intended for use as a basis for a
border treaty with China. Therefore, Müller was to describe not
only the Amur but also its tributaries and streams in the
greatest of detail as well as to indicate what should be
considered in a border treaty with China. Mr. Anton Büsching has
printed an exact copy of this description in the <u>Magazin fuer
neue Historie und Geographie</u> (Magazine for New History and
Geography) (II, pp. 483-518). Originally, Mr. Büsching had
included the description under General Kindermann's name because
his name was on the copy (as owner) which he had probably
obtained from Mr. Lange. Mr. Büsching corrected this error in
the preface to the description. This description also must not

be confused with the "History of the Amur River Region," printed
in the second volume of the Sammlung russischer Geschichte
(Collection of Russian History). Müller also wrote it but it is
quite different from this early description.

(1743)

On 7 October a Senate ukaz from the Chancellery was
communicated to the council. The Senate inquired whether the
professors, adjuncts, students and other persons belonging to the
Kamchatka Expedition had fulfilled their tasks according to their
instructions or whether any of them still needed to remain in
Siberia. Mr. Gmelin was given a copy of the Senate's order so
that he could discuss it with Mr. Müller and then draft an answer
to it at the next council meeting. The main points in the draft
answer to the Governing Senate's requests are as follows:

1. "Among the professors, adjuncts, students, etc., sent
to Siberia to carry out various scientific observations,
the adjuncts Steller and Fischer, the geodetic surveyor
Krasil'nikov, the artist Berkhan, the translator
Lindemann and the students Popov, Ivanov and Gorlanov are
still in Siberia. Some of them are in Okhotsk and others
in Kamchatka in order to continue the observations the
professors have assigned them.

2. The descriptions already sent from Siberia and the
ones still to be turned over attest to Professor Gmelin's
extreme diligence in describing in the greatest detail
everything belonging to natural history and the natural
sciences and to Professor Müller's in describing the
history and geography of a region, the artifacts,
customs, habits and religion of the people living there
according to the instructions they had been given.

3. We cannot say whether Adjuncts Steller and Fischer
are still needed since we have received no report from
them for such a long time. Therefore, we do not know
what they have done or still have to do. We can report
even less about the activities of the geodetic surveyor
Krasil'nikov and the students Ivanov and Popov since they
only answered to the late Delisle de la Croyère. The
persons mentioned here could be notified because of the
Senate's orders to complete their activities as quickly
as possible and return to Petersburg since it was no
longer necessary for them to stay in Siberia for such
scientific research."

This statement was given to the other professors so that they
could offer their comments. On 11 October in a special meeting
held about the matter, Mr. Siegesbeck thought they could not say
that it was not necessary for someone to continue research in
Siberia because there was still a lot of things to investigate in

the plant world. Mr. Weitbrecht countered by saying that people still there should be relieved of the continued hardships of that long journey. On 14 October, Mr. Müller's draft and several members' comments were read to the council. It was decided that it should be presented to the council once again with the suggested changes so that it could be signed by all of them. On the 17th a decision was reached to give this reply to the chancellery and, because Mr. Siegesbeck had requested some rare Siberian plants, to write Mr. Steller to collect them on his return trip. On 18 October the Academy's answer along with the appropriate appendices was sent to Mr. Nartov with a reminder that no report had ever been received from Mr. Fischer. Despite this answer sent to the Chancellery Mr. Nartov demanded another one on 29 October ostensibly because of a repeated order from the Senate. On 31 October they, therefore, requested a copy of the translation of the Academy's recent answer and of the Senate's repeated order. At the same time, the professors expressed their surprise that the Academy's recent answer to the Senate's inquiry did not suffice. A letter written by Mr. Nartov to Mr. von Winsheim showed that the Senate had issued no new order concerning the Kamchatka expedition, but rather that Senate Secretary Tsamiatin had said to the Academy's Registrar Timofiev that he should request a positive answer about the Kamchatka Expedition from the Academy Council.

The following is the response Müller drafted to the Governing Senate:

In keeping with reports recently received from adjuncts Steller and Fischer, the Academy should recall them as well as the geodetic surveyor Krasil'nikov and their subordinates. On their return trip, however, they should make as many observations as possible according to the Academy's instructions. They also should bring back the books and instruments left behind by the professors.

DOCUMENT 5

The following memoranda, decrees, and reports from the Academy of Sciences archives illustrate the problem of communications constantly faced by the explorers who remained fully reliant upon the Academy in St. Petersburg for their authority and financing. The Academy, in turn, had to apply to the Governing Senate for permission to allow any change in the original decree. Yet the explorers and the Academy were separated by thousands of miles. Translations by G. Melnikoff, Russian Department, Carleton University, and J. L. Black.

A. Korff resumé of Chancellery report to the Governing Senate. Chancellery Archives. 23 May 1737. From _Materialy_, III (St. Petersburg, 1866), p. 391.

By decree of Her Imperial Majesty, the Academy of Sciences had determined: To present a report to the Governing Senate, worded as follows:

On the past 9th of March of the year 1737, the Governing Senate received by dispatch a report presented by Captain-Commander Bering concerning the wrongs suffered by the professors of the Kamchatka Expedition, and a request to render a decision on this matter by decree. And now the professors of the Kamchatka Expedition are declaring the following by letter: Johann Georg Gmelin is reporting a fire that occurred in Irkutsk in which he lost several personal effects and is requesting to be compensated in books and other effects; Gerhard Friedrich Müller is reporting that Captain-Commander Bering informed them by letter as to how, in virtue of the decrees of the Governing Senate, he would be unable to supply them in Kamchatka with needed victuals, and demanded that the transportation of victuals, because of great difficulties, be not assigned to them, and that they not be obliged to waste time in Iakutsk; all this being represented exactly in greater detail to the Governing Senate in reports from the said professors. And at the request of Professor Gmelin, books, instruments and other items from the Academy of Sciences will be sent as soon as possible. Because of the aforesaid and of the reports sent by the said professors Gmelin and Müller, the Senate is to render a gracious decision, so that these professors be delivered from such great difficulties and shortcomings, and be satisfied in everything, in order for this expedition to be brought to a satisfactory conclusion.

Korff

B. From the Protocols of the Academy Chancellery

8 May 1738

By decree of Her Imperial Majesty, the Academy of Sciences
listened to the dispatches sent from the Kamchatka Expedition by
Professors Gerhard Friedrich Müller, dated 16 December at
Irkutsk; and by Johann Georg Gmelin, dated 2 November 1737, from
Kirenskii ostrog, in which they submitted and requested the
following:

(1) that instructions be issued in response to the reports sent
by them some time ago to the Governing Senate; (2) that the
Governing Senate grant them by general decree the power to demand
of local adminstrations that they execute, under penalty of heavy
fine, all the requests of the said professors, because the delays
and other aggravations caused by the said administrations and
other local officials are quite intolerable; (3) that another
professor of history be sent to join them; (4) that in addition
there be assigned to them two geodesists and two copyists, one
for German, the other for Latin, and also a Russian clerk with
complete knowledge of bureaucratic style; (5) that those in
charge of meteorologicl observations be granted a small salary
increase, so they would perform their tasks with great
application, for some of the observations are made so badly that
they are completely useless; (6) that professor Müller, according
to the certificate of Doctor Gmelin, herewith included, has
contracted a serious illness, that unless he gets better, it will
be impossible for him to travel to Kamchatka; this is why in the
appended petition to Her Imperial Majesty, he humbly requests
that if there should be no improvement in his illness, he be
allowed to return to St. Petersburg, but should there be some
improvement in his illness he be ordered to survey the locations
in Siberia that have not been surveyed; (7) since the decree of 1
September 1737 sent by the Governing Senate does not specify
where to obtain a ship, provisions, money and workers in such an
empty location as Okhotsk, there is a danger that the purpose of
the Governing Senate may remain unfulfilled; for which they made
a second representation to the local provincial adminstration,
and request that the Governing Senate take into consideration
their representation made at the end of last year concerning the
transportation of supplies; (8) in order to assist the Kamchatka
Expedition, in view of the shortage of supplies and the
difficulty in transporting the same, only the needed persons,
namely Professor Gmelin and Adjunct Steller, a landscapist, with
two soldiers and two cossacks should be sent there [by land], and
the provisions shipped by boat.

And the 6th of May, Johann Eberhardt Fischer, Adjunct at the
Academy of Sciences and Rector of the gymnasium declared by
petition: (1) that upon his arrival in Russia by the highest
grace of her Imperial Majesty, he was appointed an adjunct at the
Academy and Rector of the gymnasium established within the same
Academy, a position he has occupied from 1730 to this day; (2)

hat he has now been informed that the Kamchatka Expediton needs
et another assistant, who could study the history of the peoples
elonging to the Russian sceptre; (3) that he wishes to make his
ost humble and faithful services available for that purpose, and
opes besides, that in consideration of this long and very
ifficult journey, Her Imperial Majesty, as in the case of the
rofessors and other public servants previously sent on this
xpediton, allocate him a salary double of his present pay,
amely 720 rubles, with an appropriate travel allowance, and
rovide other items required by this position. And that upon
ompletion of this expedition, and by the all-merciful decree of
er Imperial Majesty, both in view of his services at the
ymnasium and at the Academy, and in consideration of such
ervices and faithfulness that may be demonstrated by him during
he expedition, he be promoted to the rank of professor of the
cademy of Sciences with a salary equal to the one he desires to
eceive on the expedition, namely: 720 rubles. In view of this
the Academy] has resolved:

To send a report to the Governing Senate to inform it, and to
equest most humbly that the Governing Senate condescend to
ender a favourable decision on the submission presented by the
forementioned professors and consisting of eight points as
ndicated, and that it order the required decrees to be sent, and
hat a contract be concluded with the aforementioned rector
ischer about his stay with the expedition as an adjunct of
istory and assigning him an annual salary of 660 rubles yearly,
n the same basis as the contract concluded with the adjunct of
istory, Steller; a copy of the said contract to be appended to
he report to the Governing Senate. And to request that the
overning Senate condescend to approve the contract concluded
ith him, Rector and Adjunct Fischer, on the strength of which
he assigned annual salary of 660 rubles per year, with, in
ddition, a travelling allowance, and that orders be given to
end the appropriate decrees: for given the present
ircumstances of Professor Müller, it is imperative to send such
 person to replace him, together with the personnel referred to
n point eight.

And in view of this, the Academy of Sciences deems it very
ecessary that the observers mentioned under point five receive
n top of their present salaries another four or five rubles for
he reasons indicated; and for those observers who do not get any
alary or credit, a special salary may be assigned according to
he circumstances of each, and paid from the funds of the
amchatka Expediton. These observers are the following: Semyon
unitsin at Kazan; Fedor Sannikov, Nikitin Karkadinov, Baron
alev at Ekaterinburg; Yakov Mirovich at Tobol'sk; Vasily
al'berg in Iamyshev; Kozma Charoshnikov in Eniseisk; Piotr
ovrigin in Nerchinsk; Nikita Kanaev in Irkutsk. But if
rofessor Müller gets some relief from his illness, the Academy of
ciences humbly requests the Governing Senate that when some of
he professors are in Kamchatka, the aforementioned Müller be

ordered to survey those provinces, districts and localities of
which no description has been made as yet.

With regard to the preparation and transportation of
supplies, as well as the dispatch of the required orders for
every possible help to be extended to the professors during their
extremely difficult journey there, the Academy of Sciences hopes
that the Governing Senate in its high wisdom will adopt such a
resolution so that the exalted decision taken by Her Imperial
Majesty concerning this voyage, which requires such great
expense, can be put into effect.

One should also write about all this to the professors of the
Kamchatka Expediton and for information to provide them with a
copy of the report submitted to the Governing Senate and of the
concluded contract. Having sealed all this in a package, one
should send it to the said professors through the Siberian
Department with an order to the offices of Tobol'sk province with
the following instruction: when this package is received by the
said office, let it be sent immediately to the professors of the
Kamchatka Expedition, and let the Academy be informed of this
fact.

C.   From the Protocols of the Academy Chancellery

9 September 1738

By decree of Her Imperial Majesty, the Academy of Sciences has
resolved to send a report to the Governing Senate, stating that:
Although the Academy of Sciences in its report to the Governing
Senate, submitted already some time ago, namely the 8th of May of
this year, stated that Professor Müller cannot pursue his journey
to Kamchatka because of illness, and therefore requested that
Rector Fischer be sent as an assistant in his place, while
Professor Müller be ordered to write a historical and
geographical description of the areas not yet visited [by him];
yet to this day the Academy of Sciences had not received a
resolution to that effect.

After that, on the 10th of April, we received from both
professors, from Irkutsk, copies of their correspondence with
local offices about food supplies, copies of which are included
here together with a petition from Professor Gmelin, addressed to
Her Imperial Majesty, requesting that he be discharged from the
Kamchatka Expedition.

Since the Academy of Sciences from the very beginning of the
expedition foresaw such occurrences, and for that reason
recommended already in its first report of 10 July, 1732, that
the number of people needed for it be doubled, [and] it humbly
requested in its report addressed to the cabinet of Her Imperial
Majesty to send more professors to Kamchatka, so that in the

vent any of them should fall ill or die, their observations and
he expenses incurred be not lost, which was most graciously
pppproved by Her Imperial Majesty, so that adjunct Steller was
ent to Kamchatka for that purpose.

For this reason it was resolved to present for the second
ime this humble request to the Governing Senate, so that the
overning Senate would condescend to give very favourable
onsideration to this report and to adopt an appropriate
ecision. And since it is evident from the mentioned reports
hat the preparation of food supplies in those regions is very
ifficult, it is requested that the assistants Steller and
ischer be sent to Kamchatka with the most needed personnel,
hile the two above-mentioned professors be sent to those regions
f the Siberian province which they have not yet visited, for a
omplete description of this land and also of its geography and
atural history. In this fashion the whole plan adopted for the
amchatka Expedition will come to a desired result and at the
ame time we will see the conclusion of an enterprise from which
he Russian Empire will derive particular honour and considerable
enefit; for it is already evident from the reports sent by the
bove-mentioned professors, that they [the professors] have made
any observations of particular use for trade and for other state
evenues, which will be translated into Russian and conveyed to
he Governing Senate.

J. A.] Korff

). __Archives of the Chancellery of the Academy of Sciences__

6 April 1739

s by decree of Her Imperial Majesty, sent from the Governing
enate to the Academy of Sciences of the 31st day of last March,
t is ordered to implement the following:

Professor Müller, who is at present with the Kamchatka
xpedition, is to be relieved from the Kamchatka journey because
f his attested illness, and sent for treatment to St.
etersburg. While travelling from Siberia through places where
e has not yet been, or through places he had passed without
isiting them for lack of time, he is to carry out appropriate
nvestigations for a detailed description of the natural history.
n order to complete the observations on this expedition, as a
elp to Professor Gmelin, Adjunct Fischer is to be sent now, with
n appropritate salary, according to the contract signed with him
n this Academy, and with a travelling allowance to be paid from
he revenues of the Siberian office. To them are to be attached
wo copyists, one for German, the other for Latin, the said
cademy to decide where to get them, and also a Russian copyist,
ith a perfect knowledge of administrative style, the said
opyist to be provided by the Siberian provincial adminstration.

Salaries of the nine observers employed for metorologica
observations, are to be determined according to the situation o
each, and are paid from the same sources as previously, but wit!
an additional four or five rubles per year. And those wh
previously did not receive a salary are to be paid by the loca
district offices the basic pay of a foot cossack, plus th
Academy increase mentioned above. In view of this and for th
execution of the above degree of Her Imperial Majesty, th
Academy of Sciences are ordered that:

(1) Professors Müller and Gmelin be informed by letters of th
decree sent from the Senate, and that the said Müller, on th
strength of the decree, upon the arrival of the adjunct Fische
would return to St. Petersburg to cure his illness. To ensure
detailed description for a proper history, [Müller] is to trave
from Siberia through locations he had not yet been to, or throug!
those he had insufficient time to visit. As to the books
letters, instruments and belongings in the possession of the sai
Professor Müller on the Kamchatka Expedition, they are to be kep
in readiness with an inventory, and upon the arrival of Adjunc
Fischer are to be transferred to him against his signature an
according to the register list, except those items needed b
Müller for his journey; but the said Müller is not to leave
before the arrival of Fischer. Adjunct Fischer is to get read
immediately for his departure to Kamchatka and to submit to th
office of the Academy of Sciences a list of items, such a
carriages and other things needed for the journey.

(2) Two copyists, one for German, the other for Latin are to be
found and hired; and two geodesists are to be requested b
memorandum, from the Member of the Privy Council, Tatishchev, an
from the Admiralty.

(3) Doctor and Professor Gmelin is ordered to fix the salary o
the nine persons designated as observers, with an increase o
four to five rubles above their pay per year; and to request th
additional funds from the Siberian provincial office, on th
account of the Academy; then give it to the observers. To thi
effect an order [ukaz] is to be sent from the Academy to tha
province, and a memorandum is to be sent to the Siberian Offic
requesting the immediate dispatch of letters by parcel to th
professors of the Kamchatka Expedition, wherever they are a
present.

(4) As soon as the geodesists are provided and the copyist
found, a memorandum is to be sent to the State Treasury Boar
requesting that a salary as well as an appropriate travellin
allowance be paid immediately by the Treasury Board, contrary t
the previous dispatch, on the account of the Kamchatk

xpedition, to Fischer, and to the geodesists and to the
opyists.

J.A.] Korff

Christian] Goldbach

.D. Schumacher

. Archives of the Chancellery of the Academy of Sciences

0 February 1740

ince last November 1739, Professors Müller, Gmelin, and Adjunct
teller have reported the following by letter:

1) Gmelin - about his return to St. Petersburg because of
llness, due to which it would be impossible for him to reach
amchatka and because according to his contract the duration of
is services had expired;

2) Müller - about the impossiblity of carrying out alone the
ask assigned to him in geographic history and in the description
f natural resources, a task requiring a great deal of work,
hile he has not even recovered from his illness. Müller also
tates that Gmelin is in very poor health, which makes him
ncaplable to remain with the Kamchatka Expedition.

3) Adjunct Steller requests the Governing Senate to issue and
rder to the Iakutsk office about sending them supplies without
elay. And on this 8th day of February 1740, in the decree of
er Imperial Majesty issued by the Governing Senate, it is
ritten that by decree Her I. M. signed by Her I. Majesty's hand,
rofessor Müller is ordered to convey to the surveys made of the
ands lying between the Amur and the river Uda and of other lands
ear the border.

n view of that, according to the decree of Her I.M., the Academy
f Sciences has decided to inform the Governing Senate of its
onsidered opinion and request that Professors Müller and Gmelin
hould be ordered to complete that task together, thus helping
ach other, and upon its completion they can be ordered to go to
t. Petersburg because of their illnesses, since the work they
tarted can be carried out by their assistants Steller and
ischer, and fewer losses will be incurred in the interst of Her
.M., for these adjuncts receive a much smaller salary than the
rofessors. And that at the time of their return let it be
rdered that the Professors should receive confirmation by decree
hat on their way back from Siberia both should exert their
fforts in the study of the natural history of their regions and
f their animal, vegetable, and mineeral resources, for the task
ould be too difficult for one person only to carry out. For a

thorough examination, copies of the translations from the letter
received from the said professors and their adjuncts are herewit
appended.

[J.A.] Korff

J. D. Schumacher

F. Müller to the Academy of Science Chancellery from Tobol'sk*

[7 October 1740]

This journey was very profitable for a fuller study of the Ostia
[now Khanty] and Vogul [now Mansi] tribes, their manner of lif
and their customs, and similarly for the composition, on th
basis of oral accounts, of notes on everything dealing with th
Samoyeds. Soon after my arrival in Tobol'sk, I again took up m
inspection of the local archives, but in my absence it had falle
into such disorder that many volumes, or so-called ancier
stolbtsy, which formerly were in it and from which I intended t
have excerpts made, are no longer to be found. In this, as i
all other matters concerning which I had to petition th
administration office orally and in writing, I met with coolnes
and delays in execution. Although this annoys me to no enc
because it interferes with my studies to a great degree, I c
not, on the other hand, wish to have recourse to complaints, ar
keep trying to overcome through moderation, courtesy, ar
requests, the irritation that has arisen against me and m
studies.

G. Müller to the Academy of Science Chancellery, January 1742
from Turinsk**

The time spent by me in Siberia in accordance with the Imperia
command has permitted me in particular to devote myself t
bringing into full clearness the history of Siberia through th
collection of all documents belonging to it, and I had the goc
fortune to gather from the archives detailed data on all th
principal events that have taken place since 7101 (1593), afte
the Greek calendar. But concerning previous years, and eve
concerning the first colonies founded and commanded from Russi
after the beginning of the subjection of Siberia by Ermak in 708
(1577), no ancient data have found their way into the Siberia
archives, though the cities of Tobol'sk and Tiumen, astr
ordinary Siberian chronicles bear witness, were founded in 709
and 7095 (1586 and 1587). From these chronicles it appears tha
even earlier in 7091 and 7093 voevody from Moscow were i

---

    *   From Pekarskii, P., _Istoriia Imp. Akademii Nauk_. I (St
Petersburg, 1870). Extract from Chancellery document.
    ** From Pekarskii, P., _Istoriia Imp. Akademii Nauk_. I (St
Petersburg, 1870). Extract from Chancellery archives.

iberia. Since the archives in Tiumen begin with 7102 (1594), in
obol'sk with 7133 (1625), in Pelmiak, Berezov, and Tara with the
ears of their founding (7101 and 7102), concerning all this it
s impossible to learn anything more circumstantial, except what
s contained in brief form in the chronicle mentioned.   Thus
here is no hope of finding anything on this point in the
rchives which I must look over in Turinsk and Verkhotur'e,
ecause they were founded in 7107 and 7109.

ENDNOTES TO DOCUMENTS

. From Müller, _Istoriia Sibiri_, I (Moscow-Leningrad, 1937), pp.
60-61.   This was Müller's own version of the more detailed set
f instructions issued him by the Senate.   Translated by J.L.
lack.

. _Materialy_, II (1886), pp. 446-7.

. One pud = 36.11 pounds.

The following text is from a booklet published in
London in 1754, a translation of "Lettre d'un officier de
la marine russienne," by an anonymous author, published
in Berlin in 1753. Evidently commissioned by the Russian
government, it was written to counter Nicholas Delisle's
assertions that he and his stepbrother, Louis Delisle de
la Croyère were responsible for accurate charts of the
North Pacific.   Frank A. Golder [Bering's Voyages]
attributes this document to Sven Waxell, and Lydia T.
Black [The Question of Maps, [p. 32] casts some doubt on
the common attribution to Müller but most of the evidence
recommends Müller as the author. The "Letter" contains
some   clear   falsehoods;   for   example,   the   purported
author's claim to have travelled all the way with Bering,
evidently   introduced   to   disassociate   Müller   from   the
'letter'; and it reveals his harsh opinions of de la
Croyère. The official Russian position on these voyages
is carried here, and Müller's role as mouthpiece for a
European audience is demonstrated.

Except for Bering and Delisle (Beerings and de l'Isle
in the original), names are given here much as they were
in the eighteenth century edition, as are the italics.
Some very long passages have been broken up into two or
more paragraphs.

[G.-F. Müller], A Letter from a Russian Sea-Officer to a Person
of Distinction at the Court of St. Petersburg. Translated from
the original French (London, 1754). Reprint of original English
version.

A Letter from a Russian Sea-Officer to a Great Man at Court

My Lord,

Your Excellency is pleased to require my thoughts both on Mr
[Joseph N.] Delisle's new map of discoveries to the northward of
the South-Sea, and his memoir annexed to it, in which that
gentleman sets forth the motives for making that map, and chiefly
consists in accounts of the navigation of our people and their
discoveries, together with a supposed narrative of the Spanish
Admiral de Fonte,* said to have been sent in the year 1640, to
make further discoveries in that same part of the globe. Besides
the pleasure an affair of this nature must in itself give me, as
relative to a science which for some years past has been my
favourite study, your Excellency's commands carry with them such
an indispensable weight, that I shall not plead insufficiency

* "Admiral de Fonte" was most likely a fictional character.
See Lydia T. Black, "The Question of Maps", p.27.

otwithstanding there being several other officers of more
xperience, and equal diligence, who had no less than myself a
hare in the new discoveries made in the several voyages of that
xpedition, which we commonly call the Kamchatka expedition;
owever, there is one particular consideration which may possibly
ntitle me to a preference herein, which is, that
fter my return from America, I was commissioned to compare the
ournals of several ships, both among themselves, and also with
ther accounts of the countries lying in the South-Sea, and,
fter examining them with the most accurate attention, to draw up
 map in which all the new discoveries were to be set down with
he utmost exactness. And this map would have been published
efore now, had it not been delayed by the expectations of some
ccounts from the most inward parts of Siberia, to clear up
ertain doubts which arose in the very execution of that work.

I now come to the point and begin with my observations on Mr.
elisle's Memoir, as from these it will easily appear what
udgement ought to be formed of his map.

The Sieur Delisle begins with speaking of the treatises he
ublished at St. Petersburg, for the advancement of astronomy,
eography, and natural philosophy; he excuses his neglect to
ublish their continuation at the time appointed, by the voyage
f his brother Mr. de la Croyère to Kamchatka. He says, that
eing solicitous to collect fresh materials over and above those
e had aready at hand, he had waited the return of his brother,
n order to add the observations made in the last voyage to
amchatka, when the unexpected news of his death could not but
ccasion new delay, 'till such time as he might get information
f what his brother had done. These, according to Mr. Delisle's
wn words, are the reasons whereby he has been induced to put off
he continuation of the work he had begun; but, I apprehend, that
hey will appear very suspicious to your Excellency, to whom the
ules and institutes of the academy of St. Petersburg are so well
nown, and who cannot but be informed of the discontents which
r. Delisle gave to the directors of the Academy. Here lies the
rue cause of his delay; besides, that any expectation from his
rother was extremely ill-grounded; I was myself an eye-witness
f this gentleman's manner of living, and, after his death, how
ery few observations of his own were foundamong his papers,
esides what he was assisted in by lieutenant Krasilinkov [sic,
.D. Krasil'nikov]. It is to this ingenious pupil of Mr.
erquarson [Henry Farquharson], formerly geographer* to the navy,
hat those observations, which have been delivered in to the
cademy under the name of la Croyère, are to be rather ascribed,
nd without whose information little, very little indeed, could
e expected from Mr. de la Croyère's diligence.

---

*   Henry "Farquarson" was not a geographer; rather he was a
avigational expert who, as a very young man in 1701 had been
ppointed first director of Peter I's Mathematics and
avigational School in Moscow.

The Sieur Delisle further pretends that the materials with
which he would enrich his work, he had collected from other
channels; nay, even from other countries; if so, why has he
deprived us of them, as they, of right, properly belong to us
Why was he not pleased, at least, before his departure, to
acquaint the academy of his writings, that a copy of them might
have been taken: so far fom it (and I have not been wanting to
make the best enquiry after it) there is not a single member of
the academy, to whom he has vouchsafed to give a sight of the
relation of the Admiral <u>de Fonte</u>, which, he says, he received
from <u>England</u> in the year 1739. This is a piece of jealousy
utterly unbecoming of a man of letters, but is greatly aggravated
by his being a member of a learned society, where all discoveries
ought to be common.

Mr. <u>Delisle</u> would have the world believe that it was by
express order of our court that he entered upon his researches in
<u>Russia</u>. This is but a very slender circumstance, and I should
not so much as have mentioned it, but that it tends to introduce
a kind of confusion in the history of geographical works in
general, which relate to our territories; and particularly in the
second <u>Kamchatka</u> enterprise. As to the former, nobody knows
better than your Excellency, that <u>Peter the Great</u> referred to his
senate the care, that plans and charts should be taken of the
several parts of his vast dominions; and for this, the senate
were to receive all the reports of the surveyors, who have been
employed in this work ever since the year 1715.

Mr. [Ivan K.] <u>Kirilov</u>, who at that time worthily filled the
office of first secretary in this commission, a man of great
activity and zeal for his country, had begun, before Mr. <u>Delisle</u>
came to <u>Russia</u>, to collect the plans sent by the surveyors, and
had them engraved under his immediate inspection; and out of
these he completed a general map of <u>Russia</u>, which was the first
ever seen among us, and is very well known. <u>Zealous</u>, in the
prosecution of <u>Peter the Great</u>'s design, he, some time after
published a collection of particular maps, under the title of
<u>Atlas of the Russian Empire</u>; and these he likewise intended to
augment, but he found himself under a necessity of discontinuing
his scheme, being, after his promotion to the state council in
the year 1734, employed in a commission which would admit of no
avocations.

It is true that Mr. <u>Kirilov</u>'s maps have in them many marks of
the infancy of geography among us at that time, yet no other
objections lay against them, than such as are common to all
beginnings; and, besides the singularity of them, there are other
very good reasons which maintain them in esteem. To these we
were afterwards indebted for the resolution of the academy, to
have new maps done; and with this view it was that they engaged
the Sieur <u>Delisle</u> to come to <u>Russia</u>, where he entered into a
contract with them, not only as an astronomer, but likewise as a
geographer; and who, immediately after his arrival, which was in
the year 1726, was not by the court, but by the Lord President

[of the Academy], ordered to draw such maps as were specified to him, there being no necessity for the court to interpose in matters which were already in hand, and in their proper channel.

Here I could produce another passage in the memoir which I am now examining, as it has some affinity with the preceding; but as I am for following the Sieur Delisle, step by step, before I come to it, several other particulars do occur, not less deserving of animadversion:*   "Mr. Delisle promises to perform general and particular maps of Russia, far superior to those of the Academy; these, said he, speaking of his own, are taken from the obeservation which I have collected for that purpose;" whereas in truth he should have said, from those with which the academy furnished him, but of which he has been far from making the use for which they were given him: on this head I heard frequent complaints of Mr. Delisle's dilatoriness of his work, and of his excuses; that he stood in need of some informations, which could not be settled but by astronomical observations, without which it was an utter impossibility for him to form a general map, much less a complete set of particular maps.   I cannot help thinking that it was wrong in him to aspire at a perfection, which was no more required of him, than it could be expected in such a first attempt; yet after all this scrupulous exactness of Mr. Delisle, and after the space of twelve years, so far was the work from being brought to any forwardness, that there were scarce the first outlines to be seen of it.   Hereupon the Academy, in the year 1740, very justly thought fit to employ others of their members, who exerted themselves with that assiduity, that, about the close of the third year, the maps which constitute the Russian Atlas, published in the year 1745, began to be engraven. Had these been taken only from the observations which were in Mr. Delisle's keeping, yet is it highly probable that in a capital city, which had this design so much at heart, they could not have wanted opportunities of daily getting such informations, to have added them to the new plans expected from the different provinces; tho' I am far from pretending, that this new Russian Atlas is as perfect as to preclude all future improvements of the geography of this kingdom, which would be contrary to the sentiments of the academy itself, who, upon the first appearance of this new Atlas, had come to a resolution of having amended, in a new set of more correct maps, what mistakes they had observed in these.

The illustrious person [K.G. Razumovskii], who is at the head of the academy, (the Hetman of Little Russia) shows himself no less attentive to promote this affair, than he is in all other points, which tend to the honour of that respectable society; and from hence we cannot but hope a much greater success in this than in the first attempt; and the rather, from the numerous supplies of many maps and geographical accounts, particularly of the Asiatic Russia, and the neighbouring countries, of which, before

---

*   Here, and elsewhere, punctuation belongs to the original translater of Mr. Müller, 1754 [Ed.].

the return of those academicians, who had been sent thither on
purpose to procure better and more complete informations, we had
but an imperfect knowledge.

Mr. Delisle, speaking of what Peter the Great had done to get
intelligence of the northern limits of Tartary, and to find out
whether they did not join with America, or at least were but a
small distance from it, says, "That the Emperor, for this
undertaking made choice of Mr. Beerings [Vitus J. Bering], who,
after receiving his order in the last years of that great
Emperor, on the 5th of February, had received again the said
order ratified by the whole senate." Here is a mistake of the
day, Mr. Bering having set out of his first enterprise on the 5th
of February, 1725. After that, Count Apraksin, lord high
Admiral, had given public notice that all sea-officers who were
inclined to go on that voyage should repair to him. Upon which,
Mr. Bering having presented himself to the lord high Admiral, he
received from him his instructions, which were indeed, very
short, but all written with the Emperor's own hand a few days
before his demise.

What I advance here is no more than I have often heard from
Mr. Bering himself, nay, whose instructions I myself have seen,
which were as follows:

First, to make the best of his way to Kamchatka and there to
build two small vessels. Secondly, with these to reconnoitre the
furthest northern part of the eastern coasts of Siberia and to
see whether in any part they joined with America. Thirdly,
afterwards to enquire on the American coasts after some European
settlements and plantations, or to try whether he could not meet
with a ship, to learn the names and the bearings of the coasts.
Fourthly, to draw up an exact account of all his proceedings and
then to return to St. Petersburg.

On the first of March 1730, Mr. Bering returned to St.
Petersburg, bringing with him a complete narrative of his voyage,
in which, he says, that after tracing the eastern coast of
Kamchatka, and of the land of Tschutschi [Chukchi], as far as the
latitude of sixty-seven degree and a half, he perceived the coast
to stretch away to the West, in the manner as some of the
inhabitants, who came aboard his ship, had before informed him;
from whence he had concluded that there could be no continent by
which Asia and America were joined, and that, having thus
executed his mission, he returned. This voyage lasted from the
14th of July, 1728, to the 2nd of the following September. Since
which, it has been found by a second expedition from Kamchatka,
that, although, as to the separation of the old and new world,
Mr. Bering is right, yet is he mistaken when he says that, at the
elevation of sixty-seven degrees and a half, it appeared to him
as if the coast fell off to the westward; there being at that
latitude but one single promontory, which the Anadyrsk-Russians
called Serzekamen, and beyond which the coast continues its
northern direction, as it does from Kamchatka, till near the

great Tzsukochkoi-Nos [Chukotskii], where it actually inclines westward, and where at a place betwixt the 70th and 71st degree of latitude it makes out the northern extremity of Asia.

Another proof of the separation of the two continents, which Mr. Bering is said to have given information of from Kamchatka is (according to Delisle's opinion), "That the inhabitants of the said country have seen a vessel which came from the river Lena." It is true, indeed, that there is a tradition among the people of Kamchatka that some Russians were arrived among them long before the conquest under Vladimir Atlasov,* but, by what way, they knew nothing of. During the second Kamchatka expedition, a member of the academy [Müller] found among the records of the town of Iakutsk that the Russians had come thither by sea, that they had sailed thence beyond the great Chukotskii-nos and were afterwards cast away to the southward of the river Anadyr; this event is said to have happened in the year 1648; and has been inserted since, with an abstract of this narrative and what relates to it, in the observations of the Petersburg newspapers, published inthe year 1742; from whence I conclude that Mr. Bering could have had no account at Kamchatka of a vessel coming thither from the river Lena; especially as there is not the least intimation of any such thing in all the narrative of his voyage; to that this account of Mr. Delisle's is owing to his too precipitate judgement, who, no doubt, took it from the above mentioned observations in the St. Petersburg newspapers; from which it was erroneously conjectured that such an event hath been known to inhabitants of Kamchatka, and that they must have informed Mr. Bering about it.   .

I shall carefully avoid any critical animadversions on Mr. Delisle's expressions and confine my reflections to his meaning only: he talks of I know not what harbour at Kamchatka, from whence Mr. Bering set out on his journey; whereas he should have rather mentioned a river of that name, there being no harbour there properly so called; and in the second expedition they could meet with no harbour at all till they came to Avacha Bay, which is about 60 sea-leagues southward of the river Kamchatka. "After his return to Kamchatka harbour (these are Mr. Delisle's very words), Mr. Bering was told of land to the eastward, which in very clear weather was discernible; that having refitted his vessels, which had been damaged by a storm, he attempted to go thither, but that this second trial was unsuccessful, for that after sailing about 40 leagues to the east without discovering any land, he met with asecond storm, and the wind being directly contrary, drove him back to the harbour from whence he had setout." Would not one, from this account, be inclined to think, that this second attempt of Mr. Bering was immediately after the first? Yet, that was very far from being the case, for Mr. Bering, before he went upon it, had wintered at Kamchatka, not sailing from there till the 5th of June, 1729, and then, without

---

*   Atlasov was the first man to systematically explore Kamchatka and bring it and its people into the Russian Empire, 1697-99 [ed.].

any intention of returning to the place of his departure, having
sailed beyond the south point of <u>Kamchatka</u>, he steered directly
for the mouth of the river <u>Bolshaia-Reka</u>, and from thence to
<u>Okhotsk</u>.

    It may possibly appear strange to many, that Mr. <u>Bering</u> did
not, in this voyage, fall in with the island where he was
shipwrecked in his second expedition; but this may have been
occasioned by the fogs, which in these seas are very frequent and
thick: as to marks of a neighbouring country, of which, Mr.
<u>Delisle</u> says, that captain <u>Bering</u> had himself told him, nothing
is more certain than this; the little attention that was given to
it will give me an opportunity of speaking again about it. It is
ceratain likewise, that Mr. <u>Bering</u>, and his Lieutenant Mr.
[Alexei I.] <u>Chirikov</u>, had in the years 1728 and 1729, observed at
<u>Kamchatka</u> two eclipses of the moon, but, that by these
observations, Mr. <u>Delisle</u> was enabled to determine with precision
the longitude of this most eastern part of <u>Asia</u>, and that the
same had been confirmed in the second expedition, by careful
observations of the satellites of <u>Jupiter</u>, is what I cannot well
conceive. Mr. <u>Delisle</u>   is pleased to ascribe these observations
of <u>Jupiter</u>'s satellites to his dear brother, and some <u>Russians</u>
skilled in those kinds of observations; all this must in justice
be understood of to be the work of Lieutenant <u>Krasillnikov</u>
[Krasil'nikov] alone, who by the Senate's order accompanied them
and who in these matters was the most expert of them all.

    And   now   we   come   to   the   circumstances   of   the   second
expedition, for which, as Mr. <u>Delisle</u> pretends, we are beholden
to a map of his own, and that the whole was conducted according
to a plan laid down by him: "In the year 1732," says he, "I had
the honour of laying before the <u>Empress Anna</u> and the Senate this
map of mine, in order to incite the <u>Russians</u> to prosecute their
discoveries, wherein I also succeeded." Is it to time, or age,
that we are to impute this error of Mr. <u>Delisle</u>'s? Has he lost
all rememberance of that order by which he was bound to draw the
map he here speaks of?   Had this occured to his thoughts, I
believe he would have hardly ventured to say that he himself laid
this map before the <u>Empress</u>, and much less that his view in it
was to animate the <u>Russians</u> to new discoveries. At that time, I
much conversed with Mr. <u>Delisle</u>.   I was a witness of his
geographical labours as far as they related to new discoveries; I
was also Mr. <u>Bering</u>'s interpreter in the conversations that
passee between them, and I do confidently affirm that when Mr.
<u>Delisle</u> began his second map the orders for the second expedition
had already been given.   Captain <u>Bering</u>, sensible of the
deficiency of his first discoveries, had offered himself to
prosecute them, and so did his lieutenants, for which they were
all rewarded by a higher rank.   It is plain, therefore, that this
work of Mr. <u>Delisle</u> must be ascribed to superior orders, and I
remember perfectly well that the <u>Empress Anna</u>, having directed
her senate to give captain <u>Bering</u> his directions and orders for
his second voyage, it was his opinion that it would be highly
conducive to the better success of it, if the academy were to

furnish him with proper informations concerning the situations of the countries, and of the seas whither he was bound; upon which the senate gave her orders to the academy accordingly, and Mr. Delisle was appointed by the academy to form the map of which I am now speaking, together with the additional observations relating to it. No sooner were the map and the observations finished than they were both delivered to the senate by the academy; so that the truth is, that so far was Mr. Delisle from inciting the Russians to fresh discoveries, or setting Mr. Bering's second voyage on foot, that he did no more than work as he had been bid; and then, whether this performance of his did more good, or harm, to the expedition is another question which shall be discussed in the sequel.

However, the senate gave Mr. Bering copies of the observations and of the map; of both which I also procured a copy, which now enables me to compare them with what Mr. Delisle says in his last treatise published at Paris.

He advances, "That he had struck out three different ways for discovering what had hitherto remained unknown; First: a direct course to Japan, through the land of Jesso [Jedso], or rather to sail through those narrow seas, which separate it from the State's Island and the Company's Land, to cruise on discoveries north of the land of Jedso, and to endeavour to find out again the way that lies between this land and the eastern coast of Tartary."

This is what may be justly called a good advice after the thing is done. In the original of Mr. Delisle's observations, there is not a single word relating to any such enquiries; all that Mr. Delisle does there is to propose three different ways for finding out the neighbouring countries eastward of Kamchatka, the two first must be allowed to agree pretty well with the second and third, exhibited in the Paris relation; wherein they are thus expressed.

First. "If one should reach the most northern, and at the same time the most eastern parts of Asia, as far as Captain Bering went (this, as I have already said, is a conditional proposition) one could not miss a falling in with America, whatever way one would choose betwixt northeast and southeast, since the farthest distance would be about 600 leagues." (This is a very considerable error in the computation of the distance of the land betwixt Asia and America, they begin towards the north, separated only by a narrow strait, which sailing southward is found gradually to widen.)

Secondly, "Without venturing so far, possibly, it were better, and more convenient, to set out from the eastern coast of Kamchatka, and steer due east, in quest of that neighbouring country, of which Captain Bering had found some appearances in his first voyage. As to the third way, Mr. Delisle conjectured, that the lands of which Don Juan de Gama had sight, might

possibly be discovered sooner, and with more certainty, by
sailing in quest of them towards the southeast of Kamchatka."

The bad success of this proposal was undoubtedly what brought
him to see his mistake, and what may have put it into his mind,
to alter it into a project of the way to Japan, and from the land
of Jesso.

Nothing can be more foreign to this purpose, and at the same
time more jejune, than the narrative Mr. Delisle has thought to
give us of Mr. Bering's voyage itself. He makes him to have
sailed in the year 1741, in quest of those countries towards the
east of Kamchatka, of which in his first voyage he had got some
vestiges. "He did not proceed very far (saith he) for, being
overtaken by a violent storm, and the weather being extremely
dark, his vessel was rendered unable to keep the sea any longer,
and was cast away on a desert island, in the latitude of 54
degrees, not far from the harbour of Avacha, the place he had set
out from."

Thus it seems, all that Mr. Bering did, was nothing but just
to shipwreck, and that immediately after he had left the harbour.

And here I am obliged to give to Mr. Delisle's dry and
slender account a little more nourishment, by adding a relation
of the voyage of Mr. Bering and the other officers in this
expedition. I am the better able to do it, as I myself had a
share in it, and can appeal to the journals and charts of each of
the ships.

Mr. Bering, the commanding Captain Mr. [Martin] Spangenberg,
Captain Mr. Chirikov, and some other sea-officers, set out from
St. Petersburg in the spring, 1733. They stayed at Iakutsk and
Okhotsk till the vessels were ready, which, at this last place,
were building for them. When everything was in readiness for Mr.
Spangenberg's voyage, he, agreeably to the senate's orders, set
out first from Okhotsk in June 1738, with three ships under his
command; to which was added a great covered chaloupe of twenty-
four oars which he got to be built at Bol'sheretsk-ostrog, in
Kamchatka, where he wintered. This sloop was designed to enter
within such narrow straits, between islands, as they might chance
to meet with, where larger ships could not enter.

In the summer of 1739 he went to Japan. The long row of
isles between Japan and Kamchatka served him for a guide. He
landed in Japan in two places, where the inhabitants received him
very civilly; but he did not come (as Mr. Delisle wrongly
asserts) to Matsmai, the chief place in the isle of Jesso,
thinking that without going there he had executed his prescribed
orders. He returned to Okhotsk and wintered at Iakutsk.

When a particular account of this voyage came to St.
Petersburg, upon a presumption, judging by the course he had
steer'd, that he might have been deceived by the coast of Korea,

he was ordered to make a second voyage for the confirmation of the first, which accordingly he undertook in 1741 and 1742; but his ship, built in haste of wood not dry enough, growing leaky, he was obliged to come back.

Messieurs Bering and Chirikov sailed from Okhotsk on September the fourth, 1740; they had both the same destination. The first was to follow the streamer of the other, that, in case of accident they might be abler to succour one another. They sailed directly by the point of Kamchatka, without entering the river Bolshaia-Reka, as is usually done coming from Okhotsk, and cast anchor in the port of Avacha, or, as they called it, the port of St. Peter and Paul. During their wintering in that port, they got everything in readiness for their chief expedition, which had America in view, as soon as the weather should permit it. Under the undertainty which road to take, captain Bering held a sea council on the fourth of May, 1741. In this council it was determined to try, whether the land of Don Juan de Gama could be found out. It proved to be an unfortunate determination, and the cause of all the disasters that succeeded. We went to sea the fourth of June.* Mr. Bering had on board his ship, Mr. - Steller, a physician, a man very well versed in natural history, who was sent by the academy. Mr. de la Croyère was with Mr. Chirikov. but notwithstanding the orders directing Mr. Bering and Chirikov not to part from one another, they could not possibly avoid it, being parted by storm and fogs eight days after they set sail. Their design to look out for the supposed land of Gama had carried them directly towards southeast. They went in this direction to the 26th degree, without getting the least trace of that land. They then turned towards northeast, and they both reached the coasts of America, but in different places and without knowing anything of one another. Mr. Bering, and we who were with him, after a voyage of six weeks, discovered the first land, being, as we reckoned, 500 Dutch miles or leagues from Avacha. We took in fresh water, and we had traces of inhabitants, but saw none. Having stayed there three days on the road, Mr. Bering consulted with his officers, and was resolved to turn back. On the 21st of July, before sun-rising, we weighed anchor. We had only to follow the coast, which turned westward, but the number of islands we met with made the navigation very troublesome; and when we took to the sea, we were overtaken by storms and contrary winds, which occasioned daily retardations. In the meantime, in order to take in once more fresh water, we were obliged to return to the coast, which we had kept from as much as possible. We soon got sight of it, and were still about ten leagues off, when we cast anchor between the islands. The island whence we fetched the water from, we called Shumagin-strov. The water there appeared to be good, notwithstanding being taken out of a lake, but was mixed with sea-water, which the flood, that sometimes overflowed the island, had brought

---

    *   The "We", of course, is to add more authenticity to his story. Müller did not accompany Bering [ed.]

there.   Of this we felt very sad effects, viz, distempers, and
the loss of many of our people who died of it.

During three or four days we endeavoured in vain to descry
any of the natives, whose fires we saw by night along the coast.
On the 4th of September these savages came of their own accord on
board of our small vessels, and after giving us notice of their
presence by great shoutings, they showed us their Calumets, that
is, their sticks with falcon's wings on their top.   By the signs
they made us, we understood that they invited us to come on shore,
to supply us with provisions and fresh water.   We took advantage
of it, and some of our people ventured to follow them, but some
misunderstanding soon arising, all commerce with them was broken
off.

Having, on the 6th of September, proceeded on our voyage with
a tolerable good wind, we soon found, as we went on, our
impediments increased from the continued coast and the adjacent
isles we met with.   Mr. Bering, in order to avoid them, turned
more to the south, and, in effect, the sea proved for some days
to be quite free; but our joy was of a short duration, for on the
24th of September, at the height of 51 degrees, we found again
some coasts with many islands, when at the same time such a
violent storm arose, which lasted seventeen days, that it drove
us back eighty miles.   An old pilot assured us, that in fifty
years sea-service, he had never met with such a storm.   Well
might therefore the name of the Pacific Ocean be spared; or if it
deserves to be so called towards the tropic, as it possibly may,
sure it does not deserve that name in this plae.

The weather indeed grew calm again, but our provisions were
considerably diminished, and of all our hands we had first, we
had but one third part left us that remained in health after all
disasters.   We had still half the way before us to reach the port
of Avacha, so that several of us were of the opinion to winter in
some place in America, rather than to expose ourselves to still
greater mischances than those we had before; but they who were
for trying their utmost to recover the harbour of Avacha, and who
judged that it would then be time enough to look out for some
other place of safety, when all hopes were lost of bringing this
to bear, carried it against the first opinion; and thus the month
of October was spent to as little purpose as the former.

On the 30th of the said month we descried two islands, which
appeared to be like those which stretched themselves from the
south foreland of Kamchatka towards Japan; upon this we stood to
the northward, and having got to the height on the 4th of
November, we found ourselves under the 56th degree; at last, the
5th of November proved the fatal period of our voyage, for, as we
were making sail westward, we struck upon a desert island, where
we saw nothing but death before us, the ship was beat to pieces
upon one of the sands with which the island was surrounded;
however, we got safe ashore, and with such things as we thought
were indispensably necessary to our subsistence, and moreover by

a particular mercy of providence, soon after our own landing, we had the pleasure to see the remainder of our ship drive ashore, which we carefully gathered together, in hopes of being able, by the assistance of God, to make it the instrument of our removal from this dismal habitation.

The island, on which we were cast, had not so much as a tree growing on it, and we were obliged to build huts, and to make firing of the wood which the sea drove ashore from other places. This is the desert to which we gave the name Bering, from that of our leader, and where, from excess of grief, and that he could not recover Kamchatka, he expired on the 8th of December; he refused to eat or drink, and would not suffer himself to be brought into one of our huts, so that in this condition, a man of his age, joined to the infirmities that naturally attend it, could not but sink under the weight of such a complication of distress. We young folks recovered our spirits, and took courage, resolved on preserving our lives to the utmost, and to use all possible means for getting clear of this unhappy confinement. Before our coming to the island, it had only been the resort of sea-animals for taking the air, copulation, and breeding their young ones. At first these creatures suffered us to come pretty near in sight of them, without being in the least disturbed; but after they had seen some of their species killed by the shot of our people, they made off at the first sight of us.

We shot several of these animals, which served us for food and raiment, and the valuable beaverskins, which we got by these means, made us some amends for our sufferings.

The spring coming on, we fell to the execution of the great project for our deliverance, and with the remains of the vessel made shift to build a large tight-decked sloop, fitted with sails and anchors, and proper tacklings, to bear the sea, in case it were not our misfortune to meet with very bad weather. In this boat we committed ourselves to the sea the 17th of August, 1742.

From this narrative may be corrected the error of Mr. Delisle, who places Bering's Island in the 54th degree, and not far from the harbour of Avacha, whereas its true situation is in the 56th degree, at sixty miles distance from Avacha and forty Dutch miles from the mouth of the river of Kamchatka.

As to the voyage of Mr. Chirikov, although he did not suffer so much from the sea and other difficulties one may meet with on such an expedition, it was nevertheless attended with much hardship, and especially from the tenderness of his heart, which his profession as a seaman was far from having hardened to insensibility. After his being separated from Mr. Bering, steering to the northeast, on the 15th of July, he came to sight of a land, whose shore was surrounded by steep lofty rocks, with a deep sea beating against them; he prudently kept at some distance, and on the third day sent the master, Abraham [Avraam]

Dementiev, with ten hands, to take a view of the country; but
neither Dementiev, nor any of the people that went with him, were
ever heard of again. This man deserved our tears; he was of good
family, young, well made, a man of virtue and singular knowledge
in his profession, and a zealous lover of his country.

Six days after, Mr. Chirikov sent the boatswain, Sidor
Savelev, with three men, but no more was heard of them than of
the former. All this time a continual smoke was seen on shore,
and the second day after the boatswain's departure, two men in
different canoes, or little boats, came off from the place where
Dementiev and Savelev had landed, and when they came within
hearing, they cried out with all their force, "Agai! Agai!" and
immediately made for the shore again.

Mr. Chirikov was at a loss what to make of it, but despairing
of ever seeing his men again, and having no other boat to send
ashore, he left that place on the 27th of July, determining to
continue on the coast as long as he possibly could, and
afterwards to return to Kamchatka; therefore Mr. Delisle commits
a mistake in saying, that during the whole month of August, Mr.
Chirikov had kept cruising in that part, waiting the return of
his people; he kept continually within sight of land for above
one hundred miles, amidst the difficulties of frequent contrary
wind and fog; once particularly he found himself in extreme
danger, being got near the shore, on which he came to an anchor,
but lost it; no less than twenty-one small leather boats, with a
man in each of them, made towards him, but that was all, as he
was not able to converse with them. The want of fresh water and
the scurvy carried off many of his people; among these were the
lieutenants Chikhachev and Plautin, two very useful persons, and
expert seamen, and from whose longer life many more good services
might have been expected.

Mr. Chirikov himself, on the 20th of September, felt some
symptoms of a disorder, but his prudent diet, and the land air
soon set him rights again; with Monsieur de la Croyère it went
otherwise, imagining himself to be well enough, nay, even almost
to his dying moment. It was wondered, that the great quantity of
brandy which he swallowed every day had such a good effect, but
it was soon perceived, that all advantage he reaped from this
inflamatory liquor, was to forget for some time his pain, while
the iquor was working in his body. He died on 10th of October,
just at his coming into the harbour of Avacha; having dressed
himself in order to go ashore, and after having given once more
an extravagant vent to his joy at his safe return; however, one
important service of his is not to be omitted, which was, that
upon the Americans showing themselves at some distance to Mr.
Chirikov, he assured him that they were very like the inhabitants
of Canada, where, before his coming to Russia, he had served
seventeen years in the French troops.

Mr. Delisle mentions another discovery made by the Russians,
who, in the year 1731, ventured to take the same course which Mr

ering had taken two years before the first voyage. Here, it is
o be observed, that in the year 1730, Mr. [Dimitrii I.]
avlutski, at that time Captain of foot, and one [Afanasii]
hestakov, chief of the Cossacks of Iakutsk, were appointed to
educe the Chukchi, a wild refractory people, who had revolted
gainst our court; and in order to have in readiness all
ecessaries for the army's subsistence, Mr. Pavlutski sent Mr.
Mikhail] Gvozdev the surveyor, to find out those provisions,
hich were remaining of Mr. Bering's first expedition, with
nstructions to bring them to Chukchi in the vessel left by Mr.
ering at Okhotsk.

    Gvosdev acquitted himself perfectly well of his commission,
ringing his vessel to Serdtse Kamen without the least mischance;
ut there he neither found Mr. Pavlutski, nor could get any
idings of him, which obliged him to put back for Okhotsk; but
ere, though he had no thought of making new discoveries, he was
arried by the wind on the coast of America, opposite to the land
f Chukchi, and at no great distance from it. I never have heard
hat he got sight of any one of the natives of that country,
hich renders very doubtful that narrative of Mr. Delisle, about
 conversation held between the captain and the Americans, and
etween people too, who could not understand one another's
anguage. But be this as it will, this fortuitous voyage
onfirmed what we were informed of before, only from the
elations of the Chukchi, viz, that the great continent of
merica reaches to within a small distance of them; and thus the
onjecture which Mr. Delisle ascribes to Mr. Buache proves to be
ell founded; and, though it was not till after a general
nowledge of the structure of the globe, that he had supposed
hat the north parts of Asia must be joined to America by a ridge
f mountains and a shallow sea, I make no difficulty to add an
pinion which may corroborate what he has advanced; which is,
hat I am of the opinion that formerly the land of Chukchi and
he part of America opposite to it, were joined, but separated by
n inundation, a volcano or an earthquake, as has happened in
ther places; and thus the peopling of the vast American
ontinent is more easily accounted for than on any other
ypothesis.

    As to the discoveries made on the coasts of the Frozen-Sea,
r. Delisle is contented with his very French-fashioned
onciseness, to tell us that he formed his map of these coasts
rom observations taken at sea, from Archangel to the river
olyma; but would it not have been much more candid and honest to
ave owned that he drew them from the new Russian Atlas? For had
e known anything farther, he would not, it seems, so far
eviated from the generous custom of the learned, to assign to
ts right owner what is not properly their own; and this act of
iterary justice would have been much to his credit here on so
ine an occasion. It is true, that the discoveries of this
oast, or rather of the road through the Frozen-Sea, as far as
hose places are accessible, was a work of vast labour and time.

Two ships sent from Archangel to Berezov and two more fro
Berezov to Turukhansk at length reached the place of thei
destination; but the other two, which were fitted out at Iakutsk
of which one was to go from the mouth of the river Lena, to th
mouth of the river Enisei, and the other from the Lena, eastwar
to attempt a passage to Kamchatka, had not the like success; th
former not being able to prosecute its voyage further than
little beyond that part where the river Taimura runs into th
sea.   A ridge of islands, running north-westwards from the coas
obstructed their passage, and the prodigious pieces of ice, tha
were immoveable, not permitting them to get to the end of thes
islands, all this labour came to nothing and the vessel itsel
was lost.   The experiment to be made with the other vessels
which were come from the Ob into the Enisei in order thence t
meet that vessel expected from the Lena, met with no bette
success.   They were obliged to wait at the river Piesid
[Piasina]:   so that the coast betwixt the Piesida and the Taimur
would have remained unknown had they not been discovered by land
On the other hand, the vessel which was to sail from the Len
eastward on a passage to Kamchatka, perished among the ice nea
the river Indigirka.   From so many unfortunate voyages it ma
well be concluded what account is to be made of the passag
through the Frozen-Sea, which the English and Dutch formerl
attempted with so much zeal and eagerness; But unquestionabl
they would have given over any such attempts had they bee
acquainted with the insurmountable dangers and difficulties o
this boyage; and after all, which of us are more likely t
succeed in such an attempt, they, or we Russians who are mor
inured to cold and fatigue than the former and are able to bea
the want of a thousand things, and who, though powerfull
supported, yet failed in our enterprizes.   To what purpose the
were all these charges and labours of so many trials?   Why, it i
to find a shorter cut to the Indies, a considerable advantage
own, were one not obliged to go through a severe winter of thre
or four months by the way; after all, the nearest way to th
East-Indies is to be found only on our maps and globes.

Lastly, Mr. Delisle speaks of a large country which he say
was discovered in the year 1723, lying northward of the Frozen
Sea in the 75th degree of latitude; but without giving us on
word of where, or by whom it was discovered: it seems that h
was borrowed this mistaken account from that of the voyages i
the Frozen-Sea published in the observations on the St
Petersburg news-papers for the year 1742; which observation
contain such accounts as were got from Iakutsk; but what stres
can be laid on them, as they consist only of reports of th
meanest of people, some saying that they had discerned a countr
over-against the river Kolyma, and others went so far as t
affirm that they had been there, whilst others again said tha
the land lay opposite to the river Iana.   In a word, they wer
for having it believed that those parts were full of larg
islands; but when skilful persons came to be appointed to ge
certain intelligence of them, they met with insuperabl
obstacles: from whence I conclude the aforesaid reports to hav

een very precarious, although Mr. <u>Delisle</u> had unhappily given so
ar into them as to talk with positiveness of those lands, and
ven to assign them a latitude; an error which he would not have
ommitted could he have read the originals.   I shall close the
resent with some thoughts on the supposed narrative of the
<u>panish</u> Admiral <u>de Fonte</u>, which, being one of the fundamentals on
hich Mr. <u>Delisle</u>'s maps are built, deserves a more strict
nquiry than the particulars we have hitherto considered of: a
panish narrative, of which there is only an <u>English</u> translation,
ithout being able to come at any <u>Spanish</u> orginal and without any
nformation from history, that such an Admiral was on the voyage
scribed to him, or even so much as that ever such an Admiral was
n being; such a relation, I say is at first extremely
uspicious.

However, let this be thought to amount to no more than a bare
uspicion; yet without dwelling any longer on those
ircumstances, I think, I am able to discover very manifest marks
f falsity in the relation itself by showing some of its contents
o contradict the most common and received truths, and proving
thers to shock all probability, and that throughout it is a very
nsufficient basis for a map, unsupported as it is of all other
uthority.

<u>First</u>.   One could hardly think it possible, if we had not
ere an instance of it, that a <u>Spanish</u> admiral should have
eckoned by the years of <u>King Charles</u> of <u>England</u>'s reign, just in
he manner as is used by the <u>English</u> in their public
ransactions.   Does not this favour a conjecture, that possibly
ome Englishman, under the borrowed name of a <u>Spanish</u> Admiral,
ad taken the liberty to introduce his own conceits into the
orld; or, supposing he had found the materials in some <u>Spanish</u>
elation, that at least he dressed them up his own way?

<u>Secondly</u>.   According to this narrative, Captain <u>Hudson</u>
erformed his voyage for the discovery of a northern passage in
he first years of the reign of King <u>Charles</u>. But what an
versight is here in a consumate seaman and an Admiral?   Was he
nacquainted with the history of the maritime discoveries in his
ime?   <u>Hudson</u> died in the 1610, and it was the year 1625 when
harles the first began his reign. Let it not be objected here
hat it was Captain's <u>James</u>' voyage, to which is to be referred
hat is said in the narrative of King <u>Charles</u>.   For even this
ould not quite remove the difficulty, since Captain <u>James</u> did
ot perform his voyage till the sixth year of the reign of that
rince.

<u>Thirdly</u>.   And what becomes of the voyage said there to have
een undertaken by the inhabitants of <u>Boston</u>, which no soul ever
eard a word of?   I have made it my business particularly to
nquire whether any mention was made of it in any collection of
oyages, and particularly of the <u>English</u>, most of which we have
n hand; but to no effect.   Mr. Arthur <u>Dobbs</u>, whose zeal for the
iscovery of a north-west passage is very well known, is the

first who has made a mention of the affair; his intention herei
was to encourage his countrymen to perform that which, accordin
to the contents of the narrative in question, is not only no
impossible, but even very easy.   Here is a circumstance whic
very much increases my suspicion; it is relating to what Mr
Ellis says in his account of his voyage to Hudson's Bay, p.70
Besides, says he, that the Boston undertaking is not absolutel
incredible; which words Mr. Delisle interprets as if Mr. Elli
means that Admiral de Fonte's relation contained nothing in i
which is not at least very probable; whereas there is not a wor
of this in his whole book.   And when, p. 72, he mentions a
instance of a voyage performed from Boston to Hudson's Bay, ye
he adds nothing of its being undertaken with the view of findin
a passage, nor does he so much as know the time of this voyage
on which account he finds himself obliged to own that thi
account cannot be made use of as a proof of the question.

Fourthly.   Upon their arrival at St. Helena, the Admiral an
the ships company provided themselves with rosin, which issues i
great quantities out of the earth; chiefly to make use of as
preservative against the scurvy and dropsy; against whic
distempers rosin is reckoned a sovereign specific: this
indeed, is something of no small importance, and does grea
honour to the bishop of Cloyne's tar-water; that one would almos
imagine the reason of its being inserted was purely to convinc
unbelievers of the transcendent virtues of the bishop'
medicament.

Fifthly.   And what is to be thought of the geographica
errors; such, for instance as that of a Cape Abel, which he make
a harbour of, and placeth it upon the coast of California, in th
20th degree of north latitude, while it is known that Californi
does not reach so far.   It is not an easy matter, indeed, t
persuade one's self that such descriptions were taken upon th
spot.

Sixthly.   Let us now follow captain Bernardo, one of th
Admiral's fellow-adventurers; who, after traversing a large sea
called Valasco, sails to the height of 79 degrees north; one o
his crew is carried, by the natives of the country, to Davis'
Straits; there he sees how the junction is interrupted and quit
obstructeed by a chain of prodigious mountains, lying north an
northwest; notwithstand which, they showed him ice no less tha
100 fathoms deep in the sea, and which was to have been ther
since the creation; the land stretches away northward and the ic
remains upon the land.   Are these not manifest contradictions an
at the same time sufficient warrants for the Admiral to say tha
no passage had been found from northwest into the Frozen-Sea
And yet others have been introduced, clearly to prove that ther
is such a passage.

Seventhly.   But now comes the more improbable place of th
whole narration: the Admiral, after passing through severa
seas, which all have a communication with one another, meets wit

an <u>English</u> ship, which was upon finding out this northwest
passage; he goes up to her in one of his sailing vessels; and
could not the <u>Englishman</u> have taken the same course that the
<u>Spaniard</u> had?   No: but instead of that he is contented to
deliver up his charts and journals to the <u>Spaniard</u>, and at once,
for what reason we are to seek, breaks off his voyage and very
friendly parts from the Admiral. Now let anyone bestow the least
reflection upon all this insipid stuff, and all the other
incidents to be met with in this narrative, and then judge
whether it be worthy of any credit, or calculated only for
amusement.   Mr. <u>Delisle</u>, carried away by his fiery impatience to
come at this northwest passage, imagines the two ships to have
met in a narrow strait joining to <u>Hudson's Bay</u>; but was there
ever such a strait found out thereabouts; although no small pains
have been taken to find it?   and on this very account it is, that
Mr. <u>Delisle</u> has been led to say that the Admiral's course ended
in the bay of <u>Baffin</u>, which yet is as improbable as the rest, and
contradicted by the very narrative itself; for it was at the bay
of <u>Baffin</u>, where Captain <u>Bernardo</u>'s sailor is said to have been
carried, and where they showed him nothing but a prodigious ridge
of mountains and heaps ofice: this part is by mistake called
<u>Davis's-Straits</u>, but I don't know how it came about that Captain
<u>Bernardo</u> found things there quite contrary to what the Admiral
found.

These observations I do think are sufficient to show that it
is a vain and fruitless attempt to make use of the pretended
account of Admiral <u>de Fonte</u>, for filling up the vast and hitherto
unknown space betwixt <u>California</u> and <u>Kamchatka</u>.   And now from the
premises, I am led plainly and impartially to deliver my opinion
on Mr. <u>Delisle</u>'s map, which, as may already be perceived, will
not perfectly harmonize with the description he gives us of the
coasts of <u>America</u>.   As to the appelation of these coasts, I see
no reason why he should not have made use of that given them by
their first discoverers; such as Captain <u>Drake</u>, who names them
<u>New Albion</u>:   however, as it is not thoroughly proved that ever
Captain <u>Drake</u> was in those parts, those names at least should be
used which we find in the old maps and globes; as, <u>Niewada</u>,
<u>Sierra</u>, <u>Guiura</u>, and <u>Anian</u>, which are names of provinces and
kingdoms, and certainly not without some derivation, and which,
perhaps, a <u>Spaniard</u> may have given them in some narrative unknown
to us; tho', for my part, I should rather have been inclined to
have made use of the name <u>New Russia</u>, in imitation of other
nations, who have called countries <u>New-England</u>, <u>New-Spain</u>, <u>New-</u>
<u>France</u>, <u>New-Holland</u>, etc.   It may be said we are not in
possession of them; but as to this, it is purely in our
discretion, for, at least it is certain, that these vast
countries belong to no power able to dispute the possession with
us.

How little acquainted Mr. de l'Isle is with our sea-
discoveries, must be manifest to everyone from his marking but at
one single place, betwixt the 235 and 240th degree of longitude,
some coasts, for the discovery of which the public is indebted to

us: now, if he has done this only to find a more convenient
place for Admiral de Fonte's Archipelago of St. Lazare, as it is
called, it would have been much worse; but so far from admitting
of this Archipelagus, it is rather the northwest and western
bounds which must be carried farther to join them to that land,
which was seen at 51 degrees; since there wanted but very little,
but that this whole district had been discovered by one or other
of our ships.   It will not be amiss here to observe that the
coast of this latter country lying under the 51st degree, is in
Mr. Delisle's map made four times longer than it should be.   This
land hath been seen, not only by Mr. Chirikov, but also by Mr.
Bering, as we likewise have formerly seen it.

This Mr. Delisle knew nothing of, as having no knowledge of
Mr. Bering's voyage; yet does Mr. Delisle turn it to the praise
of his brother to show that he has done all he could to
immortalize his dear name: A country, these are his words while
he is speaking of his brother Mr. Delisle de la Croyère, which
was seen by Mr. Chirikov, and by Mr. Delisle de la Croyère; again
you find the way from Kamchatka to America by Capt. Chirikov, and
Mr. de la Croyère.   This might pass well enough if Mr. de la
Croyère had been any ways instrumental in finding that way; but
having been no more than an idle spectator, what title has he to
any mention in that affair?   He must have been blind not to have
seen the coasts, which were visible to everyone else, and, not to
speak of us officers on both ships, who, as such, had our share
in the execution of the affair, I take liberty to affirm, that
our common sailors deserve much more than Mr. de la Croyère   to
have their names perpetuated as having been really useful and
laborious hands, but that a list of their names would take up too
much room in this short piece.

It has already been noticed, that Mr. Delisle has fallen into
a mistake in his memoir, by placing Bering Island in the latitude
of 54 instead of 56 degrees, and this error is also brought into
his map; the manner also of his placing the islands, which lie
betwixt Kamchatka and Japan, would deserve a remark, if I could
not refer myself to the map of Capt. Spangenberg, the essential
part of which may be seen in the last leaf of the Russian Atlas.
A judicious connoisseur and judge of such naval experiments will
not hesitate to give the preference to the informations of this
complete and indefatigable seaman, namely, Capt. Spangenberg, who
made his voyage on purpose to take a particular view of the said
islands; such a judge, I say, will always prefer this man's
observations to those of other ships, who made theirs only by the
way, and as it were accidentally.

Mr. Delisle is of another opinion; he is pleased to stick to
the situation of the island Jedso, and the other islands
discovered by the Dutch ships, called the Castricom.   He
contradicts our informations, and to invalidate them, maintains
his pretended land of Gama, which he brings a little more to the
southwest than in his map of 1732.   This is being a man of
learning with a witness, to endeavour to impose further on the

world, rather than retract a former assertion. How much more
becoming were it ti leave everyone in the possession of what is
his proper right, than to go about to bias the reader and favour
one to the prejudice of another.

I conclude with a general remark upon the part of <u>Siberia</u>, as
it appears in Mr. <u>Delisle</u>'s map. It is entirely taken from the
<u>Russian Atlas</u>, and that without any amendment of the faults both
of the engraver and writer. It would therefore be an egregious
mistake to presume that in <u>France</u> better and more exact maps
should be made of our country than we ourselves in avoiding the
imputation of slowness; it will be an addition to the glory of
our illustrious <u>Empress</u> and the whole nation; than which there
cannot surely be a more prevalent motive to each true-born
patriot heart. This I am confident would quickly be effected by
the countenance of the most eminent personages in the nation; and
I particularly flatter myself, that as your <u>Excellency</u> is
pleased, in a distinguished manner, to interest yourself herein,
it will prompt us to retrieve our past remissness. It depends
upon you to procure me the advantage of contributing to this
work; and, if you will be pleased to invest me with that care, I
shall undertake it with the utmost ardour and cheerfulness.

I now submit these observations to your Excellency's superior
judgement! My wish in this affair will not prove fruitless, if,
agreeably to your views, I can be so happy as to be employed
therein and deserve your approbation: I shall always think it a
great happiness to be permitted to call myself,

My Lord,

Your Excellency's, &c., &c.

                              N.N.

BIBLIOGRAPHY

The following list includes only those titles which are relevant
to Müller's experiences in Siberia, and to the Academy contingent
with the Second Kamchatka Expedition.

Muller's Publications on Siberia:

Bering's Voyages: The Reports from Russia by Gerhard Friedrich
Muller. Ed. by Carol Urness. Fairbanks: University of Alaska
Press. 1986.

Conquest of Siberia and the History of the Transactions, Wars,
Commerce, &c., &c., carried on between Russia and China from the
earliest period. London, 1842.

Ezhemesiachnye sochineniia. 20 vols. St. Petersburg, 1755-1764.

Istoriia Sibiri. 2 vols. Moscow-Leningrad, 1937-1941.

Leben Herrn Georg Wilhelm Stellers... Frankfurt, 1748. See
Steller, G.W., below.

A Letter from a Russian Sea-Officer, to a Person of Distinction
at the Court of St. Petersburgh: Containing His remarks upon
Mr. de l'Isle's Chart and Memoir, relative to the New Discoveries
Northward and Eastward from Kamtschatka. London, 1754. Translated
from the French edition of 1753.

Opisanie o torgakh sibirskikh. St. Petersburg, 1756

Opisanie zhivushchikh v Kazanskoi gubernii iazycheskikh narodov,
iako to Cheremis, Chuvash i Votiakov... St. Petersburg, 1791.

Opisanie Sibirskago Tsarstva i vsekh proizshedshikh v nem del,
ot nachala a osoblivo ot pokoreniia ego Rossiiskoi derzhave po
sii vremena. St. Petersburg, 1750

Sammlung russischer Geschichte. 9 vols. St. Petersburg, 1732-
1764.

Voyage et decouvertes faites par les Russes le long des cotes de
la Mer Glaciale & sur l'Ocean Oriental, tant vers le Japon que
vers l'Amerique. On y a joint l'Histoire du Fleuve Amur. 2 vols.

Voyages from Asia to America, for Completing the Discoveries of
the Northwest Coast of America. London, 1761.

"Zur Geschichte der Akademie der Wissenschaften zu S. Petersburg,"
in Materialy dlia istorii imperatorskoi akademii nauk. Vol. 6.
St. Petersburg, 1890.

Documents, Memoirs and Contemporary Works:

"Akademiki Miller i Fischer i opisanie Sibiri." Chteniia v Imperatorskom obshchestve istorii i drevnostei Rossiiskikh pri Moskovskom universitete. Bk. 3, section V (1866), 15-30.

Coxe, William. Account of the Russian Discoveries between Asia and America. 2 Vols. London, 1787, Reprint 1955.

Gorin, P.O., ed. "Iz istorii osvoeniia severnogo morskogo puti (Ekspeditsiia Beringa 1732-1743 gg). Krasnyi arkhiv. 72 (1935), 137-143.

Gmelin, J.-G. Reise durch Sibirien von dem Jahr 1733 bis 1743. 4 Bks. Göttingen, 1751-1752.

..., Voyage en Sibérie. 2 Vols. Paris, 1767.

Golder, Frank A. Bering's Voyages: An Account of the Efforts of the Russians to Determine the Relation of Asia and America. 2 Vols. New York, 1922-1925.

Krasheninnikov, S.P. Opisanie zemli Kamchatki. 2 vols. St. Petersburg, 1755; with foreword by G.-F. Müller; reprinted in Moscow, 1949.

..., S.P. Krasheninnikov v Sibiri: neopublikovannye materialy. Moscow-Leningrad, 1966

..., Explorations of Kamchatka. Report of a Journey Made to Explore Eastern Siberia in 1735-1741. Translated and edited by E.A.P. Crownhart-Vaughan. Portland, Oregon, 1972.

Locatelli, Francesco. Lettres moscovites. Paris, 1736.

Materialy dlia istorii ekspeditsii Akademii nauk v XVIII i XIX vekakh: Khronologicheskie obzory i opisanie arkhivnykh materialov. Ed. by V.F. Gnucheva. Moscow-Leningrad, 1940.

Materialy dlia istorii imperatorskoi akademii nauk. 9 Vols. St. Petersburg, 1885-1900.

Protokoly zasedanii konferentsii imperatorskoi akademii nauk s 1725 po 1803 goda. 4 Vols. St. Petersburg, 1987-1911.

Russian Penetration of the North Pacific Ocean, 1700-1799: A Documentary Record. Vol. 2. To Siberia and Russian America: Three Centuries of Russian Eastward Expansion, 1584-1867. Ed. by Basil Dmytryshyn, E.A.P. Crownhart-Vaughan & Thomas Vaughan. Portland: Oregon Historical Society, 1986.

Sokolov, A. "Istoriia Severnaia Ekspeditsii, 1733-1743." Zapiski. Gidrografricheskoe upravlenie. Pt. 9 (1851), 190-469.

[Steller, Georg]. The First Official Report from Russian Sources

concerning Bering's Voyage to America: or "Life of Mr. Georg
Wilhelm Steller..."   Frankfurt, 1748.   Ed. by Frost, O. W.
Translated by Olga M. Griminger.   Alaska Historical Commission
Studies in History, No. 223, 1986.   Frost attributes authorship of
this work to Müller.

General Works:

Andreev, A. I. "Trudy G.F. Millera o vtoroi Kamchatskoi
ekspeditsii." Izvestiia: Vsesoiuznoe geograficheskoe obshchestvo.
91:1 (January/February, 1959), 3-16.

..., "Trudy G.F. Millera o Sibiri." In Istoriia Sibiri, vol. 1.
Moscow-Leningrad, 1937. Pp. 57-144.

..., Ocherki po istochnikovedeniiu Sibiri. Vypusk vtoroi: XVIII
vek (pervaia polovina). Moscow-Leningrad, 1963.

Bagrow, Leo. A History of Russian Cartography up to 1800.   Wolfe
Island, Ontario, 1975.

Bakhrushin, S. G. "G.F. Miller kak istorik Sibiri."   In bk:
Istoriia Sibiri, Vol. I. Moscow-Leningrad, 1937. Pp. 3-56.

Barratt, Glynn.   Russia in Pacific Waters, 1715-1825   Vancouver,
1981.

Bashkatova, Z.V.   "Sibirskaia gorodskaia promyshlennost' v
dvorianskoi istoriografii pervoi poloviny XVIII v."   In Istoriia
gorodov Sibiri dosovetskogo perioda (XVII-nachalo XX).
Novosibirsk, 1977. Pp. 26-44.

Belov, M.I. "O sostavlenii general'noi karty Vtoroi Kamchatskoi
ekspeditsii." Geograficheskii sbornik, 3 (1964).   131-145.

Berg, L.S. Otkrytie Kamchatki i ekspeditsii Beringa 1725-1742.
Moscow-Leningrad, 1946.

..., Ocherki po istorii russkikh geograficheskikh otkrytii.
Moscow-Leningrad, 1946.

Black, J.L. "G.-F. Müller and the Russian Academy of Sciences
Contingent in the Second Kamchatka Expedition, 1733-43. Canadian
Slavonic Papers, 25:2 (June, 1983), 235-252.

..., G.-F. Müller and the Imperial Russian Academy.   Kingston-
Montréal, 1986.

Black, Lydia T. "The Question of Maps: Exploration of the
Bering Sea in the Eighteenth Century."   Unpublished paper read at
The Sea in Alaska's Past.   A Maritime History Conference.
Anchorage, Alaska, 1979.

Breitfuss, L. "Early Maps of North-Eastern Asia and the Lands

Around the North Pacific: Controversy between G.-F. Müller and N. Delisle." Imago Mundi, 3 (1939), 87-99.

Büsching, A. "Gerhard Friedrich Müller." In Beyträge zu der Lebensgeschichte denkwürdiger Personen, insonderheit Gelehrter Männer. Vol. 3. Halle, 1785. Pp. 1-160.

Collins, David N. "Russia's conquest of Siberia: Evolving Russian and Soviet Historical Interpretations." European Studies Review, 12:1 (1982), 17-44

Crownhart-Vaughan, E.A.P. "Eighteenth Century Russian Scientific Expeditions to the North Pacific Ocean." Paper read at the Third International Congress for Soviet and East European Studies, Washington, D.C., 1985. See also the proceedings of the conference volume edited by D.K. Rowney, Imperial Power and Development: Papers on Pre-Revolutionary Russian History..., 1987.

Dioszegi, V., and M. Hoppal, Shamanism in Siberia. Budapest, 1978.

Dmytryshyn, Basil. "Privately-financed Russian expeditions to the North Pacific in the Eighteenth Century." Paper read at the Third International Congress for Soviet and East European Studies, Washington, D.C., 1985. See also the same conference proceedings as above.

Fischer, Raymond H. Bering's Voyages: Whither and Why. Seattle, 1977.

..., The Voyage of Semen Dezhnev in 1648:   Bering's Precursor. With Selected Documents. London, 1981.

..., "The Early Cartography of the Bering Strait Region." Arctic, 37:4 (1984), pp. 579-589.

Fradkin, N.G. S.P. Krasheninnikov. Moscow, 1954.

Gmelin, Otto.   Johann Georg Gmelin, 1709-1755. Der Erforscher Sibiriens. Ein Gedenkbuch. München, 1911.

Golder, Frank A. Russian Expansion to the Pacific, 1641-1850: An Account of the Earliest and Later Expeditions made by the Russians along the Pacific Coast of Asia and North America, Including Some Related to the Arctic Regions. Cleveland, 1914.

Grekov, V.I.   Ocherki iz istorii russkikh geograficheskikh issledovanii v 1725-1765 gg. Moscow, 1960.

Gur'ev, V.V. "Istoriograf Miller v Tomske." Russkii vestnik, no. 11 (1881), 62-72.

Istoriia Sibiri drevneishikh vremen do nashikh dnei v piati tomakh. Vol. 2. Leningrad, 1968.

Kirchner, Walter. A Siberian Journey. The Journal of Hans Jakob
Fries, 1774-1776. London, 1974.

Kosven, M.O. "Etnograficheskie resul'taty Velikoi Severnoi
Ekspeditsii 1733-1743 gg." Sibiriskii etnograficheskii sbornik, 3
(1961), 167-212.

Lauridsen, Peter. Vitus Bering: The Discoverer of Bering Strait.
New York, 1889. Reprint, 1969.

Maier, L.A. "Gerhard Friedrich Müller's Memoranda on Russian
Relations with China and Reconquest of the Amur." Slavonic and
East European Review, 59:2 (April, 1981), 219-240.

Mirzoev, V.G. "G.F. Miller kak istorik Sibiri v otsenke russkoi
dorevoliutsionnoi i sovetskoi istoriografii." Uchenye zapiski
Kemerovskogo pedagogicheskogo instituta, no. 5 (1963), pp. 45-71.

..., Istoriografiia Sibiri (Domarksistskii period), Moscow, 1970.

Pekarskii, P.P. Istoriia imperatorskoi akademii nauk v Peterburge.
2 vols. St. Petersburg, 1870-1873. On Müller see especially vol.
1, 308-430.

Pypin, A.N. Istoriia russkoi etnografii. Vol. 4. St. Petersburg,
1892.

Radlov, V. "Iz sochinenii akademikov G.F. Millera i I.G. Gmelina."
Materialy po arkheologii Rossii. XV (1894). "Prilozhenie" to
Sibirskiia drevnosti. Vol. 1:3. St. Petersburg, 1894. Pp.
55-126.

Robel, Gert. "Der Wandel des deutschen Sibirienbildes im 18.
Jahründert." Canadian/American Slavic Studies, 15:3 (Fall, 1980),
406-426.

Schottenstein, Isaac M. "The Russian Conquest of Kamchatka, 1697-
1731." Unpublished Ph.D. dissertation. University of Wisconsin,
1969.

Sokolov, A. "Severnaia ekspeditsiia, 1733-43 goda." Zapiski
gidrograficheskago departamenta morskogo ministerstva, Pt. 9. St.
Petersburg, 1851, 190-469.

Stewart, John Massey. "Early Travellers, Explorers and
Naturalists in Siberia." Asian Affairs, 15:1 (February 1984), 55-
64.

Vorob'eva, T. "Izuchenie vostochnoi sibiri uchastnikami vtoroi
kamchatskoi ekspeditsii." Sibirskii geograficheskii sbornik, 3
(1964), 198-233.

Zinner, E.P. Sibir' v izvestiiakh zapadnoevropeiskikh
puteshestvennikov i uchenykh XVIII veka. Novosibirsk, 1968.

INDEX

Abasheva R., 85
Abagaitu, Mt., on Chinese border, 100
Abakanskoe, 15, 58
Abintsy (Abalar), 39, 84
Ablakit (Ablaikit), 82-83, 90
Academie des Sciences, Paris, 35
Academy of Sciences, St. Petersburg, Chancellery, 7, 25, 119;
     Conference, 18, 35; Historical Assembly, 21-22
Admiralty College, 74
Aga R., Onon R. tributary, 102
Aginskii zavod, 102
Alekseev, Fedot, vi
Alcohol, 11, 54, 59, 65
Altai Mts., 78, 82, 89
Ammann, Johann, Dr., 64
Amur R., vii, 11, 29, 48, 61, 93, 97
Amur Valley, Russian need for, 97
Anadyr R., vi, 127
Angara R., 11, 57, 58
Anna, Empress, 61, 72
Apraksin, Count, Lord High Admiral, 126
Archeographical Commission, 37
Archeology, 66
Archives, Tara, 79; Tobol'sk, 18, 74, 76; Tomsk, 15, 18, 59, 87;
     Ilimsk, 53; Iakutsk, 18, 54; Krasnoiarsk, 90; Nerchinsk, 97;
     Irkutsk, 104; Eniseisk, 18; Verkhotur'e, 18
Arctic Ocean, vi, vii, 54, 73
Argun R. 99-100
Argunskii (Nerchinskii) silver mines, 92, 98, 107-109
Argunskii ostrog, 88-96, 98
Arkhangel'sk, 73
Astrakhan, 69
Astronomical observations 89, 90, 105, 128
Arintsy, 90
Atlasov, Vladimir, 127
Auteroche, Chappe d', Abbe, ix
Avacha Bay, 127, 131
Avsianikov, Stepan, 48

Bachmeister, H.L.Ch., 34
Baikal, 53, 57, 92, 102
Balagansk, 78, 91
Bandits, 16
Banks, Joseph, vii, viii
Bantysh-Kamenskii, N.N., 34
Barabinsk Steppe, 79
Barabinsk Tatars, 86
Barluzka sloboda, 91
Barguzin, 110
Barnaul, 83-84

147

Barsak Tatars, 85
Barsov, A.S., 22
Bayer, G.-S., 2, 4
Bell, John, of Antermony, x
Belozersk, 17
Berezov, Ob R., vii, 16, 59, 136
Bering, Vitus J., vi, 1, 4-5; assessment of, 12, 14, 55, 63, 65,
    67, 73, 76, 77, 91, 92; voyage, 4 September 1740-17 August
    1742, 131-133; death, 14, 126, 130
Berkan (Berkhan), Johann, 6, 18, 48, 77, 81, 111
Bernardo, Capt. 138-139
Betskoi, I.I., 49
Bilimbaevsk iron works, 71
Birds, 58
Biron, Ernst, Johann, Count, v, 5, 63
Bogorodskoe selo, Ob R., 87
Bol'shaia R., 128
Bol'sheretsk ostrog, 130
Bonpland, Aime, vii
Borsa R., cave near, 101
Bougainville, Louis Antoine, viii
Braun, Joseph-Adam, 21, 88
Bauner, surgeon, 67
Breitfuss, L., 34
Brevern, Karl von, 14
Braun, Joseph, 88
Bribery, 54
Bride price, 50-51
Bronnitsy, 8, 66
Buache, Philippe, 135
Bucholz (Bukholz), Ivan D., 11, 53, 92
Bukhara, 29; language, 11, 79
Bukharans, 10, 82, 87
Bulgars, 68, 70
Bura R., 94
Burial mounds, 66
Buriats, 10, 53, 56, 90
Büsching, Anton-Friedrich, 28, 32, 37, 49, 110

Camels, 10
Cantemir, Demetrius, 69
Catherine II, ix, 29, 83
Cedar-nuts, 60
Chagatai Steppe, 101
Chailar R., Argun R. source, see Hailar
Charoshchnikov, Kozma, 88, 115
Cheboksary, 7, 67
Cheremises (Mari), 7, 50, 67, 69-70
Chekin (Shchekin), Nikifor, geodesist, 48, 73
Chikoi R., 93-94
China, 53, 56, 95, 100

Chirikov, Aleksei, 4, 63, 77-78, 130 131; death, 14; voyage, 1740-1741, 133-134
Chita R., 96; ostrog, 96, 101
Chitinsk, 98
Chukchi, 126, 135
Chukotka, Cape, 4
Chukotka, Peninsula, early voyage around, 54
Chukotskii Nos, Cape, 127
Church, 59
Chulym R., 87
Chumysh R., 84
Chuvash, 7, 27, 67, 69-70
Circumcision, 52, 75
Clark, William, vi
Cold, 11, 54, 60
Cook, James, viii
Copper, 89-90, 102
Cossacks, 29, 84
Coxe, William, Rev., ix, 35
Cuper, Gisbert, 86

Dalai-Lama, 53, 86, 91; religion, 100, 103
Dalai Nor L., 100
Dames, Peter, at Argun silver works, 98
Decker, Johann, 18
DeFonte, Admiral, fictitious discoveries of, 15, 122, 136-139
Delisle, Guilaume, 3, 64
Delisle, Joseph Nicolas, 3, 4, 25, 26, 27, 64, 102, 122 ff.
Delisle de la Croyère, Louis, 6, 8, 9, 19, 27, 48, 49, 55, 64, 69, 70, 71-74, 76-78, 88, 91-95, 104-106; death, 129
Dement'ev Avraam, 134
Demidov, Akinfii, 76, 83
Demidov, N.A., 17
Demidov, Vasilii, 71
Demidovs, 60
Dezhnev, S.I., voyage of 1648, vi, 13, 66
Dolgoi waterfall, Angara R., 78
Dolonskii ostrog, 82
Dzungar Mongols, 28, 93

Education, 60
Ekaterinburg, 16, 28, 60, 71-73, 75, 107
Elizabeth, Empress, 14, 25, 65
Engel, Samuel, 34
Enisei R., v, 74, 78, 88, 90
Eniseisk, 13, 53, 57, 73,87-88
Epidemic, livestock, 10
Eravninskoe (Eravna), ostrog, 96, 98, 102
Erintsei, taisha, of Buriats, 96
Ermak Timofeevich, 16, 22, 29, 51
Euler, Johann-Albrecht, 32
Euler, Leonhard, 16, 25, 26, 32-33

Evreinov, Ivan, 3

Fairs, Eniseisk, 86; Irbit, 9, 16
Falk, I.P., 33
Farquarson, Henry, 123
Fischer, Johann Eberhardt, ix, 13, 15, 21-22, 27, 31, 33, 59, 70,
    107-108, 110-112, 114-118
Fisher, Raymond H., vi
Forster, Georg, viii
Frost, O.W., ix

Gama, Juan de, fictional navigator, 131
Garlamov, 77
Georgi, J.-G., 2, 3, 33, 99
Gerber, J.-G., 31
Germans, 60-61
Gmelin, G.-G., viii, ix, 5, 6, 8-12, 16, 24-25, 27, 49; house
    burns, 55; illness; 56, 63-65, 69-71, 73-75, 79-80, 84-85,
    92-93, 95, 107, 109-110, 113-114; death, 19
Gmelin, Samuel, 33
Goldbach, Christian, 104, 119
Golder, Frank A., ix
Golubtsov, Ivan, 20, 22
Gorlanov, Aleksei, student, 18, 48
Gorodishche, sloboda burial mounds at, 97-98
Gottschied, Johann, 11, 30, 32
Graves, 58
Great Kamchatka Command (1716), 3
Great Northern Expedition (First Kamchatka Expedition), 3, 14
Guldenstadt, J.A., 33
Gvozdev, Mikhail, 135
Germans, 61

Hablitz, K.I., 33
Hailar R., Argun source, 100
Halberg, Vassili, 81
Health problems, bloodletting, 51, 56; syphilis, 10; scurvy, 55,
    134; pneumonia, 16; 115
Hennin, George v., Gen.-Lieut., commandant of Ekaterinburg, 8,
    51, 71-73; replaced, 75, 107
Herdebol, mining sampler, 72
Hessen-Homburg, Prince v., 68
Humboldt, Alexander v., in Siberia, 1829, vii, viii

Iablonovyi khrebet (Apple Mts.), 96
Iakhontov, Il'ia, translator, 18, 48, 77, 86, 89
Iakuts, 54
Iakutsk, vi, 10; fire at, 12; 54, 74, 76, 87, 103
Iamysh, L., salt lake, 11, 80
Iamyshevskaia, fort, 9, 52, 80, 84
Iaroslavl, 6, 67
Ilim R., 78

Ilimsk, 11, 53
Illness, 55, 57, 60, 64-65
Imperial Art Museum (Kunstkamera), 83, 100
Indigirka R., 136
Ingoda R., 96
Irbit, 16, 73
Irgenskoi zavod, 71
Irkutsk, 53, 73, 78, 86-87, 89, 90-92, 95, 102
Iron smelting, 87
Irtysh R., 10, 76-78, 81-82; forts on, 79
Iset R., 16
Iusupov, Boris, Prince, 20
Ivanov, Aleksandr, surveyor, 48, 98, 110
Ivanov, L., student, 77, 111

Japan, 4
Jasper, on Argun R., 99
Jedso (Yezo), 129, 130

Kalmyk language, 11
Kalmyks, 80-83, 85, 95
Kamchadals, revolt, 1730-1731, 4, 14
Kamchatka, 4
Kamchatka expeditions: First, 12; Second, vi, viii, 5, 13,
    See also Great Northern Expedition
Kamenskii zavod, ironworks, 8, 73
Kan R., 91
Kankaragai region, 84
Kansk ostrog, 90
Kantemir, Demetrius, 68
Kazan, 7, 50, 67-71; Tatars of, 69-71, 75
Ketsk ostrog, 90
Keyserling, H.-G., Baron v., 14, 105
Khilok R., 96
Khrushchev, voevoda, 88
Kiakhta, vii, 11, 53-55, 90, 92-95, 97; Treaty of, 27-29,
Kindermann, Gen., 110
Kirenskii ostrog (Kirenga), 12, 55-56
Kirenskii zavod, 14
Kirghiz-Kazakhs, 68, 79, 82
Klenovskaia zastava, 71
Klenovskoi fort, 71
Kirilov, Ivan K., 4, 63, 65, 124
Kolyma R., 54
Kolyvan, 52, 84
Kolyvan mining works (Kolyvano-voskresenskie zavody), 80, 82-4,
    90
Kondoma R., 84-85
Korff, J.-A., Baron, 14, 104-106, 113, 116-117
Korolev, Andrei, 97
Koshelev, fleet master, 74
Kostroma, 67

Kotovtsy, 90
Kovyrin, Petr, 98; also as Petr Kovrigin, 115
Koz'modem'iansk, 50, 67
Krasheninnikov, Stepan P., viii, ix, 12, 18, 27, 48, 54, 57, 90, 98; death, 19
Krasnoiarsk, 10, 53, 58-59, 87-89; archives, 16
Krasil'nikov, A.D., Lieut., geodesist, 48, 63, 69, 77, 106, 111, 123, 128
Krasno-slobodskii ostrog
Krekshin, P.I., 26
Kuchum, Khan, 77
Kungur, 9; alabaster caves at, 71
Kurile Islands, 14
Kutuzov, Mikhail, 72
Kuznetsk, 17, 52, 84, 86

LaMothe, Major, 7, 50, 68
Lange, Lorents, vice-gov. of Irkutsk, 17, 61, 90, 110
Lead, at Argun silver works, 99
Leather work, 69
Lebedev, V.I., 22
Lefort, Francois, 2
Legislative Commission, 32
Leibniz, G.W., 2
Lena R., 10, 12, 54
Lepekhin, Ivan, x
LeRoy, P.L., 21
"Lettre d'un officier..." (1753), 28, 122-141
Lewis and Clark expedition, similarity to Bering exped., vi
Libertus, Johann-Christopher, 106
Lindemann, 111
Lindenau, Jacob, 13
Locatelli, Francesco, ix, 68
Lomonosov, M.V., 19, 21-22, 24, 28, 31
Lopsan, Mongol taisha, 93, 103
Lowitz, G.-M., death, 33
Lugasa, stream, 90
Lursenius, J.W., 48, 77, 81
Luzhin, Fedor, 3

Mackenzie, Alexander, viii
Makar'ev cloister, 67
Makovsk ostrog, 78
Maksimovich, L., 37
Mammoths, 89
Mangazeia, 57
Martini, adjunct, 59
Medical treatment: bloodletting, 51, 56; syphilis, 10; scurvy, 55
Messerschmidt, Daniel, ix, 3, 90, 100
Meteorological observations, 71, 73, 81, 109
Meyer, Jeremiah, Capt., 2

Midwives, 59
Miklaev, merchant, 70
Mirovich, Jacob, 76
Mishukov, Z.D., Vice-adm., 20
Mordvins, 7, 70
Mosquitoes, 10
Müller, Gerhard-Friedrich, vi, and passim; marriage, 1742, 16,
    60; at St. Petersburg, 1743, 17; permanent secretary of
    Academy Conference, 28; illness, 56; Director of Archives,
    and death, 35
Mungatskoi ostrog, 86
Murder of husband, punishment for, 15
Musin-Pushkin, P. I., commandant of Kazan, 7, 50
Musk-deer, 89

Nartov, Andrei K., 19, 111
Narym, vii, 59, 70
Naun, 98-99, 101
Nerchinsk, vii, 11, 91, 96, 98
Nerchinsk, salt lake, 101
Nerchinsk, Treaty of (1689), need to replace, 97
Nerchinskii (Argunskii) silver mines, 92, 97
Neva R., 65
Nikolskaia, 92
Nizhne-Kamchatsk, 4
Nizhnii Novgorod, 7, 67
"Normanism," 25
Novaia Mangazeia, 15
Novaia Pristan, 65
Novgorod, 65
Novikov, 34
Noza (Nitsa) R., 59

Ob R., 16, 73; Ob gulf, 74, 78-79
Okhotsk, 4
Old Believers, Tomsk, 53
Olearius, Adam, 29
Omsk, 9, 79, 80
Olonets, 72
Ona, trib. of Uda R., 95
Onon R., 94, 96, 98, 101
Orenburg Expedition, 63
Orlenga R., 72
Osa, 50, 71
Osokin, Balakhnishch merchant, 71
Osterman, A. I., Count, 4
Ostiaks (Khanty), 16, 59
Ovtsyn, D.L., Lieut., 73-74

Padun, waterfall, Angara R., 78
Pallas, P.S., 32-33, 36-38, 91, 93, 95
Pavlutskii, Dmitrii I., 135

Pelmiak (Pelym?), 121
Permian speech, 87
Peter the Great, 2, 32, 52-53, 63, 68, 70-71, 76, 79, 81, 124, 126
Piasina R., 136
Pictographs, 88, 91
Pisarev, Maj. Gen., harbor-master at Okhotsk, 10
Plautin, Mikhail G., Lieut., with Chirikov, 134
Pleshcheev, Aleksei L'vovich, Governor, Tobol'sk, 8, 74
Pleshcheev, Andrei, Vice-Governor, Irkutsk, 11
Polevskoi zavod, 72
Papov, Feodor, 48
Popov, N. I., student, 7, 22, 77, 111
Posotskoi monastery, 92
Postal service, 8
POWs, 61

Publications:

Atlas rossiiskoi (Russian Atlas), 125, 135, 141
Drevniaia rossiiskaia vivliofika (Ancient Russian Library), 37
Commentarii Akademiei Scientiarum Imperialis Petropolitanae, 1, 11, 21
Flora Sibirica (Gmelin), 25, 94-95
Magazin für neue Historie und Geographie, 110
Memoriae populorum (J.G. Stritter), 37
Monthly compositions (Ezhemesiachnyia sochineniia), 31-32, 39
New monthly compositions (Novyia ezhemesiachnyia sochineniia), 38, 87
Neue Nordische Beiträge, viii
Sammlung russischer Geschichte, 2, 37?-38, 70, 111
St. Petersburg Gazette, 1, 4
Siberian chronicle, 8-9

Pus, J.-W., translator, 4

Raguzinskii,Savva Vladislavich, Count, 29, 93
Razin, Stenka, rebellion, 33
Razumovskii, Kril Grigor'evich, Count, 20, 25-27, 62, 125
Reiser, mining councilor, 83
Remezov chronicle, 74
Rentel, Johan, 3
Romanov family, 11
Rycaut, Paul, Sir, 68
Rychkov, P.I., 31-32

Saian, 89
Salamatov, Petr, 87
Salt, 60, 80, 98
Saltykov, F.S., 2
Samarovskii iam, 32, 78

Samoyeds, 16, 58, 90
Savelev, Fedor, 134
Schlözer, A.-L., 32
Schumacher, J.-D., 1, 3, 11, 13,-14, 19, 25-26, 49
Schumacher, von, Secretary of Danish delegation, St. P., 61
Shchekin, surveyor. See Chekin.
Selenginsk, 29, 53, 55, 92, 94-95, 07, 102
Semipalatinsk fort, 9, 52, 79-82, 90
Senate, Supreme Governing, 18, 61-62, 64, 66-67, 73, 88-89, 104, 119
Serdtse Kamen, Cape, 126, 135
Shaitanskie iron works, 71
Shamanism, 53
Shamanskoi waterfall, on Angara R., 78
Shestakov, Afanasii, 135
Shetilov, Vasilii, surveyor, 91, 93, 97
Shmalev, Timofei I., Capt., 33
Shmalev, Vasilii I., 33
Sibir, Tatar fort, 9, 11, 77
Siegesbeck, J.-G., 111
Silantov cloister, 69, 71
Silver, 72, 95, 98
Silvo R., 9
Sisertskoi zavod, 72-73
Skobel'tsyn, Petr, surveyor, 17, 91, 93
Soimonov, F.I., 2, 14, 31
Sokolovskii, Andrei, 89
Soksunskoi zavod, 71
Solikamsk, 16, 60-61
Solonaia R., 91
Sorcery, 50, 53, 55, 85-86, 95, 97-98, 100-102
Sosnovskoi ostrog, 86
Spangenberg, Martin, ix, 4, 12, 14, 63, 130
Spanish, 63
Stanovoi Khrebet, 96
Steller, G.W., viii, 13, 36, 57, 111-112; death, 19
Stol'btsy (records), 9, 16, 74, 120
Strahlenberg, Ph.I.T., ix, xii, 3, 71, 84
Stritter, G.-G., 37, 110
Stroganov, Baron, 71
Strube de Piermont, F.H., 21 ?
Surgut, 16, 78
Svistunov, Ivan, surveyor, 91
Swedes, 59, 67, 75
Swedish Academy, Stockholm, 38 ?

Taimyr R., 136
Tanguts, 52, 102
Tara, 9, 11, 52, 75, 78-79
Tasseeva (Tosseeva) R., 91
Tatars, 3, 7-8, 10, 15, 50-52, 58-60, 69

Tatishchev, Andrei, mine surveyor, 73
Tatishchev, V.N., 16, 31, 33, 65, 70, 82, 107
Teleut Tatars (Telengits), 52, 85
Teplov, G.N., 21, 26
Tess R., 90
Tevkelev, Aleksei, 68
Thompson, David, viii
Timofeev, Academy Registrar, 112
Tiumen, 16, 59, 75
Tobol R., 79
Tobol'sk province, 80
Tobol'sk, double sloop, 10, 73
Tobol'sk, v, 3, 8-9, 11, 16, 51-52, 55, 59, 71, 73, 75, 77-78,
    82, 87, 92
Tom R., 84-88, 90
Tomsk Ostiak dialect, 87
Tomsk, 10, 15, 59, 75, 83-84, 86-87; archives, 16
Trediakovskii, V.K., 21-22, 24
Tret'iakov, Vasilii, student, 18, 48, 77, 90, 94
Troitskii, fort, near Kiakhta, 94
Trutnev, Gerasim, Udinsk cossack, 93
Tsamiatin, Senate Secretary, 112
Tsurukhaitu, 53, 100
Tübingen, 9, 25
Tulun village, 91
Tumanskii, Fedor, 28 ?
Tungus, 53-54, 57, 81, 96
Tunguska R., 78
Tunguska, R., 57
Tunkinsk ostrog, 106 ?
Tunkiskii ostrog, 110
Turinsk, 16, 59, 121
Turukhansk, 136
Tutern, 95
Tver, 6, 66-67

Ubinskaia fort, 82
Ud R., Okhotsk Sea affluent (Udskoi ostrog at mouth), 91
Ud R., Okhotsk Sea, 11
Uda R., trib. of Selenga R. (with Udinsk at mouth), 91, 95
Uda-Chumna-Tasseeva R., trib. of Upper Tunguska R., (with
    Udinskoi on Uda), 91
Udinsk, 53, 92, 98
Uglich, 6, 67
Upper Tunguska R., 91
Ural, Mrs., 51, 60
Ushakov, Moisei, geodesist, 48, 73
Ust'-Kamenogorsk, vii, 9, 52, 80, 82-83

Verendrye, Sieur de la, vii-viii
Verkhne-Irtyshskie, 11
Verkhotomskoi ostrog, 86

Verkhotur'e, 16, 60, 71, 78
Voguls (Mansi), 9, 16
Vologda, 17, 61
Voskresnie, 84
Voskresenskaia gora, 84
Votiaks (Udmurts), 7, 50, 70
Vyshnii Volochek, 66

Waxel, Sven, Lieut., 9
Werden, Karl van, 3
Weitbrecht, Josia, 112
Winsheim, C.N., 112
Witsen, N., 4

Zeia R., 97
Zhelezinskaia, 9, 80
Zyrians, 87

Measurements cited

zoll - 2 1/2 cm., or 1 inch

ell - about 2/3 of a meter or 7/10 of a yard

verst - 0.66 mile

klafter - a fathom

groschen - a farthing, or 1/10 of a penny

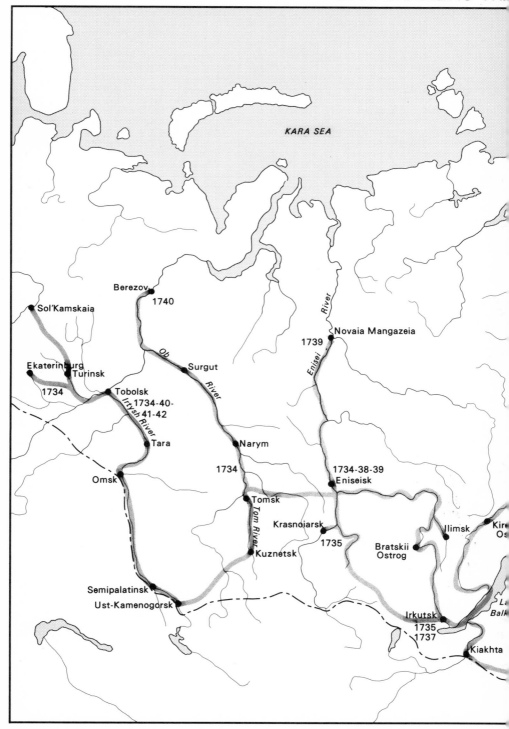